GREAT ASIAN RELIGIONS

GREAT

ASIAN ⛩⛩⛩
RELIGIONS

C. George Fry, James R. King,
Eugene R. Swanger, and Herbert C. Wolf

Baker Book House   Grand Rapids, Michigan 49506

ISBN: 0-8010-3511-2

Library of Congress Catalog Card Number: 84-70029

Printed in the United States of America

Unless otherwise indicated, all Scripture quotations are from the King James Version of the Bible.

The authors wish to acknowledge permission to quote excerpts from *Creativity and Taoism* by Chang Chung-yuan, copyright © 1963 by Chang Chung-yuan, reprinted with permission of Crown Publishers, Inc; *The Spirit of Islam* by Syed Ameer 'Ali, reprinted by permission of the author's literary estate and Chatto and Windus Ltd.; *The Way and Its Power* by Arthur Waley, reprinted by permission of George Allen and Unwin Ltd. and Grove Press, all rights reserved; *The Reconstruction of Religious Thought in Islam* by Sir Mohammad Iqbal, reprinted by permission of Oxford University Press; and *The Complete Works of Chang-Tzu*, translated by Burton Watson, reprinted by permission of Columbia University Press.

In addition, the authors wish to acknowledge the use of illustrations from the Los Angeles County Museum of Art: anonymous gift, page 59; the Cleveland Museum of Art, purchase, John L. Severance Fund, page 133; Japan National Tourist Organization, pages 2–3, 10, 69, 145, and 211; Bibles for India, pages 2–3, 62, 168, and 180; the Christian Reformed Church Board of Missions, page 146; *A Chinese View of China* by John Gittings, used by permission of Pantheon Books, page 89; and *Symbols, Signs and Signets* by Ernst Lehner, used by permission of Dover Publications, pages 33, 65, 87, and 193.

Photographs on pages 82, 84, and 157 are of amulets from the collection of Eugene R. Swanger and appear by courtesy of James R. King, as do those on pages 38 and 137.

Contents

68422

Introduction

C. George Fry

A community whose life is not irrigated by art and science, by religion and philosophy, day upon day, is a community that exists half alive.

—Lewis Mumford

In the major Midwestern city in which I live we have a proud motto: Fort Wayne, City of Churches. For almost two centuries that has been the case. From Roman Catholic to Congregationalist, much of the Christian spectrum has been represented in our population. A vibrant Jewish community also has been present. Christianity and Judaism—two of the great religions of western Asia—have been transplanted to the American Midwest with relatively little difficulty. No sense of peculiarity attaches to their presence in the North American heartland. These Asian religions are now seen as American faiths and are so named—Southern Baptists, Indiana Yearly Meeting of Friends, or Missouri-Synod Lutherans.

Recently, however, other Asian religions have come to Fort Wayne. We have a Hindu fellowship, a Muslim society, and a number of Buddhists. Although India, Iran, and Indochina may seem far from Indiana, the reality of the 1980s is that these nations have contributed immigrants to the new America. With them they have brought their faiths. In my classes at a local college I have had students who were Zoroastrian, Shintōist, Confucianist, or Taoist. I need not go more than five miles from my home to be in conversation with representatives of most of the great religions of Asia. This is a new phenomenon for many Americans. While it has

7

never seemed a long way from Indiana to Israel (many local churches and synagogues sponsor annual pilgrimages to the Holy Land), it does appear to many that the physical and spiritual distance from China, Japan, and India is much greater. Contact with Buddhists or Hindus was previously made only by watching a television documentary, listening to a missionary sermon, or reading the *National Geographic*. These occasional glimpses of the Asian world were supplemented by the impressions of soldiers returned from Vietnam, the accounts of businessmen who had visited Japan and Thailand, or the slides shown by tourists who had been to mainland China. Now East Asia is as near as a Hindu community center beside a United Methodist church, or a Muslim prayer meeting convening at noon in the campus center of a local university. Middle Americans are now in the midst of rediscovering the religions of Asia.

This book, *Great Asian Religions*, has been written by four Midwesterners of the Protestant tradition to share their impressions of the faiths of our neighbors, whether they live in Chicago or Singapore, Columbus or Kyoto. In this introduction let me suggest two things that we have attempted. One of them is explicit. It is to introduce Asia and its religions. The other is implicit. It is to suggest a style of Christian contact with those of other faiths.

An Introduction to Asia

It is impossible to overestimate the importance of Asia. If we can imagine the story of humankind having been lived within the three dimensions of space, time, and spirit, we must, in fact, conclude that Asia has been the dominant influence upon the human saga.

There is, to begin with, the simple fact of space. Asia, the largest of the continents, has a land surface larger than that of the moon. The continent contains nearly seventeen million square miles of land, one-third of the land on the earth. Asia, moreover, is strategically located, which is another way of saying that it has always been at the center of the human drama. Europe has been described as Asia's largest peninsula, a fact that has given rise to the useful coinage *Eurasia*, and, when we view Africa in the same way, we achieve the novel term *Eurafrasia*. Ancient maps, moreover, sometimes suggested that this huge landmass was an island surrounded on three sides by oceans—the Atlantic, the Pacific, and the Indian. Even the discovery of the Americas has not done much to alter that perception. One scholar noted that "earth is Eurafrasia. Off its coasts are two large islands—North and South America."

The space that is Asia is filled with an almost infinite variety. These varieties give rise to superlatives: earth's highest peak, Mount Everest, and its lowest point, the Dead Sea. The world's broadest plain is the great Eurasian steppeland extending from the Ukraine to the horizons of Mongolia, and the world's highest and narrowest passes link China and India through the Himalayas. Asia embraces some of earth's driest places, like the Gobi Desert, and some of its wettest, like the rain forests of Borneo; Asia, moreover, is also dotted with gardens—in Persia, in China, in Sri Lanka, and in Japan—that are reminiscent of Paradise, as well as austere landscapes such as the almost lunar-like wastelands of Iran—the Dasht-e-Kavir—and the great tundra of Siberia. Size and situation combine with diversity and complexity to make Asia the world's most astonishing continent.

Asia is a matter of time as well as place. Here the human family is thought to have originated, and even today Asia remains the habitat of almost two-thirds of our race. Approximately 2.5 billion people are said to live on this continent. Asia not only is "the Mother of Man," but also must be seen as "the Teacher of Man." While historians debate whether civilization originated in the Nile Valley or that of the Tigris and Euphrates rivers, the reality is that those two riparian civilizations, together with those that developed in the Indus Valley and that of the Hwang Ho, came to form a gigantic "cultural crescent" that stretched from Thebes to Sumer and Akkad to Mohenjo-Daro and Changan. That broad belt of civilized living that girded together so much of Asia was, many contend, the most startling fact of antiquity, suggesting that Asia is, indeed, "the Mother of Civilized Man." Much of what we associate with civilization, from agriculture to literary culture, from legislation to meditation, from technology to theology, grew out of an Asian context. To read this on a printed page perhaps makes very little impression. To experience it, however, in the Asian situation is another matter, one that is sensed by standing near ancient burial mounds or before shrines, or strolling through

The Torii Gate at Miyajama (Inland Sea), Itsukushima Shrine.

crowded bazaars or impressive palaces, or walking in manicured gardens or sitting in quiet mosques. One realizes the truth in the saying that "all civilized men and women are Asians." Each day, in a thousand and one ways, our lives are rendered pleasant and useful because of the legacy of Asia to human civilization. This legacy has been given to us across time and space, through a myriad of transmitters and interpreters, but its origin remains evident: Asia.

Asia is, however, more than a place on a map or a chronology of events in a history text. Asia is a state of mind, a religious experience, a quickening of the human spirit. Asia is a constant reminder of the truth uttered by Jesus: "Man shall not live by bread alone" (Matt. 4:4). Mankind may live in time and space, but humans live by moral and religious values as well. Nowhere is this more evident than in Asia. No great world religion has originated outside Asia. Theologically the whole human family, to the extent that it adheres to a higher religion, is Asian. This is evident in little ways, as common as the word *amen* spoken often in the Christian service, yet of Asian origin, being the Hebrew word for "certainly" or "verily." It is obvious in major ways: the Jewish synagogue, the Catholic cathedral, the Methodist chapel, the Presbyterian church, the Hindu temple, the Buddhist shrine, the Muslim mosque—all now so much a part of the American landscape— have their ultimate origins in Asia.

The explicit purpose of this book is to introduce seven great religions of Asia: the Hindu, the Buddhist, the Confucian, the Taoist, the Shintō, the Islamic, and the Christian traditions. This is done by proceeding regionally. We start in South Asia with the faiths that originated in India—the Hindu and the Buddhist. Next we move to East Asia to consider the philosophical religions of China—Confucianism and Taoism—and the national faith of Japan—Shintōism. Finally we turn to the two major world relig-ions that started in West Asia—Islam and Christianity. Judaism is excluded not because it lacks significance, but because it lacks size. Other faiths of Asia that are qualitatively great but numerical-ly small—such as Zoroastrianism and Jainism—have also been excluded. Our concern has been to consider those Asian religions which are quantitatively important.

Four authors have collaborated on this book. They represent three different disciplines—theology, history, and literature; two different Protestant traditions—Lutheran and Presbyterian; and two diverse academic contexts—a liberal-arts college and a theo-logical seminary. All, however, share one common concern—a love for Asia and its peoples and cultures, and a desire to interpret these for their fellow Americans. All the authors have lived and labored in Asia. In this volume Herbert C. Wolf authored the chapter on the Hindu tradition; Eugene R. Swanger wrote the material on the Buddhist and the Shintō traditions; James R. King prepared the sections on the Taoist tradition and Islam and served as editor; C. George Fry did the introduction and the chapters on Asia and the Confucian tradition, and collaborated with the other three contributors on the section about Christiani-ty. All would like to express their appreciation to readers and editors at Baker Book House, especially Dan Van't Kerkhoff, for encouragement at every juncture in this venture. To colleagues at Wittenberg University and Concordia Theological Seminary they also extend a heartfelt thank you for assistance at many places and for counsel on numerous occasions. Any faults or errors remaining in the text the authors own.

Our attempt in this book has been the scholarly study of religion, not its advocacy. We have tried to provide up-to-date information and to convey something of our personal experience of each of the religions discussed. For more than two decades each of us, now in midlife, has listened carefully, respectfully, and critically to the voices of Asia. The material shared in this book is the result of that listening. Our primary purpose, therefore, is one of reporting, as objectively and honestly as is humanly possible, what we have seen and heard. Because each of us is also a member of an affirming community, a body of Christian believers, that listening has occurred within the context of Protestantism. We have tried, however, to maintain the distinction between teaching and preaching, between reporting and affirming, between description and prescription. Although that has been our central concern as professors, implicit in our whole effort has been our own grounding within the heritage of historic Reformation Protestantism. For that reason it is also necessary to introduce some assumptions.

An Introduction to Religions

Introductions occur between strangers. They are crucial because they provide first impressions which may become permanent attitudes expressed in relationships. For that reason we feel that it is crucial that in our introduction we provide some perspective on our attitudes toward the opportunity and the challenge confronting American Christians today—that of living in a religiously pluralistic society.

Contact with persons of other religions immediately poses a paradox for the practicing Christian: How can I, like Paul, be found "speaking the truth in love" (Eph. 4:15)? On the one hand it is a biblical imperative to show love for the stranger, not to "vex . . . nor oppress" (Exod. 22:21), for the Hebrews were "strangers in the land of Egypt" (Exod. 22:21) and Jesus himself, a member of a minority people, spent part of his childhood as "a stranger in a strange land." Hospitality, not hostility, is to be the Christian attitude toward "thy stranger that is within thy gates" (Exod. 20:10). On the other hand it is also a biblical imperative that Jesus Christ has an ultimacy that can be shared with no other. Once the Master said, "I am the way, the truth, and the life: no man cometh unto the Father, but by me" (John 14:6).

Every Christian believer will have his own way of dealing with this paradox, the paradox of the openness and the exclusivity of Christianity, and obviously the more intensely one is involved with people of other religions, the more painful the paradox is: it is more immediate in India than in Indiana. Three ways of dealing with this dilemma seem to us to be less than satisfactory. One is the way of the cynic, who looks at the problem and decides that the claims of no religion have priority, that all religions are the same, that no religion has a greater share of the truth than any of the others. Curiously enough, this rejection of the life of faith sometimes takes the form of a very aggressive assertion that "I am right." A second response to the great paradox is that of the secularist, who seeks an answer in the least common denominator, asserting that all that is required is that a person live a good life. And a third common response is that of confrontation: arguing about religion, trying to force one's position upon others. In each of these strategies the mystery and grandeur of the Christian position, and the need to speak the truth in love, get lost.

To resolve the paradox that is Christian discipleship we must consider the world of the New Testament. From a survey of the world of Jesus and the apostles, the prophets who preceded them, and the Fathers who followed them, three things become obvious to us.

First, religious pluralism was a reality in New Testament times. Sometimes it is asserted that religious pluralism as known in contemporary America is a recent phenomenon. In one sense, of course, it is new to the West. For centuries Europe and Europe's possessions beyond the oceans were considered Christendom. Normally one type of Christianity prevailed within each country: Lutheranism in Sweden, Catholicism in Ireland, Presbyterianism in Scotland, or Anglicanism in England. Even the minorities that existed were often Christian minorities—Huguenots in France,

Waldensians in Italy, Lutherans in Austria. Only within the last two centuries has the old Christendom fragmented before the forces of secularism and pluralism. In another sense, however, such pluralism is not new. The world of early Christianity was one filled with religious diversity. The Christian churches lived alongside many philosophical systems, such as Platonism and Epicureanism; many mystery religions, such as Mithraism; and many forms of local polytheism, such as the cult of Diana in Ephesus, or that of Athena in Athens. Even the land in which Jesus lived and labored knew pluralism. Magi, possibly of the Zoroastrian persuasion, visited the infant Jesus. Greeks sought the Master just prior to his passion. Between cradle and cross Jesus encountered Samaritans, Syrophoenicians, and Roman centurions. As the people of the Old Testament lived amid the polytheism of Egypt, the philosophy of Greece, the Zoroastrianism of Persia, and the varied religions of Canaan, Babylon, Assyria, and Arabia, so Jesus ministered among those of many faiths. From our study of the New Testament we feel that religious pluralism is an experience that we share with the people of apostolic times.

Second, the people of the Bible reflect a variety of attitudes toward those of other faiths. These responses, which differ considerably, were conditioned by the context in which the believing community found itself. On occasion there was open hostility. Elijah on Mount Carmel slaughtered the priests of Baal; Joshua commanded the extermination of the Canaanites. Later Ezra the Scribe forbade intermarriage between Hebrews and Gentiles. Behind this hostility were, undoubtedly, a fear of syncretism and a dread of the extinction of the Jewish community through assimilation. More common than hostility, however, was an attitude of hospitality and ministry. Joseph, savior of his people from famine, was married, with God's approval, to the daughter of an Egyptian priest. Moses, the liberator of the Hebrews from Egyptian oppression, was wed to a daughter of Jethro, a Midianite priest whom he asked for counsel. Ruth, the Moabite, became an ancestor of Christ. Bilquis, Queen of Sheba, consulted Solomon, the sage of Israel. This attitude of friendship and witness continues into the New Testament. On occasion Jesus commended those of other traditions: he praised the faith of a Roman centurion and that of a Syrophoenician woman; he employed a Good Samaritan (not an orthodox Pharisee) as an illustration of charity, or love in action;

Christ himself ministered in compassion to Samaritans, whether physical lepers by the roadside or moral ones by the well. Christ did so, however, without compromising his own message or mission, insisting, even in the moment of graciousness by Jacob's well, that "salvation is of the Jews." We believe that it is in this spirit—hospitality and ministry—that the church went out into the ancient world. By the miracle of Pentecost it was not Jewish cultural hegemony that prevailed, but a new catholicity, a cosmopolitan attitude, for on the birthday of the church the good news was heard not simply in Hebrew or Aramaic. Rather, each person heard "them speak in [his own] tongue the wonderful works of God" (Acts 2:11).

Within the biblical literature several possible relationships between Christianity and other faiths are explored. This means, in our opinion, that it is both simplistic and dangerous to prescribe any one of these approaches as *the* biblical model that is always normative. The apostles and prophets of the New Testament era, inspired by the Holy Spirit, showed great sophistication in their interaction with persons of other traditions. They did not regard all religions as equal, nor did they feel that all contexts were identical. The posture of the Christian apologete was conditioned by the needs of the situation in which he found himself and the persons to whom he was speaking. For that reason, at times in the New Testament we are informed that certain other religions are to be regarded as part of divine revelation. Theologians later referred to this as natural revelation (given in nature, society, and personality), in contrast to special revelation (conveyed in Christ and the Scriptures). Peter, having met Cornelius and his family, said, "Of a truth I perceive that God is no respecter of persons: But in every nation he that feareth him, and worketh righteousness, is accepted with him" (Acts 10:34–35). The philosophy of natural law was developed by Christian thinkers as diverse as Thomas Aquinas and Ulrich Zwingli, Dante Alighieri and John Milton. At other times in the New Testament certain religions are seen as a preparation for the coming of Christianity. Paul, speaking on Mars' Hill to Athenian adherents of the philosophical religions, quoted, with approval, the writings of their "poets" and "prophets," saying, "For in him we live, and move, and have our being; . . . For we are also his offspring" (Acts 17:28). During his discourse Paul contended that his God was not a strange one to his auditors but instead "the Unknown God, whom therefore ye ignorantly worship, him declare I unto you" (Acts 17:23). Church fathers (for example, Eusebius) regarded other faiths as "the Old Testament of the Gentiles."

Yet at other times within the New Testament literature the apostles, like Paul, are compelled to condemn, not condone or commend, the practices of certain other faiths. In the opening chapters of Romans, where Paul makes a compelling case for justification by grace alone through faith, the apostle attacks in uncompromising fashion the perversions of the natural man and the aberrations produced as "sick religion" by "sick men." In such a context certain other religions—such as the temple prostitution connected with some types of classical paganism—are seen as temptations to evil, causing damnation. It is interesting, however, that when Paul informs the Romans of the "demonic" character of such religion, he does so in the name of natural law (the testimony of the true God in cosmos and conscience). Yet at other times the New Testament writers praise those of other faiths. At points there is even an indication that they may be among the elect. Zwingli, one of the fathers of the Reformed faith, marveled at this, hoping against hope that "whosoever is good can be eternally of God." To us, as to the Zurich reformer, one of the most moving chapters of the Canon is the seventh chapter of Hebrews. Nowhere is the priesthood of Jesus Christ taken more seriously, and nowhere is his vicarious atonement taught more clearly. But it is precisely in that setting that the author takes "Melchisedec, king of Salem, priest of the most high God" (Heb. 7:1) as a paradigm or model of the Savior. Melchisedec is commended as a foretype of Christ. He was not, however, a Hebrew, nor was he a member of any Jewish synagogue. We have found no indication that Melchisedec was an adherent of the family of Abraham or a cleric of the church that met in his household.

This priest, like the mysterious Jethro, father-in-law of Moses, or the equally baffling Job, righteous patriarch but no Hebrew, is one of those "outside the visible covenant" to whom God gave "wisdom and grace" and who is numbered "within the invisible church." One should neither overstate this possibility nor understate its significance, for the Christian walk today is filled with mystery. The mystery is that God has not left himself without witness to his righteousness, his love, and his graciousness, but that at times he chooses to veil himself, or present himself in ways that we cannot immediately understand. Our mission is to witness in love to the truth he has given us and to work and testify, as best we can, to "the grace of our Lord Jesus Christ." It is not to judge, for that is the task of Christ, to whom individuals and nations must give account.

Each of the religions of Asia regards itself as possessing ultimacy; none views itself as penultimate. None of these faiths would see itself as consciously preparatory for another faith, in the way in which Christians traditionally have regarded Old Testament Judaism. As systems, non-Christian religions, we feel, do not point to Christ. But we also believe that God is not absent anywhere in the world he has made.

I remember the way the late Herbert Leopold, a conservative Lutheran preacher, reprimanded an ardent brother who was rapidly increasing the population of hell by his sweeping condemnations. "God," he said, "has limited the church to the means of grace—Word and Sacrament; God has not limited himself to these means. Possibly he has other ways to work out his will."

In thinking about the Christian approach to other world religions, it is clearly important that we keep before us all the texts of the New Testament, gathering from all of them a composite and complete picture of the biblical attitude toward other faiths, remaining open all the while to the "mysterious ways" in which God may move. It is also important that we read each verse in context, keeping in mind the specific situation out of which it grew and applying it to modern conditions with the greatest care. In this way we can begin to live within the great paradox of our faith—the absolute claims of Christ and the openness of God's love to all.

1

Asia:
A Survey

C. George Fry

One of the central facts of human experience appears to be religion. Paul observed that the ancient Athenians were very religious (Acts 17:22), for as a man who came from Asia Minor—modern-day Turkey to be specific—he appears to have been attuned, from his earliest days, to religious questions. His interest many Asians seem to have shared, for most of the great religions of the world—in Paul's day and in ours—have their roots in this greatest of all continents. We can, moreover, associate them quite clearly with three separate geographical areas of Asia.

First of all, there are the religions of West or Southwest Asia, the faiths that had their inception in Mesopotamia and their development in Israel and Arabia. Sometimes these are called the Abrahamic faiths, for all honor Abraham, the primordial patriarch, the great exponent of monotheism, as their forefather.

There are three Abrahamic faiths—Judaism, with more than fourteen million adherents; its offspring, Christianity, with nearly one billion followers; and Islam, which embraces perhaps eight hundred million faithful. Collectively these three faiths incorporate more than half the human family, fulfilling, in a strange and startling way, the promise to Abraham that he would be "the father of a multitude of nations" (Gen. 17:4, RSV) and that God would make his descendants as numerous as the stars of heaven or the sand of the seashore (Gen. 22:17).

Although major differences, which ought not be minimized, divide these religions, Judaism, Christianity, and Islam share

19

many principles, perspectives, and practices. All are radically monotheistic faiths, addressing God as El, or Elohim, or Allah, and believing that God has spoken to man in a Revealed Book. A prophetical succession from Adam onward is an integral feature of these faiths. Exclusivistic, calling for an absolute and unshared allegiance, these religions also manifest themselves in great evangelistic and ethical fervor. Islam and Christianity are ardently missionary; they regard themselves as having a universal significance for all persons. With an apocalyptic sense and a strong eschatological flavor, both await the coming of God's kingdom and the day of judgment as the climax of human history. We can assert, then, that a substantial portion of the human family finds its ultimate loyalty and spiritual allegiance in value systems that originated in West Asia.

There are, secondly, the religions that originated in South Asia—Hinduism, which has from time immemorial been linked with the Indian subcontinent, and Buddhism, which originated in India and migrated to Sri Lanka and China. Even though there is something of a parent-child relationship between the Hindu and Buddhist traditions, these two religions diverged radically when Buddhism migrated, so that they no longer bear to each other the kind of family relationship that Judaism and Christianity or Judaism and Islam have. In part this divergence is due to the vast distances separating the river valleys of India and China. In part it is due to the fundamental differences in attitude between Indian and Chinese society. In part it is due to the long period of time involved in the development of these value systems. In part it is due to the fact that each of these faiths has tended to meet a different need and to fulfill a somewhat divergent function in society. In part it is due to the complexity and subtlety of the human spirit, as each saint or sage sought to interpret a dimension of reality that was especially significant to him. There is, furthermore, throughout South and East Asia a "principle of plenitude" at work, which impels people to receive each of several religions as meeting certain perceived needs, but which regards no one of them as meriting total or exclusive loyalty. Often the faiths of South and East Asians are intermeshed in a way quite astonishing to a Christian or a Muslim (there is even some melding, in India, of Islam and Hinduism, despite their bitter differences, at the levels of ritual and social structure), and Hindus and Buddhists find it difficult to comprehend the radical exclusivity of the Abrahamic faiths.

The older of the two great religious traditions of India is Hinduism, linked to the subcontinent even in its name. Today approximately six hundred million people profess loyalty to this tradition, and its influence pervades every aspect of Indian life—art, literature, family organization, social structure, diet, dress, rituals of birth and death, and national and international policy. Of all the great religions of the world, Hinduism is the most "spiritual" in its view of reality, and its stress on the power of the unseen world, on reverence for life, and on the interconnectedness of all things has made it a very popular force among young people today who are protesting the secularization and the materialism of Western society. Thus the coral-brown robes and the shaved heads of Krishna followers are a familiar sight in nearly every large city of the world.

The Buddhist tradition began as a reformation of Hinduism and indeed has sometimes been described as a kind of "Protestantism within Hinduism." In spite of its Indian roots, however, the religion associated with the Buddha found its real home elsewhere—in Sri Lanka, Southeast Asia, China, and Japan. It counts more than 250 million adherents, most of them of course in East Asia, but others scattered in places as remote as London, Chicago, and São Paolo. Certainly the influence of the Buddhist tradition upon Western life and thought within this century has been impressive. Buddhism undeniably has a life of its own, but its indebtedness to the older faith remains obvious. Thus some scholars insist that the two faiths should be regarded as but opposite sides of the same coin, twin manifestations of one common reality. Together, these two religions present a spiritual force comparable in numbers to Islam or Christianity.

Third are the great religions of East Asia, two of which, the Taoist and the Confucian traditions, had their start in China. Both of them, because of the character of Chinese thought, are deeply philosophical. From time immemorial the Chinese have been concerned about right relationships, especially about the relationship of the ego or the self to nature and to society. Seeking harmony with nature is a major focus of Taoism, a faith that is said to have about thirty-two million followers (because of conditions in China today, the accuracy of that figure can be disputed).

However, the actual influence of Taoism on the popular level is greater than statistics would suggest. As an intellectual force, Taoism has attracted the attention of German physicists, French novelists, American philosophers, and Spanish poets.

While Taoists sought to create concord between man and nature, Confucius and his followers strove to establish yet another network of satisfying relationships, those between the self and society. Confucius was a contemporary of Lao-tzu, the father of Taoism. Venerated as a great sage, Confucius devoted much of his thought to what we would call the public philosophy. His moral and social thought still commands the allegiance of at least 160 million men and women throughout the world. Furthermore, the extent of the influence of Confucius goes beyond the confines of his creed. One of the most celebrated Confucian scholars of this century was a devout Presbyterian, Lin Yutang. His contention was that Confucian moral values are generally compatible with the spiritual claims of Jesus Christ, the Savior. Regardless of the merits of that argument, one must remember that the two philosophical faiths of China—Taoism and Confucianism—have never regarded one another as being mutually exclusive (as are Christianity and Islam), and that both have coexisted for centuries with the Buddhist tradition. More than one author has suggested that the Chinese relate to nature through Taoism, to society through Confucianism, and to transcendent reality through Buddhism.

In many respects, Japan is a child of China, for much of her culture was borrowed from the continent. Indebtedness, however, did not rule out ingenuity. Japan has steadfastly maintained her own unique identity, in spite of two great periods of foreign influence—that of China in the seventh century and that of the West in modern times. Although Japan is predominantly Buddhist in belief, she has a national religious tradition of her own— Shintōism, a creed to which sixty million Japanese pay allegiance. Like the other East Asian religions, Shintōism is not exclusivistic and readily permits concurrent membership in other systems. Furthermore, one does not "belong" to a Shintō shrine in the same way that one would hold membership in an American Presbyterian church or a Lutheran parish. Nor does one frequent a Shintō temple in the same way an American Baptist would "go to meeting." Instead, the Shintō tradition is an all-pervasive influence, taking many forms, both civic and cultic, in Japan. As a national faith, it provides a necessary supplement to the Buddhism or secularism by which the Japanese order their daily lives.

The term *Southeast Asia* embraces both countries of the Asian mainland such as Vietnam, Laos, Kampuchea (Cambodia), Thailand, and Burma and island republics such as Indonesia (including Sumatra, Java, part of Borneo, and the Celebes) and Malaysia (including peninsular Malaysia and part of Borneo). The complexities of this region's history are readily reflected in the complexity of the religious and racial situations. For in addition to constant migrations, often motivated by commercial interests, of people native to the region, there have been powerful influences from outside the area, by the Dutch and Chinese among others, for purposes of colonization. Thus, in addition to Buddhists in Thailand, we find Roman Catholics in Vietnam, Protestants and Catholics alike in the Philippines, Muslims in Indonesia (indeed, the Javanese constitute the third largest ethnic bloc of Muslims in the world), and traces of animism everywhere.

Geographical Factors

Without asserting geographical determinism, we do feel that a case can be made for the influence of geography on culture and thus on religion. Islam was given its distinctive shape by the urban environments that nurtured it in the Middle East; the concern of Taoists with fitting into the flow of nature seems to reflect the Chinese environment, which is sometimes harsh and sometimes benign—an environment that requires some effort at adjustment by the human beings who live in it. And surely the luxuriance of the Hindu tradition bears some relationship to the luxuriance of the Indian subcontinent that nurtured it. There is some justification, it would seem, for a few words about the physical qualities of the regions from which the great religions of Asia sprang.

India

"India is not a place—it is a state of mind." Or perhaps we should say innumerable states of mind, for the subcontinent itself does not present a unified picture to the observer. To the west, situated along the Indus River, is the state of Pakistan, a third again larger than France and with a population numbering more than eighty million. Created as West Pakistan in 1947, and thus separated from the Hindu majority of India, it is properly treated as part of the Islamic world, for which it has supplied art and theological scholarship since the period of the Middle Ages. To the east of India proper lies Bangladesh, separated from India in 1947 as East Pakistan and since 1971 an independent country—one of the world's poorest and most tragic. North of India lies Nepal, with only fourteen million people. Its capital is the legendary Katmandu and within its borders lies Mount Everest, the world's highest mountain peak. The great majority of the people are Hindu, and throughout history they have been pawns in various political struggles between India and China. Tiny Bhutan, with fewer than two million inhabitants—most of them Buddhist—is also tucked away in the Himalayas. And far to the south, hanging like a pendant from the Indian peninsula, reposes the lovely island of Sri Lanka, once known as Ceylon or Serendip (from which comes our word *serendipity*). About half the size of Alabama, Sri Lanka has a population of more than fifteen million, the majority of whom are Buddhist. There are also Hindu, Christian, and Muslim minorities.

The present Republic of India, which occupies most of the subcontinent, is a vast land about one-third the size of the United States but with a population three times as large—estimated at 640 million. The population density is more than 530 people per square mile, and there is incredible crowding in the cities. The Republic of India is today the most intensely Hindu country on our planet.

India's geographical diversity lies behind the enormous diversity of experience that she has provided for her people. The fact that she faces great seas—the Arabian to the west, the Bay of Bengal to the east, and the Indian Ocean to the south—has put her in constant contact for millennia with the people of Indochina; with the people of Indonesia and Malaysia; and with the people of the east coast of Africa, bordering on the Indian Ocean. And favorable wind patterns made trade with the Arabian Peninsula possible at a very early date. Moreover, India boasts the world's highest mountains to the north; three of the world's mightiest river systems—the Indus, the Ganges, and the Brahmaputra; deserts; jungles; and thickly populated plains. India's spiritual odyssey cannot be separated from these features of geography.

Moreover, India exhibits a rich and exotic ethnic mixture: her people match her geography in complexity. Many colors, castes, and cultures exist on the subcontinent, even though modern Indians are essentially a blend of the native Dravidian folk and descendants of the Aryan invaders who entered India from the north (modern Soviet Turkestan) or from the west (present-day Iran) in the second millennium before Christ. Since that time, British, Portuguese, Persian, Turkish, and Mongol strains have been added to create a simply overwhelming anthropological variety. Hindi is the official tongue, but English is still widely used and hundreds of dialects are spoken.

India also displays a multifaceted climate and economy. In the north, within sight of the Himalayas, the climate is temperate. In the south, within sound of the Indian Ocean, it is tropical. Altitude and latitude are both important factors. One constant feature in much of the country is the monsoon, a seasonal or periodic wind and the rainy season associated therewith. In one day during the monsoon season, it is possible to experience a dust storm in the morning, a tropical rainfall in the afternoon, and a brilliant clear sky by evening. Equally complex is the economy connected with this climatic diversity. The majority of India's people are villagers, making their living from agriculture—raising jute, tea, and food-stuffs. Yet India also has some of the world's largest cities— Calcutta (9,100,000), Bombay (8,200,000), and Delhi (5,200,000). In such urban centers, heavy industry challenges labor-intensive agriculture, high technology threatens native handicrafts.

India's people have always expressed a profound and variegat-ed spirituality. Within the milieu of this peninsula, so packed with people and history, promise and necessity, two of the most influential of the world religions—Hinduism and Buddhism— have developed, and here it is, also, that two other great religions —Islam and Christianity—have developed in ways that constitute fascinating variants on the form these religions have taken in the Middle East and the West. One of the purposes of this book is to explore this spiritual diversity.

China

Given its geographical extent, its vast population, and its complex history, China is an overwhelming reality that arouses speechless wonder. There are, in fact, only two other nations in the world—the United States and the Union of Soviet Socialist

Republics—with which comparisons can be made. Indeed, some similarities between the United States and China can perhaps appropriately be suggested here.

As the United States dominates North America, extending some four thousand miles from east to west, so China straddles East Asia, reaching westward from the Pacific for almost three thousand miles. Unlike the United States, which is bounded by two major oceans, China confronts only one large body of water; wilderness and steppeland comprise the western frontier. As the United States has southern neighbors in Mexico and the Caribbean of a distinctively different culture, so China looks across the forbidding Himalayas toward India, a peninsula half her size and worlds removed in culture. Unlike the Mexican peninsulas, which are separated from the United States by—at most—a river, the Indian and other peninsulas of southern Asia are cut off from China by significant geographical barriers. Chinese influence, however, has reached Burma, Thailand, Malaysia, Singapore, and Indochina. To the north China has no friendly Canada, but instead the Soviet Union, separated by a border that is ill-defined, contested, and a source of repeated conflict. Around China are several smaller states—the two Koreas, Mongolia, Hong Kong, Taiwan, and the city-state of Macao (a Portuguese territory). As the United States is pivotal to all portions of North America, so China is crucial to all the states of East Asia, including Japan, her neighbor offshore.

Within her frontiers China contains some 3,691,502 square miles, making her slightly larger than the United States, and one of the six largest countries on earth. This superstate comprehends many distinct districts, including twenty-one provinces that constitute the heartland of China (or core China, historic China, inner China), and five autonomous regions that make up the fringeland of China (or peripheral China, newer China, outer China). Among these autonomous regions, several—Inner Mongolia, Tibet, and Sinkiang—have had a long history of their own. Traditionally these borderlands of Chinese civilization have been engaged in a struggle with the heartland, so that a tension between the center and the periphery is a constant in Chinese history. When the state has been weak, these regions have gone their own way; when the government has been strong, they have been integrated more into the mainstream of Chinese life.

China occupies a position in latitude comparable to that of the United States, and, therefore, enjoys a similar range of climate, but the topography is different. Much of China tends to be mountainous, although there are rich valleys along the major rivers and an astounding plain to the north. The Himalayas merit the name *the spinal cord of Eurasia,* and terrible wastelands, like the Gobi Desert, add yet another kind of variety and splendor to the Chinese landscape. However, the mighty rivers, forming three chief systems—the Yellow River in the north, the Yangtze in the center, and the Si Kiang to the south—are perhaps the outstanding memory for many visitors. Traditionally, the Yangtze, Earth's fourth largest river, has been the gateway to the South for Chinese, just as the Mississippi has been for Americans the gateway to the West.

As the United States has been divided historically between the North and the South, so China too has been split into a northern and a southern sector. At times this difference has been expressed politically; always it is shown linguistically; and it is visible physically. One traveler called it the contrast of "the brown" and "the green." Northern China is the "brown land," with fertile plains, ferocious deserts, fearsome steppes. Rain comes mostly in July, but there can be dry spells of two or three years. In "the land of red-brown earth" and "red-brown houses" there are "red-brown crops," mostly grains. Southern China, south of the Yangtze, is the "green land," with mountains and valleys filled with forests and teafields, rice paddies, cypress, bamboo, so that one visitor wrote, "Mist, rain, and green fertility—that is southern China." No wonder Sir Robert Hart remarked, "China has the best food, rice; the best drink, tea; and the best clothing, silk." In a famous novel, Pearl S. Buck called China *The Good Earth,* fecund beyond belief.

In China live about one billion people, at least a quarter of the human family. Forty years ago it was but one-fifth. Within the not-so-distant future it may be one-half, for projections of 1.5 billion people in the early twenty-first century are probably not in error. Although the government of China has done much to encourage late marriage, family planning, and one-child families, China's population will grow—from the mere force of momentum—for decades to come. The inhabitants of China belong to the Mongolian (or yellow) branch of the human race. Chinese differ greatly in appearance, however, and as much physical variation can be found between northern and southern Chinese as between Swedes and Sicilians, Scots and Armenians. Cultural diversity is also evident in language, for the different dialects of China—Mandarin to the north, Cantonese to the south—are virtually separate tongues. Along with Spanish, Arabic, English, French, and Russian, Mandarin is a major world language.

As China differs from the United States in its population density and composition, so it also varies in terms of its history and economic development. Myths and legends surround the origins of China, and "divine emperors"—some half-human, half-demonic, all with supernatural wisdom and strength—are said to have set the stage for humans in East Asia. By 1500 B.C. an advanced civilization, comparable to anything in India, West Asia, or Europe, existed in North China. Great dynasties developed, and Chinese history came to be measured by them, as United States history is divided by presidencies and national elections. Sometimes the rulers came from the north and at other times from the south, and China also endured periods of rule from without—most notably by the Mongols (the Yüan Dynasty, 1271–1368). Living in relative isolation from Byzantium, Europe, and Islam, China came to regard itself as the center of the universe, the Middle Kingdom, an island of culture in an ocean of barbarism. Periodic overland invasions only confirmed this image. But eventually Europeans began to approach China over the ocean and by the nineteenth century China had faced or was having to face the British, the French, the Russians, and the Germans. During the Boxer Rebellion, at the beginning of the twentieth century, the Chinese had to fight off American influence; later the Japanese, now modernized, occupied China. These shocks set off the first Chinese revolution in 1911, and led to the overthrow of the empire and the founding of a republic. This first republic, a victim of two world wars, the Great Depression, and persistent threats from the Japanese, was replaced by the People's Republic of China, led by the Marxist Mao Tse-tung. Under Mao's leadership, China attempted to transform itself economically from an agricultural to an industrial society, and culturally from an imperial, traditional civilization to one dominated by the proletariat. Still very much of a Third-World country, China in the early 1980s is pursuing a more pragmatic, less ideological approach to her economic and political problems.

One observer recently remarked that India was intoxicated with religion whereas China was "dead sober with reality." The creativity of the Chinese spirit has lain in the realm of natural philosophy and social ethics, and the supernatural has usually been relegated to the realm of fairy tales and folklore. Thus, while Indian thought has been obsessed with the spiritual and the metaphysical, the concern of the Chinese has been with this world and the present moment. Later we will see how, in the teachings of Taoism and Confucianism, the Chinese have struggled to come to terms with the good life on this earth.

Japan

Recently I was traveling by train in Japan. Surprised to see so many Australians on board "the bullet," I finally asked one for an explanation. "To us from down under it's like going home to Britain—only not so far," he replied. My Japanese train ride was the final leg of a trip across the Old World from Canterbury to Kyoto, but it had not occurred to me to compare Japan and Britain.

Indeed, at first glance the two countries appear extremely different. They are at opposite ends of Eurasia; one is predominantly Mongolian, the other Caucasian. One is Altaic in speech, the other Indo-European. The heritage of one is Buddhist and Shintō, of the other predominantly Christian. I could continue to list the contrasts. But then the similarities begin to intrude upon our attention. Both Japan and Britain lie off the coast of Eurasia, Japan being an archipelago composed of more than five hundred islands, Great Britain, at least traditionally, made up of two large islands and many small ones. Although located in different latitudes and composed of different dimensions, both Japan and Britain share a similar orientation. Each nation is located between a great ocean and a great continent. Japan is situated between Asia and the Pacific, Britain between Europe and the Atlantic. Across significant seas both countries confront the mainland: Japan is separated from Asia by the East China Sea, Britain from Europe by the North Sea. Because of the maritime situation of each empire, both Japan and Britain are seagoing states, and both have impressive naval traditions.

Undoubtedly the topography of Japan is more rugged than that of Britain. Visitors often speak of the Japanese Alps, mighty snow-capped mountains, the most famous of which is Mount Fuji (12,388 feet). The green hills and fertile plains of both countries, however, are similar. Furthermore, because of the Gulf Stream in Britain and the Japan Current in Nippon, both empires share a somewhat similar range of climate. Both have a northland of snowy winters; both a southland of semitropical summer opulence. To visitors from other countries they present vast manicured gardens, often shrouded in fog and rain, then dazzled by the splendor of an afternoon sun.

It has been suggested that geography is destiny, and insularity has affected the history of both Japan and Britain. Both hold on to the tradition of kingship—although their near continental neighbors, France and China, have had radical revolutions. Japan's royal family traces its origins to antiquity. Mythology explains the arrival of the offspring of the sun goddess to become the initial emperor of Japan. Japan is still called Dai Nippon, Great Land of the Rising Sun; at one time it was a point of pride that the sun never set on the British Empire. An amazing continuity has characterized Japan's royal family; and Britain's institution of monarchy continues to be strong. It is significant that the notion of monarchy has survived and thrived in each nation even though various dynasties have occupied the throne.

Both Japan and Britain are populous kingdoms, although Japan's inhabitants outnumber those of Britain by about two to one (112 million as opposed to 55 million). Furthermore, the population of each monarchy differs in composition. Japan's inhabitants are relatively homogeneous (99 percent Japanese); Britain, since ancient times, has had a composite population. Celts, Romans, Anglo-Saxons, Scandinavians, and Norman-French have all contributed to the make-up of the British people. Since World War II large numbers of immigrants have arrived from the Third World, making Britain a multiracial and pluralistic society.

Today, both Japan and Britain are predominantly industrial. This is not to deny the existence of fishing, forestry, farming, and herding. Japan remains noted for its rice fields; before the Corn Laws of the nineteenth century Britain was farmed for wheat. Japan and Britain are now noted mostly for manufacturing. It is often said that Britain invented the Industrial Revolution in the eighteenth century, but Japan perfected it in the twentieth century. Both kingdoms are celebrated for textiles and automobiles, steel and utensils, machinery and technology. Both Britain and Japan rely on exports to earn capital to feed their vast populations. Japan enjoys economic prosperity and Britain confronts financial austerity, but the future for both countries is in industry.

These parallels in their historical pilgrimages bring yet another comparison to mind. Both Japan and Britain share a strong heritage of feudalism. Feudalism was introduced into Britain by William the Conqueror (1066); it flourished in Japan under the Fujiwara (858–1160). A strong sense of aristocracy survives in each kingdom, in spite of the rise of democracy. As a result of the feudalization of Britain and Japan, both states endured long civil wars. Britain emerged from her War of Roses to see the rise of a united England, Ireland, and Wales under the Tudors (1485–1603) and finally, in spite of civil war under the Stuarts, the union of Scotland with the rest of Britain as the United Kingdom. Japan, as a result of civil war (celebrated in the novel and the television series *Shōgun*), entered the Tokugawa Synthesis, a period of isolation lasting until 1854. It is significant that when Japan emerged from isolation, it was due to incentive provided by the United States, a child of Britain, and that Japan, although incorporating elements from many Western countries, most consciously imitated America and Britain. It was not strange, therefore, that when Britain ended a period of "splendid isolation" after the death of Victoria, she chose as her first ally, Japan.

Both Britain and Japan are more than the products of geography and history. In each society piety and morality have been major factors in national development. As Christianity entered Britain in the sixth and seventh centuries after Christ, so Buddhism, a faith born in India and nurtured in China, was introduced to Japan. Japan embraced this universal faith, seeking in it answers to ultimate questions. Concurrently, as a result of deliberate imitation of the Chinese court, Confucian and Taoist thought came to Japan. The advocacy of Buddhist metaphysics and Confucianist ethics, however, did not undermine Shintōism —"the way of the gods," the civil and cultic faith of the Japanese. How the Shintō tradition has survived, finding for itself a significant role in modern Japan, is a topic that will be explored in a subsequent chapter.

Hilaire Belloc once noted that "every major question in history is a religious question." How valid or universal that observation may be we will let others decide. What is evident is that Asia, the mother of man and of civilization, has also been the mother of faith. From west and east and south have come the belief systems by which most humans order their lives and contemplate eternity. Within the vast reaches of Asia great traditions have developed— Hinduism, Buddhism, Taoism, Confucianism, Shintōism, Islam, and Christianity. To these living religions of Asia we now turn our attention.

2

The Hindu Tradition

Herbert C. Wolf

Six hundred million people, most of them living in the Asian subcontinent of India, are called Hindus. The name is not one of their own choosing. It is derived from a foreign word used by ancient Indo-European invaders to designate the great river in the northwest section of the subcontinent. The word *sindhu* means "river," and from that word come derivatives such as the Persian *hindu*, Greek *indos*, and English *India*.

Few people in India and elsewhere think of themselves as Hindus. The word is used by others to designate an incredible variety of people and practices. The Hindu tradition is like a luxuriant jungle teeming with vitality and variety; it is like the bewildering maze of sculptures on the towering gateways of Indian temples. In India alone it speaks sixteen major languages and hundreds of dialects. It encompasses immense masses of pilgrims and solitary yogins in remote Himalayan caves. It includes secularized businessmen who seem to outdo their Western counterparts in commercial skills but who still make an annual pilgrimage to the Ganges. It is the religion of those who live outside village limits and were once known as untouchables because they perform the dirty, polluting tasks of society, like cleaning latrines and removing carcasses: Gandhi called them *harijans*, the children of God.

Some Hindus perpetuate obscure and repulsive practices from thousands of years ago. Animal sacrifice is still a part of the tradition, although technically forbidden by law. Once I saw a man walking in a trance, his naked body covered with purple ash, a butcher knife piercing his unbleeding, unfeeling cheeks. Anything in nature, like the sun, two intertwined trees, an anthill home of a cobra, may become a bearer of the holy. Hinduism is also taught by sophisticated philosophers who may make no reference to God, yet there are millions of gods and goddesses among ordinary people. One can be a good Hindu and never set foot in a temple. There are Hindus who have intense devotional love for a savior god who delivers them from bondage; they have no trouble incorporating Jesus among the incarnations of the supreme God. Others obey the ancient law, which prescribes in minute detail how one does what is right according to one's stage and place in life.

Hinduism has no creed, no criterion for doctrine, hence there is no distinction between truth and heresy. There is no hierarchy of bishops or general assembly of clergy and laity. There are no universally accepted rites, no official membership lists. There is no founder like Abraham or Jesus or Muhammad. There is no single ultimate reality like Yahweh or Allah. If you ask someone, "Are you a Hindu?" few would answer yes. It might be appropriate to say that anyone in India who does not reject the name is indeed a Hindu.

Yet with all of this rich multiplicity, something gives unity to this tradition. One scholar has suggested that religion is the substance of culture and that culture is the form of religion; they are together like the inside and outside of the same phenomenon. In no place is this more apparent than in India. We might call this the Hindu view of life.

The Hindu View of Life

Most religions thrive by telling stories that express their perception of their life experiences. Here are some Hindu versions.

A man was wandering at dusk through a beautiful forest, a peaceable kingdom. Gradually he began to realize that he was alone, that he was lost—and that the forest of beauty was becoming a forest of fear. Anxiously he started running for his life. Trees and vines reached down to grasp him, lions and tigers roared defiance. He smelled the breath of the god of death. Then he caught a vision of the divine mother waiting for him with open arms. As he raced toward her embrace, he tripped into a massive hole, an abyss with sweet-smelling jasmine vines at its mouth, but a foul-smelling odor rising from its depths. As he fell headlong into the pit, the vines caught his feet and suspended him, head downward. Beneath him a dragon awaited his fall; above him elephants trumpeted their potential victory. As he hung there, suspended upside down, his eyes became accustomed to the dark. He saw a beehive dripping with honey. Forgetting his plight, he reached out to enjoy the honey. "I'm alive!" he shouted. But he saw black and white rats gnawing away at the vines that entangled his feet and kept him from falling into the grasp of the monster beneath. "I'm alive!"—but his fall into the pit was inevitable.

Another story tells how the god Indra had slain a titan and all his forces, and was building a magnificent city appropriate for the victorious king of the gods. In a single year he built beautiful palaces, towers, lakes, and gardens. But he was not satisfied; this must be the greatest city of the gods. So he sought the aid of Brahma and Vishnu to enhance its splendor. One day a pilgrim boy appeared at the gate and inquired of Indra how he expected to build so great a city when no Indra before had done so. Indra was astonished at the question and asked, "How many Indras have you known?" No sooner had they spoken than a procession of ants four yards wide and extending as far as the eye could see marched in military precision across their path. "The secret that with an axe smites the tree of worldly vanity, hews away its roots, scatters its crown—the secret of all woes and wisdom—is hidden and revealed in these ants. Each of them was once an Indra," said the boy.

Yet another story reports that Narada and the god Vishnu were traveling at the edge of a desert. Suddenly the Lord Vishnu slumped down in the heat of the day. He gave his brass jug to Narada, and, pointing to an oasis in the distance, asked how long it might take to fetch some water. Narada replied confidently that it would take at the most half an hour. Across the desert he went. At the oasis he found a hut. His knock on the door was answered by a beautiful young woman with black hair and mysterious Vishnu-like eyes. Narada urgently asked for water to serve his lord. But the woman, observant of the tradition of hospitality, invited him into the house. Her parents appeared with food for the guest, and he, responding to their hospitality but worried about his task, ate gratefully. So satiated was he that he dozed off. When he awoke the next day he was angry. One voice within told him to take the water to Vishnu; another wanted to see the beautiful woman again. He stayed a week; he asked for her hand in marriage. The years passed; the couple had a son and then a daughter. Occasionally the voice within reminded him of the service owed his lord, but he did not heed it. His in-laws died and he inherited the house and the oasis. In the twelfth year the floods came and swept away the houses and the oasis, his children, and his beloved wife with the Vishnu-like eyes. Then he was swallowed up by the waters. But when he opened his eyes he was on dry land. His head was cradled in the lap of Vishnu, who smiled compassionately at him. "Where is the water you promised you would bring me?"

Like most myths, these stories have many levels of meaning, some of them ambivalent, even contradictory. The first suggests that the world is not what we imagine it to be; that ultimately one is trapped in a kind of catch-22. We eat, drink, and are merry. We follow the way of our ancestors and enjoy life as best we can under the circumstances. But tomorrow—or some day—we plunge into the depths. However, the story also raises in the hearer's mind the question whether there might be another way, a way of escape. The impossible might happen: one might be delivered from the ultimate peril and from the temporary pleasant respite—as well as from the illusory world of the peaceable kingdom.

The story about the parade of ants is less ambiguous. It clearly points out the vanity of human ambition, that pride goes before the fall. But it adds another dimension. Each of the ants was once an Indra. Many are the reincarnations which the self endures, from the most earthbound insect to the heavenly deities. Even the gods are subject to fall if they fail to perform their duty properly without attachment to rewards and glory. And hidden in the story are hints at unlimited earths and galaxies—so be forewarned.

The third story adds a further dimension. Instead of serving our God we get caught up in a life that is real, but not ultimately real: love, family, property, security, success. But when the floods come and destroy this world, we may find ourselves in the arms of the lord who smiles compassionately despite our failure to serve him.

The Hindu view of life arises from stories like these. Life is an infinity of times and spaces. Time is measured by a day in the life of Brahma. The creative imagination depicts one such day as the time it takes a bird flying over a Himalayan mountain once a century, brushing a bit of dirt with its wings, to reduce the mountain to a plain. Pundits describe it in almost geological terms: more than four trillion human years. One hundred years of 360 days and nights of Brahman constitute a lifetime of one Brahma. There are, moreover, innumerable Brahmas in innumerable coexisting galaxies. Each day of Brahma begins and ends with the evolution and dissolution of all things. The age of darkness in which we live in our universe is part of the last of the recurrent four ages which mercifully spiral downward in fewer years; but thousands of centuries still remain before its dissolution.

Time and space are like the cosmic ocean on which the god Vishnu sleeps—the ocean of *samsara,* the ocean that changes yet is always the same. Time is like an immense wheel, incessantly turning, with no beginning, no end, endlessly repeating its cycles of evolution and dissolution. Time is the goddess Kali, the great destroyer who is also the beautiful mother. It is the cosmic dancing god Siva, ceaselessly drumming worlds into existence and burning up all things while he remains aloof and impassive. This sense of the enormity of times and spaces perpetually evolving and dissolving is basic to the Hindu view of life.

What is true of the cosmos is true of everything within it. What Hindu sages said about ages and galaxies, ordinary people see in the recurring seasons of the year, the monthly phases of the moon, the incessant alternation of day and night. They assume that the highest mountains will some day be washed into the sea and new mountains arise out of the sea. Everything operates according to cosmic law or *dharma.* Despite the variety and multiplicity of appearances, all things are essentially one, for all things are subject to a single dharma. All things act in accordance with dharma, so that the cosmos and all within it function in an orderly way.

What is seen in the world of nature is experienced in the lives of people, birds and animals, insects, vegetables and fruits, and even what we call inanimate objects. Something—a life, a self, a soul—continues throughout innumerable universes and ages, passing from one body to another like a caterpillar interminably eating one leaf and moving to another, or like a person casting off

The great wheel representing
the endless cycle of evolution
and dissolution.

old clothes and putting on a new set, or like a sense of identity
running through the various phases of our lives from infancy to
old age. Each birth is really a rebirth, each death a redeath. There
is no beginning or end of the wheel of life; there is only a change in
the forms in which life is reincarnated. This too is a part of eternal
dharma, the eternal order that enables all things to function
harmoniously.

The form of life which one assumes in a particular existence is
determined by one's *karma*. Karma is the principle of cause and
effect, the doctrine that every action in existence has its consequences: no action goes unrewarded or unpunished. Every act is
the effect of a previous act and the cause of a new effect. Karma is
the burden we carry from one existence to another. Some actions
in past lives have already produced their effects in previous lives,
or they may be endured or enjoyed in this life. Others may not yet
have begun to produce their effects in this life or in future
existences. Karma is the principle that determines what one is. It
explains the universal variety in the world and in human existence. Some things are inanimate objects, others gods; some are

useful creatures like the cow, others unclean scavengers like a pig. Human beings are born unequal: intelligent and stupid, healthy and diseased, twice-born caste and outcaste, rich and poor. Millions of forms of existence are available, all dependent upon karma, how one lived in previous incarnations.

But karma implies opportunity, not just fate. As past deeds have ordained what one is, so present deeds will ordain what one becomes in future lives. One may progress from lower forms of existence to higher; from inanimate to animate, from animal to human, from one human form to another, from human to divine—or in the opposite direction. Throughout this great chain of rebirth, the self, the soul, the principle of life continues without memory or hope, always imprisoned in some new higher or lower form of existence. So while the law of karma may provide opportunity for progress, more often than not it means misery and bondage. Thus Indras returned as ants. In this age of darkness few live in such a way as to have a good karma. Life is more than a crushing burden. To exist means to go on living eternally in one form or another, always in accordance with one's karma.

But the Hindu view of life is that existence ultimately has an illusory quality about it. It is *maya*. The word refers to what a magician does when he creates an illusion before our eyes, what a politician promises when he seeks election. It refers to the honey we enjoy temporarily, the fascinating beauty of the woman whose eyes are like those of the divine Vishnu, or the futile magnificence of our power and creations. Philosophers quibble over the relative realness and illusory quality of existence, but the popular Hindu view of life is that it is not ultimately real.

Samsara, the sea of endless change, the crushing wheel of time; dharma, the cosmic law according to which all things evolve and dissolve without beginning and end; karma, the effects we carry from one life to another; and maya, the sense that all is ultimately vanity—these constitute the Hindu view of life.

The Hindu Way of Life

Most Hindus accept this view of life with a mixture of resignation and action. One cannot extricate oneself from the ocean of samsara; one cannot stop the world's wheel and get off. One learns to live with what is given. When one has innumerable lives to live, suffering and tragedy in one life are not final. One accepts one's place in society as what one has deserved. What appear to be injustices are not the actions of an unjust god or an arbitrary fate; they are one's just reward in accordance with the law of karma, which acts as impartially and harmoniously as the laws of the universe. I have seen people in India bear with incredible patience things which Westerners would strike out against. One seeks to perform one's dharma—one's particular duty—just as the sun and moon, gods and demons, birds and beasts of burden perform theirs. A water buffalo is not a cow; a demon ought not perform the good deeds of a god; a tenant farmer ought not try to govern. It is better to perform poorly one's own dharma, one's duty according to one's place in existence, than to do well the duty of another. The proper performance of one's own dharma in this life may possibly give pleasure and happiness now, but it is sure to lead to a better karma and a higher dharma in the next life. In this age of darkness society is given some stability by those who perform their appointed dharma patiently and with determination.

A second quality of lifestyle follows from these perceptions. It is *ahimsa;* negatively, it means doing no injury by word or deed to another; positively, it is having compassion for all things. If everything in the world has its own place and dharma, then everything, particularly everything living, is to be respected. Few Hindus go to the extreme of the Jains, who wear masks lest they accidentally inhale a gnat; but most will not knowingly harm other living creatures. Different styles of life and thought are accepted with remarkable tolerance. Live and let live is an apt response when everything is a part of the universal process, each having its karma from the past and its dharma to perform in the present.

For many Hindus, however, life and the unending series of lives have become a crushing burden from which to escape. Their ultimate concern in life is *moksha;* to transcend samsara and arrive at the other shore, to "eat up" their karma, or "to get off" the wheel of rebirth and redeath. Moksha means release, emancipation, escape, deliverance, liberation—as when a snake is freed from its old skin, or the arrow of the self is released from the bow.

It is liberation, not from sin, guilt, or death, but from embodied existence. It is release from bondage to recurring lives in time and space. You want to move beyond the maya-like, illusory quality of "reality." You want to enter the endless night of dreamless sleep, like Vishnu asleep on the ocean of samsara, beyond pain and pleasure, in absolute peace and quiet and darkness. The goal is liberation from time. And you have endless time to escape time.

The ways of moksha are many, but traditionally the Hindu community has spoken of three *margas* or paths to moksha, three *yogas* or disciplines of liberation: *karma marga*, the way of action; *jnana marga*, the way of knowledge; and *bhakti marga*, the way of devotion.

Karma Marga, the Way of Action

If any way may be considered "orthodox" in the Hindu tradition, it is the ancient way of the brahmins, the twice-born males of the highest caste—although it may be followed in varying degrees by others. It is karma marga, the way of action, or *karma yoga*, the discipline of action. Basically karma marga means performing one's dharma according to one's place in life. Certain duties are required of all people, such as ahimsa and abstention from alcohol and meat, but the specific dharma of each individual depends on that person's caste and stage in life.

First, karma marga is determined by one's caste. Hindu society is structured into four main communities: brahmins, who were traditionally teachers and priests; rulers and warriors, or what we would today call governmental leaders; craftsmen, agriculturalists, and merchants; and finally the servant or laboring caste. These four traditional castes are subdivided into thousands of subcastes, sometimes distinguished by what appear to be insignificant differences, potters who squat at their wheels and those who stand, fishermen who mend their nets from the right and those who mend their nets from the left.

Although these occupational distinctions are traditional and ideal rather than actual, they do illustrate the exchange of services and duties that is intended to produce a harmoniously functioning society. It is assumed—and clearly observed—that people are not equal. Some are "twice-born," with the status and, possibly, the personal characteristics of social and religious leaders. Often these are people of lighter skin, descendants of the Aryans who invaded the land millennia ago. They have special privileges and responsibilities, particularly if they are brahmins. At the opposite extreme are the outcastes, "untouchables," who perform the menial services of society and may, in the minds of some, exhibit the characteristics often associated with "lower" persons.

The chief ingredient of the caste system is purity. This refers not to individual or moral purity but to the need to preserve the solidarity of each particular caste vis-à-vis others. This is done by avoiding intermarriage and interdining (the two most intimate personal relationships) between castes: if possible one marries and eats only with those of one's own caste. But purity also refers to the avoidance of certain "unclean" or ritually polluting tasks by twice-born castes. By absorbing the pollution that comes from performing objectionable tasks, like cleaning latrines and gathering carcasses, sweepers and scavengers, for example, make it possible for brahmins to avoid defilement and preserve their caste purity. Brahmins are thus freed to be the teachers and priests of society.

The dharma of brahmins is the result of their knowledge of the Vedas, the ancient scriptures of the Aryans, and their access to the sacred formulas which elicited the powers of the universe, deities like Indra and Agni, the god of fire. Brahmins have what is called a triple debt to pay: to the gods by making sacrifice; to their ancestors by having sons to perpetuate the monthly ancestral rites; and to their teachers by learning the Vedas and reciting portions of them daily. *Kshatriyas*, the second caste, were the secular powers who enforced the dharma laid down by brahmins. It was they who provided protection to society, especially to brahmins with whom they share many privileges and responsibilities. The *vaishyas* are the bourgeois, the businessmen and farmers: often extremely wealthy people but generally treated as low caste by those above them. The *sudras* serve the twice-born castes. They may not recite or listen to the Vedas. They have no daily rites, are generally freed from dietary regulations, and have fewer restrictions placed on them. Females of all castes have a subservient role, which gives them their own dharma distinct from males in their own caste communities. In addition an estimated 15 percent of all Hindus, mostly of darker skin, are from the "excluded" castes. They are outcastes because of illegitimacy, crime, or their tasks which are considered unclean by the traditional castes: scavengers, workers in leather (the product of a cow), barbers (who remove polluting hair). In fact, caste persons often do not consider outcastes to be Hindus at all.

It should be recalled that karma marga according to caste is not to be considered unjust but an appropriate fulfilling of the law of karma. One is not a brahmin or a "carcass eater" because of one's birth; one is born such as a result of one's karma. The proper performance of one's own dharma in this life will make for a higher karma in the future. But one should work "without attachment" to such a goal. One does what is right because it is right—not because of a reward. The reward will be given, but it ought not be sought.

In addition to one's dharma according to caste, karma marga encompasses one's duty according to one's stage in life, again only for males of the twice-born castes. Each of the four stages in life has its own duties and privileges as well as its own rites of passage.

The first stage is that of the student or (as the Sanskrit word literally means) celibate. Brahmin males are initiated into this stage of life between the ages of eight and fourteen. The rite of passage by which they are born again as brahmins and become twice-born males is called thread investiture. Family and friends gather while the family's hereditary priest whispers into the boy's ear a specially chosen *mantra* or sacred utterance which he will use in his daily worship from that day on. The sacred thread of three strands of rope is looped over his right shoulder to be worn the rest of his life as a sign of his uniqueness, his yoke as a brahmin. In the past the student would go to live with his *guru*, his spiritual teacher and guide, study the Vedas, learn the fundamentals of ritual and conduct, and honor his guru with humble service. Obedience and celibacy are fundamental to the dharma of this stage in life.

Between the ages of twelve and twenty-four the twice-born male assumes the dharma of the second stage in life, that of a householder. This is the most important stage in life, for the family and caste are the basic economic and social structures of Hindu society. Marriage is arranged as a social contract by the families of those involved. Its goals are social, not personal: duty, not love, is basic.

Within this context the householder pursues the three ends or goals of life prescribed by the brahminical tradition. First, there is the particular dharma of a householder. This includes daily worship of his household deity, reading or reciting from the sacred texts, giving alms, and above all bringing sons into the world. His second goal is material success and prosperity in his occupation as a teacher, priest, businessman, government official, or whatever. The householder's third goal is sexual pleasure—not just having children, but experiencing the special joys that husband and wife share in their sexuality. The dharma of a householder involves disciplined participation in whatever is not forbidden in life which gives him pleasure—like Narada with his beautiful wife and family.

According to the Hindu tradition, however, even the household-er remains unfulfilled. He is all too aware of the burden of existence and yearns for deliverance. The final end of life is moksha. But moksha is not attainable for him. Even the one who follows karma marga perfectly as a householder fails to achieve release.

In the traditional Hindu way of life, therefore, there are two other stages in life besides those of the student and the house-holder. These lead more closely to moksha. When a householder sees his face wrinkled, his hair turning white, and enjoys the sons of his own sons, he may become a forest dweller, performing with his wife the disciplines and duties of that stage in life. Finally, he may become a renouncer, one who gives up his name, his sacred thread, his family and possessions to follow the dharma of a holy man—practicing austerities which lead to the destruction of the life of illusion.

Accompanying this way of duty is a karma marga of ritual action, again intended for twice-born males only. These include old Vedic rituals which are performed daily at dawn, for example, to greet the sun and prepare one's self for a new day. Complex rites of passage commemorate the crucial junctures of life when people are subject to evil forces or need beneficent ones: concep-tion, delivery, name giving, eating of the first solid food, initiation as a student, and marriage. Today the third stage in life is often accompanied by a renewal of wedding vows and a retirement ceremony. At the fourth stage the renunciant symbolically lies upon a funeral pyre, demonstrating ritually his dying to the old life and rising in a new. Among the most important rites of passage are the complicated cremation ceremonies and the monthly and annual commemorations of death intended to provide satisfaction to departing spirits and to protect those remaining in this life from haunting by unhappy spirits of the dead.

Despite its antiquity and brahminical authority, karma marga is a difficult and confusing way, with elaborate and often contradictory regulations. More importantly, it is limited to males of the twice-born castes. Although it is a marga intended to lead to moksha, it seldom succeeds in this dark age. Indeed, in such days it is often assumed that men are so inclined to disobey their dharma that, like the Indras, they descend to lower forms of existence rather than higher in subsequent embodiments.

Jnana Marga, the Way of Knowledge

For many centuries a second marga has existed alongside of karma marga. It is jnana marga, the way of knowledge, or *jnana yoga*, the discipline of knowledge. In contrast to the way of action, karma marga, with its prescribed duties for every occasion in life, jnana marga provides a philosophical and psychological way of knowing the self and the universe. Being, not doing, is the key to jnana marga. Most importantly, this way makes moksha possible in this life for its practitioners.

We have noted that in karma marga one's dharma is determined by who one is. Jnana marga in its most common form, the philosophy or teaching of Vedanta, also begins with who one is—however, not as a statement of fact, but as a question. Who am I, really? Am I the self that is identified as a member of a particular caste or class, sex, age, or stage in life? Is the true self the I that is related to the jungle of the world by my body with its desires, actions, and attachments to objects of desire? Is the self that which passes from one existence to another carrying with it the burden of karma? Karma marga says, *"neti, neti"*—the self is "not this, not that": not an individual with a name, color, caste, or identity—not a body.

Vedanta says that if we look more deeply we will find another self, the self in a kind of twilight zone of dreaming sleep where it creates its own inner world of fantastic delights and objects. Beyond this self is a third self that exists in a dreamless sleep with no awareness, no distinguishing of itself from other realities, yet very much there, unified and alive. Vedanta suggests by analogy that beyond this self is the true self, unaware, alive in the coming and going of the breath. This self is indescribable. It is like the silence and peace which are unheard but present as a fourth after the three-in-one syllable, *A-U-M*, of the sacred mantra is spoken. A-U-M. . . . That silence, unheard, unseen, is the true self. As the breath within is one with the air without, as a drop of water is swallowed up in the infinity of the ocean, as a pinch of salt flavors the whole container of water, as a flame is inseparable from the fire, so the self, *atman*, is one with Brahman. Brahman is the Absolute, the All. It is without attributes. It is the immensity that includes all things within itself, the principle of identity, the one without a second, the reality that alone is real—the ultimate. It is the silence out of which all arises and to which all returns. *Tat tvan asi:* "That you are."

We live, however, in ignorance. We confuse the self with identity, with individuality, or with the helpless passenger in a chariot driven by a mind unable to control the senses. But all of this, the false self and the world, is an illusion. We need to know what is really real.

Jnana marga, the way of knowledge, is possible only when one withdraws in silence from intercourse with the world and people, becomes an ascetic, and practices austerities. By yoga and medita-tion one learns to control the breath, the senses, the body, the mind, and the will. One yearns intensely for moksha, for deliver-ance from the false self and the world. Then suddenly it happens. Like a lightning flash illuminating the darkness, you see, experi-ence, become aware. You know the truth—that atman and Brah-man are one, that everything is one. As a tiger that has been raised as a tame goat roars when it discovers its real self, as a peasant suddenly awakens to find himself to be the lost son of a king, so one discovers the real self. Identification with the All is the highest bliss. With this experience you cease to be you, the individual, and become All. More accurately, you have discovered what you really were all along but had forgotten in the maya-like world of ignorance. Knowing All you have become All. You have obtained, you have experienced moksha—freedom from the bondage of time and space.

This way of experiential knowledge has produced some of the world's most sophisticated philosophical systems, some of which have been particularly attractive to Westerners who have turned away from the external world of action to an inner world of contemplation. These systems are all rooted in rigorous yogic discipline which moves from external control of the body and its desires to inner control of the mind and the will. The climax of the yogin's path is deep meditation and the experience of true selfhood. For some (e.g., Shankara) the experience is one of the unity of all things, philosophically described as the nonduality of self and universe, atman and Brahman. Others (e.g., Ramanuja) interpret the nonduality in a more qualified fashion as if to suggest that *tat* and *tvan*—that and you, Brahman and atman— become one in communion but remain dual. This philosophical interpretation opens up a way for a theological interpretation of the loving relation between a devotee and a divine being. Still others (e.g., Samkhya Yoga) interpret the experience as one of the independence or isolation of the true self from the illusory self of the body/mind organism. But whatever the interpretation, all attain moksha by rigorous discipline, meditation, and sudden enlightenment: experiential knowledge, jnana marga. They cross the ocean of samsara, they get off the wheel of time. They experience moksha, are freed even while embodied in a temporary organism; but from that they will soon be released also, never to be born again. Such is the bliss, *ananda*, of no-thingness, *nirvana*.

Jnana marga, the way of knowledge, however, is for the few. Most Hindus seek moksha by a third way, the way of devotion, bhakti marga.

Bhakti Marga, the Way of Devotion

A third way has become the most popular form of the Hindu tradition today. This is the way of devotion, bhakti marga. In contrast to karma marga with its detailed rules restricted to twice-born males, this path is easier, more spontaneous, and may be followed by persons of any caste, sex, or age. Bhakti marga, in fact, often deliberately transcends caste and other traditional barriers (although no social implications are derived from this). Both individuals and groups may participate. The guidance of a brahmin priest, although common, is not necessary. In contrast to jnana marga, bhakti allows human emotions and desires to flow freely rather than to be overcome by yogic asceticism. It sees reality not in terms of identity or unity, but as communion between the human and the divine. Whereas both karma marga and jnana marga can function without specific reference to god, bhakti consists exclusively of devotion to divine beings. According to jnana marga knowledge is experiential and intuitive; according to the bhakti tradition to know is to love.

The word *bhakti* means emotional attachment to one's chosen god. This attitude involves awe, fear, loyalty, and dependence upon a divine being who by nature is superior to the devotee. But the descriptive images most frequently used are those derived from more intimate human experience: a friend with another friend, a parent (usually a mother, seldom a father) and a child, a wife and her husband, and above all a woman and her lover. The central theme of bhakti is that of risking all to be with the beloved, surrendering to him, taking refuge in him, finding one's fulfillment in him. God is *Bhagavan*, the beloved.

Devotion to one's god—like all human love—can be of two kinds. One form is that of the surrender of one's self for the sake of something that is eagerly desired, like moksha, or temporal desires such as money, success, health, sons, revenge. This is the most popular form of Hindu religiosity—prayers and offerings, *puja*, made almost as a transaction, a bargain between the devotee and god: "I'll do this if you'll do that." A higher form of bhakti is love for god for his or her own sake. In this case the goal is personal communion with the divine, perfect surrender and intimacy. Such a devotee often becomes an enthusiast (*en-theos*, "filled with God"), overwhelmed with the sense of divine love to the point of receiving special gifts such as trances and visions. The ecstatic singing and dancing seen among the saffron-robed followers of Krishna on the streets of American cities celebrate this devotion. While some Hindu leaders commend this feeling of overwhelming bliss, others are apprehensive of being "blissed out." Among the followers of the way of devotion, however, the love of God is to be sought ideally for its own sake.

The bhakti tradition also speaks about the other side of the relation between the devotee and god: God responds to the approach of the devotee. The usual word for this is *prasada*, often translated by the word *grace*. The image is that of the devotee making offerings to God of food, flowers, rupees, fire, or incense which are received and blessed by God. What is "left over," prasada, is graciously returned, to be used by the devotee or for others' needs. But God's compassion may extend beyond the response to a devotee's invocations and offerings. God may graciously take the initiative and stoop down to the devotee. God's grace may be like that of a mother monkey who carries her child while the child cooperates by holding on. Or it may be like that of a mother cat who suddenly picks up her kitten and carries it wherever she wills. "Cat grace" is most popular among South Indian *bhaktas* as the symbol of the spontaneous, self-sufficient, electing grace of God and the passive, surrendering, trusting love of the devotee.

One learns the way of devotion from one's family, perhaps from the family priest; but more frequently it is discovered in movements centered in a charismatic leader who opens up the experience of divine love. Centuries ago poets or troubadours in royal courts sang about the heroic deeds of ancient warriors who found their way into legends as gods. There were wandering minstrels, often outcastes and occasionally women, who traveled from village to village creating and embellishing the folklore by song and dance. These past and present spiritual teachers and guides are called gurus. A guru is someone who has himself entered into communion with God and initiates others into the experience. He is often said to be greater than God because he leads you to God. Gurus are often worshiped as incarnations of gods by their devotees, like the gurus Shankara and Ramanuja in the past, or Gandhi or Sai Baba in more recent years.

The most difficult aspect of the bhakti tradition is not the tradition itself but the number of gods it embraces. It seems strange to us that much of what we have already said has been without reference to divine beings. This demanded that we expand our definition of religion sufficiently to include seeking for moksha apart from God—as in the karma marga and jnana marga traditions. Now we must broaden the definition in another way to take seriously the plurality of gods: 330 million is the traditional number.

The story is told of a person who asked his guru, "How many gods are there?"

Guru: 3,003. Or is it 3,000,003?
Devotee: Which is it?
Guru: 3.
Devotee: Is that correct?
Guru: There are 6.
Devotee: Is that so?
Guru: 3. Or is it 1½?
Devotee: How many gods are there, really?
Guru: 1!

A South Indian folk song puts it this way:

Into the bosom of the one great sea
Flow streams that come from hills on every side.
Their names are various as their springs
And thus in every land do men bow down
To one great God, though known by many names.[1]

Centuries ago the great philosopher Shankara made the distinction between higher knowledge, which senses intuitively that reality is nondual, and lower knowledge, which perceives reality to be of "qualified nonduality." The words *higher* and *lower* are not intended to be terms of valuation, but simply recognitions of the fact that people perceive reality differently—as Brahman which encompasses all, or as Brahman with whom each atman may commune. The All—the Godhead, as the medieval Western mystic Meister Eckhart called it—is without attributes, indescribable, absolute, the one without a second. It is "not-this/not-that," but simply *tat*—"that"—everything that a sweep of the hand and glance of the eye can encompass, and more. The transcendent absolute, however, has "another side," a personal side with attributes ascribed to it as if it were the highest Person: a name, power, wisdom, with identifiable symbols and myths. The many gods are approximations of this one God who symbolizes the fundamental nonduality. Anything can become a bearer of tat, for Oneness is revealed by plurality. The supreme Person is known by multiple incarnations and millions of names and forms; the supreme Person is also the symbol of the All—the God above the god above the gods:

[1]From a Tamil folk song.

1. tat, the All, Brahman without attributes
2. the supreme Person, Brahman with attributes
3. gods and incarnations

For the simple villager—and possibly for us who are not part of the tradition—such philosophical and religious sophistication is incomprehensible and of little practical value. People need help and love, someone to whom to pray and to sing, to care about and to show care for them. Because of their karma, or their caste or village, or because they have found that it works, most people have a favorite god to whom offerings are made, from whom boons are sought. All that matters is that God is my God, not the world's—or my neighbor's. Although some worship one god, they are usually tolerant and accepting of others; and most will be devoted to several. The complexity of life is such that one is not likely to find a god who can care for all needs or relate to all joys and tragedies. Some gods are more powerful than others; some are more able and ready to help; some are more easily placated, even manipulated. Some are cruel, even mad, as life often is. Some are gracious and loving. Many ancient gods, like those in the Vedas, are honored more in name than in deed. The high gods, like Vishnu, Krishna, and Siva, are more universal; but they are also more distant, concerned mostly about the great issues of life and death and moksha. The deities that are closest are the local gods who deal with immediate needs: fertility, avoiding the evil eye, success in a business venture or lawsuit, bringing rain, curing smallpox, sending vengeance on an enemy. Anything can be a bearer of power and a residing place of mystery: mountains, rivers, sacred trees and rocks, a crossing in a field or forest, an anthill from which a strange sound was once heard, two "married trees" whose differing branches intertwine in the image and praise of fertility. Two almost universal gods are Ganesh, the elephant-headed man who overcomes obstacles (like student examinations), and Hanuman, the young monkey-headed warrior who upholds and defends dharma. As we have noted, holy men, gurus, teachers, legendary saints of the past or present are often revered as divine beings. Even leaders and divine beings from other religions can be encompassed within the Hindu tradition as gods: Jesus, Allah, Moses, the Buddha. And there are antigods: demons who lurk in ancient battlefields and cremation grounds, deformed or barren women who become witches at night, vampires who suck blood from the bodies of warriors. In the words of the folk song, "Thus in every land do men bow down to one great God, though known by many names."

An additional problem for Westerners is the omnipresence of images, visual representations of the gods. For the ordinary Hindu the gods are not abstract or distant but concrete and present. The same Thatness without attributes which is symbolized in story and ritual as a great god or as an incarnation is also present in the image—so a fourth level should be added to the three forms of the divine just discussed: images. Sophisticated interpreters may say the image is "just a symbol" of the divine, but for the devotee the image is divine. It conveys power and grace.

One of the most universal forms of bhakti marga is that which focuses on Krishna, the black or blue god. Stories about him are many and varied. In the most famous of Hindu poems, *Bhagavad Gita, The Song of the Beloved,* Krishna is portrayed in a magnificent vision which is one of the greatest attempts of men to express the "two sides" of the experience of the holy. He is the *mysterium tremendum,* the awe-full majestic mystery, the holy, wholly other, who arouses feelings of creatureliness and impotence in those who experience his eternal power.

Narrator:

Hari [Krishna], the great Lord of Mystic Power,
Showed unto the son of Prtha [Arjuna]
   His supernal form as God:

Wearing marvelous garlands and garments,
   With marvelous perfumes and ointments,
Made up of all wonders, the god,
   Infinite, with faces in all directions.

Of a thousand suns in the sky
   If suddenly should burst forth
The light, it would be like
   Unto the light of that exalted one.

Then filled with amazement,
   His hair standing upright, Arjuna
Bowed with his head to the God,
   And said with a gesture of reverence:

Arjuna said:

I see the gods in Thy body, O God,
  All of them, and the hosts of various kinds of beings too,
Lord Brahma sitting on the lotus-seat,
  and the seers all, and the divine serpents.

Thou art the Imperishable, the supreme Object of Knowledge;
  Thou art the ultimate resting-place of this universe;
Thou art the immortal guardian of the eternal right,
  Thou art the everlasting Spirit, I hold.

Tell me, who art Thou, of awful form?
  Homage be to Thee; Best of Gods, be merciful!
I desire to understand Thee, the primal one;
  For I do not comprehend what Thou has set out to do.

The Blessed One Said:

I am Time [Death], cause of destruction of the worlds, matured
  And set out to gather in the worlds here.

Narrator:

Hearing these words of Krishna,
  Making a reverent gesture, trembling, Arjuna
Made obeisance and spoke yet again to Krishna,
  Stammering, greatly affrighted, bowing down.

Arjuna said:

Why should not all the hosts pay homage to Thee, Exalted One?
  Thou art greater even than Brahman; Thou art the First
  Creator;
O infinite Lord of Gods, in whom the world dwells,
  Thou the imperishable, existent, non-existent, and beyond
  both!

Homage be to Thee from in front and from behind,
  Homage be to Thee from all sides, Thou All!
O Thou of infinite might, Thy prowess is unmeasured;
  Thou attainest all; therefore Thou art All!

But the "other side" of the mysterium tremendum is also
apparent in the vision of Krishna: he is experienced as the
gracious god of love.

Arjuna said:

Bowing and prostrating my body,
  I beg grace of Thee, the Lord to be revered:
As a father to his son, as a friend to his friend,
  As a lover to his beloved, be pleased to show mercy, O God!

The Blessed One Said:

Have no perturbation, nor any state of bewilderment,
  Seeing this so awful form of Mine;
Dispel thy fear; let thy heart be of good cheer; again do thou
  Behold that other form of Mine!

The highest secret of all,
  My supreme message, hear.
Because thou art greatly loved of Me,
  Therefore I shall tell thee what is good for thee.

Be Me-minded, devoted to Me;
  Worshipping Me, revere Me;
And to Me alone shalt thou go; truly to thee
  I promise it—thou art dear to Me.[2]

This second very distinctive portrayal of Krishna is best seen in descriptions of him as the child and lover who has all of the qualities and elicits all of the emotions associated with such roles. As the child he plays mischievously and wildly, stealing butter, playing with his shadow, rolling in the dirt, playing pranks on his companions. He is the fluteplaying lover of incredible beauty, grace, and joy who, when the lotus is in full blossom on clear autumn nights, entices his lovers to abandon their responsibilities and dance with him in the forest. Sensuous love poetry describes the courtship of Krishna and Radha or others of his lovers. They fall in love at first sight, arrange to be introduced, meet in secrecy, dance and sing, love ecstatically; they quarrel, are jealous, forsake each other, and agonize over the separation. In many of the stories

---

[2]*The Bhagavad Gita,* trans. Franklin Edgerton, Oriental series (Cambridge, Mass.: Harvard University Press, 1972), pp. 56–60, 90 (edited slightly).

the themes of extramarital love are present: risking one's reputation and life if caught, the impossibility of a permanent relationship, brief moments of shared ecstasy, separation, and longing for reunion. These have become the most important subjects of Indian songs and poems, painting and sculpture, drama and dance. Devotees of Krishna in Madras, for example, participate in weekly and monthly celebrations of the stories about him and play the roles of the lovers, the go-betweens and servants, the friends and companions. Annually one of the great festivals (in addition to one celebrating the birthday of Krishna) re-enacts the marriage of Krishna and Radha, with images robed in magnificent costumes, jewelry, and flowers, with great processions and parades, wild dancing and singing throughout the night.

Westerners have as much of a problem understanding this aspect of the Hindu tradition as they do trying to interpret the Song of Solomon. The symbolism, however, is not obscure. God is free, spontaneous as a little child, unencumbered by rules or laws or the conventions of morality or justice. The world is his playground where he enjoys himself and invites his followers to share in the fun, not grovel before his might. He is approachable, with all the simplicity and grace of a happy child. His devotees need not fear him or postpone their love for him or experience of his presence until future lives. They share intimacy with him now. All the emotions and experiences of human love and sexuality are expressions of the relationship with him: putting him before all others, sharing the ecstasy of his love, becoming one with him. They are also jealous when he seems more interested in others, feel neglected and abandoned, experience his absence, yearn for his return. Human bondage to samsara and karma are forgotten in the ecstasy. Deliverance—moksha—is attained and even transcended in union with him.

In the pantheon of Hindu gods Krishna is often considered to be one of the incarnations of Vishnu. They are solar or savior gods who take it upon themselves to protect and deliver their devotees. Vishnu leaves the height ("zenith" is one meaning of his name) of his mountain abode and "pervades" (another meaning) the universe. As the *Gita* says,

For whenever of the right
  A languishing appears, son of Bharata,
A rising up of unright,
  Then I send Myself forth.

For protection of the good,
  And for destruction of evildoers,
To make a firm footing for the right,
  I come into being in age after age.[3]

The words suggest that anything good in the world is the work of
Vishnu; but traditional Vaishnavism interprets them as referring to
the *avataras*, incarnations, of Vishnu. Many of these are ancient
deities, heroes, or helpful animals which have been amalgamated
into the Vaishnavite tradition. They have little importance today
except as affirming Vishnu's saving power and as beautifully
carved images on Indian temples. But among them, in addition to
Krishna, is Rama. He is the heroic kshatriya (warrior) of the
Ramayana epic which is loved still today by people all throughout
South and Southeast Asia. Rama was the preferred deity of
Gandhi, who died reciting his name: Ram-Ram, Ram-Ram, Ram-
Ram.

Vishnu (like Krishna and Rama) is usually identified by the
symbols in his four hands: a discus (a sharp-edged weapon
thrown in battle to cut down the enemy, but also a symbol of the
sun), a conch shell (the Indian bugle to call armies to battle, but
also symbolic of the womb and water of life), a mace or battle-club,
and a lotus blossom (expressing the harmony of the universe
which Vishnu's power restores). He is often portrayed as riding on
the back of Garuda, a giant bird-man. (This is the name of the
official airline of Sri Lanka, Garuda Airways.) His feminine side is
expressed in various ways, most frequently by "golden-hued,
lotus-born" Lakshmi, the goddess of fertility, prosperity, and long
life.

The bhakti tradition associated with Siva stands in sharp
contrast to that of Vishnu/Krishna. The name *Siva* means "auspi-
cious," and that word suggests the distinctive mood of the Saivite
tradition. Even more than Krishna, Siva is a transcendent god, the
mysterium tremendum, the awe-full demanding, wrathful side of

[3]Ibid., p. 23.

the divine. He is a moon god, identified with darkness, night, and death, but also with life and reincarnation. On the one hand he is the destroyer of gods, of people, of evil, of universes. But the moon wanes only to wax again: Siva destroys in order to give life again. At the same time he is the god of life, symbolized by the *lingam* (an abstract erect phallus) or by the virile bull Nandi. Siva is the divine hermaphrodite—male on one side of the body, female on the other; and in him-her originate the universes and all that dwell in them.

In the face of the awesome power and mystery of Siva, his devotees often see themselves as poor miserable creatures, slaves to evil and carnal lusts. A Saivite hymn says,

Evil, all evil, my race, evil my qualities all;
Great am I only in defects, evil is even my good.
Evil my innermost self, foolish, avoiding the pure,
Beast I am not, yet the ways of the beast I never forsake.
I can exhort with strong words, telling men what they should
    hate,
Yet I can never give gifts, only to beg them I know.
Wretched man that I am, why was I born?

To rectify themselves Siva's devotees often practice the most extreme austerities, expressing their unworthiness before the Wholly Other by extreme fasts, meditating naked in the snow, smearing ashes and dung on their bodies, inflicting wounds on themselves, lying on beds of barbed wire or nails—deliberately doing those things that are both punitive and unclean.

But this awesomeness of Siva is only one part of the portrayal. A second is that he is gracious. He is "the thief who stole my heart away," who by sudden appearances (symbolized in some images by a deer) saves his devotees from danger and worldly distractions. He is the protector who is bound to give his devotees whatever boons they ask of him. It is he who traditionally lets the Ganges flow through his matted hair so that as the melting snows cascade down the Himalayas in spring they are reduced to a gentle flow irrigating the plains instead of destroying them in floods. Another Saivite hymn says,

Thou gavest thyself, thou gainest me,
Which did the better bargain drive?

Bliss I found in infinity;
But what didst thou from me derive?
O Siva, Perundurai's God,
My mind thou tookest for thy shrine,
My very body's thine abode;
What can I give thee, Lord of mine?

Siva is also the perfect yogin, the true renunciant, withdrawn into the isolation of a cave in the Himalayas, practicing his austerities in patient rejection of the world of passion and pain. But he is always virile, storing up his seed for procreation when it is needed.

These three characteristics of Siva are symbolized in the most famous artistic creation from India, that of Nataraja, the Lord of the Dance. It is Siva, perpetually performing the frenzied dance of life and death. One hand holds a drum of male and female symbols and shaped like an hourglass, beating the rhythms of creation and productive energy. Another hand holds a tongue of flame to destroy the universes so that new ones may be brought into existence. A third hand is raised in blessing, "Fear not"; and a fourth points downward to the dwarf demon of forgetfulness under his foot. His body and pieces of jewelry show both male and female elements. Serpentine energy coils about his waist. The third eye of enlightenment is open in the center of his forehead; but his face is indifferent, unmoved by the destruction and creation he is bringing about by his dance. He alone abides with a ring of flames surrounding his body.

The third of the major bhakti traditions is that of the Goddess. Like Vishnu/Krishna and Siva, she is known by thousands of names reflecting an amalgam of stories and images past and present. Three aspects of the Goddess may be noted.

First, the goddess is creative energy—*shakti;* and by that word she is often known as the shakti or wife of Siva. In this role she is also called Parvati, Sati, or Uma. Her image is sensuous and sexual; it is she who arouses the inert ascetic god for the fertile union so avidly desired by families, farmers, and herdsmen. Their creativity is often symbolized by a male lingam with a stylized female *yoni* or sexual organs. Parvati is also the divine mother who nurses the world from her full breasts and devotedly cares for her children.

But a more malevolent aspect of life is seen in the goddess. She

Nataraja, Dancing Shiva, Tamilnadu, Chola Dynasty, tenth century.

is also the goddess of epidemic disease (e.g., Shitala, the goddess of smallpox). Westerners learned about her during an epidemic of smallpox in northern India in 1974, when fifteen thousand children died and many times that were disfigured for life. "Don't you understand," a woman said to a doctor who attempted to inoculate her child, "nature is taking its own course. Why do you fight against nature?" The goddess symbolized nature taking its course in its own mysterious way. The horrible reality of an epidemic is an awesome thing: it suddenly sweeps into a village, arbitrarily attacks some and ignores others, disfigures some and kills others, and as suddenly disappears. To some it is the wrath of the goddess which causes the diseases. She must be propitiated so that her anger might be averted or directed toward someone else. The ways of the divine may not be understood, but they may be altered by prayer and sacrifice. Others see the same things a bit differently. Since the name of the goddess is the name of the disease, she is herself suffering from it. Pouring water over her image cools her just as the same action relieves the feverish child. Such a child must be particularly and peculiarly blessed because it is possessed by the disease and hence by the mysterious goddess herself. So the child is not a victim but a sacred person. Still others see the goddess as suffering for the sake of her devotees, taking their place by enduring the pain and disfigurement.

If this Job-like wrestling with the mystery of suffering puzzles us, even more difficult to understand is the goddess Kali, the black goddess, known also as Maha-Kali, the great goddess of time. Her iconography shows her as an ugly old woman, her naked body deformed, her eyes bulging with rage, her tongue protruding grotesquely. She wears a garland of skulls; severed hands hang on a belt like a bloody skirt. One hand holds a cup made of a human skull filled with blood she is drinking. Another hand holds a rosary and prayer book, and a third is in the gesture which tells her devotees not to fear. She is often portrayed as standing or crouching over the prostrate corpse-like male (Siva), trying to arouse him. Some more complex paintings also show them in ecstatic intercourse.

More than any other image, Kali shows what life is really like: a beautiful young mother who has become ugly and gone mad. The beauty, wonder, and pleasure of life are an illusion, a false reality—they do not last. Desire, pleasure, suffering, pain, love— all end in death. Such is life. Time destroys everything. Only by meditating on the finality of death can one see beyond it. Face death, contemplate it, endure it—only then can you escape it. Life is maya, an illusion, and Kali reminds us of that. But she is also creative of a new reality beyond the ocean of samsara. Moksha, deliverance, is possible by transcending this illusory world and crossing to the other side. So Kali's devotees subject themselves to the trials of self-mutilation and walking through flaming fire, enduring no injury, feeling no pain because of their faith in her power to deliver. The fires of cremation will finally purge the illusion of this life and out of the ashes freedom will arise.

Rituals

We have noted earlier that the instrumentality for binding the relationship between deity and devotee is called puja or ritual. In India most of life is ritualized: eating, bathing, making love, or arranging a marriage or a business transaction. Ritual in itself is considered efficacious—it need not be understood nor should symbolic meanings be sought. Doing the ritual, and doing it correctly, is the important thing. Proper performance restores order and blessing to life. Behind this is the conviction that the gods also have their ritual tasks to perform: eating, sleeping, marrying, aiding their devotees, receiving offerings. Ritual unites the worlds of deities and devotees into a single whole.

Because preparation is essential to all ritual action, purification takes place before a devotee approaches the deity. This usually involves pouring water over one's head and body, or partial or complete bathing in flowing river water or in a large temple tank. Fresh clothes, often of silk, may be put on, and sacred markings of sandalwood, turmeric, or colored powder applied to the forehead and body. Sandals are removed and women cover their heads. The devotees place the palms of the hands together under their bowed heads and reverently salute the deity; or they may touch their foreheads to the ground or prostrate themselves completely before the god. During all of this mantras—sacred sounds (AUM, Krim, Hrim, Klim, Shrim)—and chants are spoken or meditated upon to establish harmony between the self and the higher vibrations of the deity. The name of God may be repeated over and over again. Other actions may be observed: fasting, breath control, sprinkling water or ghee (melted butter) or coconut milk, circumambulating the sacred image, waving a fire or incense offering—these are a few of the many ways to purify one's self for entry into the presence.

The sacred centers where the ritualized life of the gods and humans is carried out are essentially three: the home, the temple, and the pilgrimage site. In both karma marga and bhakti marga the primary locus is the home. Every Hindu has a home shrine for his or her chosen deity. It may be a small section of the wall in a one-room hut, with a faded lithograph or scratched or painted sketch of the deity and a shelf for a small oil lamp and a brass cup. Or it may be a special shrine room with one wall covered with elaborately carved wooden cabinets inlaid with silver and gold and precious stones, with highly artistic images, hand-copied sacred scriptures, and expensive ritual paraphernalia. The deity is treated as a guest in the house, and all the traditional amenities of hospitality are followed. Each day the householder, assisted by his wife, welcomes the royal guest. He is awakened, bathed, given fresh clothing and water, offered sacred fruit and flowers, incense, and light. Scriptures are recited or read, prayers and chants spoken. The morning meal which will be eaten by the family is first offered to the god for blessing and then received as sacramental prasada or grace. Members of the family may subsequently make their own offerings at the shrine of their own chosen deity, another royal guest in their home.

The temple, on the other hand, is the home of the deity, the

This Hindu girl is worshiping at the family shrine in her home.

palace of royalty, so rituals appropriate for such personages are conducted there. Temple puja—often conducted at multiple shrines within the temple compound—is household puja writ large. Throughout the day and night priests of varying ranks perform complex rituals of bathing, anointing with milk and curds, and clothing the image—often much larger than life-sized, but sometimes very small—in magnificent clothes and jewels and flowers. They entertain the image with music and dance. Devotees give offerings to the priests, who in turn offer them to the deity, giving the name, lineage, astrological sign, and request of the worshiper. The devotee receives the blessed food and perhaps breathes into his or her own body the divine power in the small flame held by the priest. The devotee may also put some colored powder on the head of the deity and then on his own forehead as a sign of devotion.

On sacred days each month portable images are taken in procession from the temple in a palanquin carried on the shoulders of a team of priests or on the back of an elephant. On very special occasions, like the annual marriage celebration of the god or to break a drought, mammoth wooden cars that are more than one hundred feet tall may be dragged through the streets by thousands of men. During festivals the divine rulers may be taken hunting, bathed in the river, or brought to a birthday celebration while enormous crowds throw firecrackers, shoot colored water at each other, and get caught up in the frenzied emotion and revelry of sound and sight. Holy days become holidays; the monotony of daily life is broken. The normal order of caste and dharma is temporarily disrupted by a higher order—the celebration of the harmony of gods and humans and of the world as it was before the present dark age.

It should be noted in passing, however, that temple puja is seldom thought of as a congregational or corporate act; each devotee brings his or her individual offering and participates as a person in the festive occasions but without a commonly-shared ritual.

The third locus for ritual action is pilgrimage places—sacred centers which horizontally gather up the power around them and vertically reach beyond time and space. There are literally thousands of such places, many of them known only to obscure villagers. The most famous of them are usually at places of running water—river sources, banks, confluences, deltas, and coastal sites. Others are hill or mountain sites or *ashrams* (spiritual communities centering around a guru). They may be associated with any of the major or minor deities. Some originated in the unknown past, others are of more recent discovery, and new ones can evolve.

The greatest of all such centers is the whole city of Benares, Siva's home on the Ganges. Every Hindu yearns to make pilgrimage at least once to Benares. Other pilgrimage places enable the devotee to accumulate merit, to identify with the sacred power and presence of God, to make offerings and seek boons. But to bathe in the Ganges is to remove the stain from a lifetime's pollution. To sip the water of the Ganges is to sip the elixir of life. To set flowers afloat on the Ganges is to set one's self in the direction of "the opposite shore." And to die in Benares and be cremated at the Ganges and have one's ashes sprinkled on the sacred river is to "eat up one's karma," to escape from maya, to get off the wheel of death and rebirth, to cross the ocean of samsara, to receive moksha.

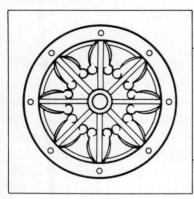

3

The Buddhist Tradition

Eugene R. Swanger

In contrast to most of the early religious traditions, Buddhism has a founder known as Siddhartha Gautama, Gautama Buddha, or Shakyamuni, and it is clear that he had a decisive impact on the nature of the tradition. It is difficult, however, to recover the historical figure. This is so for several reasons.

Following Siddhartha Gautama's death in 483 B.C., his teachings were conveyed orally for a century and a half. By the time they were put into writing, several versions of his message had developed and been institutionalized as sects or schools. Thus the earliest Buddhist scriptures reflect different positions and do not always suggest a single viewpoint. The earliest writings now in existence, furthermore, were composed no fewer than five hundred years after Gautama's death. When the scriptures were composed, inordinate praise colored the memory of the founder. For example, in the birth narrative the child comes forth from his mother while she is standing up and holding on to the branch of a sacred sal tree. He is completely free of any afterbirth and is immediately able to walk and talk. He takes seven steps in each of the cardinal directions and proclaims himself ruler of the universe.

Certainly the recovery of the historical Siddhartha Gautama is a difficult task and at best can be only partially successful. Nevertheless one can read the *Acts of the Buddha*, written by Asvaghosa in the first century A.D., and reach a few conclusions about the historical figure and his teaching with some degree of certainty. Here, as elsewhere, caution is the rule.

Buddha's Life

Siddhartha Gautama was born about 560 B.C., the son of a prince of the Shakya clan in northeastern India. His father was the ruler of a town named Kapilavastu, which might have been located near the present southern border of Nepal, although its remains have never been located. His clan was of the warrior or *kshatriya* caste, the second highest caste in the Indian social structure. Shakyamuni (Sage of the Shakyas) probably grew up in relative comfort and security. The scriptures state that his father gave him three palaces and forty thousand dancing girls. Behind these stories lie several facts: his father's interest in the affairs of this life, Siddhartha Gautama's early interest in earthly pleasures, and his father's possession of some degree of political and economic power.

According to the birth narrative, Shakyamuni was never to be allowed to see sickness, aging, or death, for his life was crossed by a double star: either he would someday become a great world conqueror or he would choose a religious vocation, becoming a monk. To steer him toward worldly success, his father made every effort to see that his son matured in an environment completely free of any suggestion of human suffering.

The attempt failed. In his late twenties Siddhartha Gautama became totally aware that every human being will grow old (unless tragedy strikes early), become sick, and die. Again, according to the Buddhist scriptures, on various outings and in spite of his overprotective father Shakyamuni saw an aged person, weak, palsied, and barely able to ambulate; a diseased person; and a corpse. Stricken and dismayed at the presence of so much suffering and death in the world, he also saw a religious mendicant during a fourth outing. This figure suggested the possibility of release from the dilemma of existence.

At this point, Shakyamuni made the decision to leave his wife and son and the comfort and security of his home to assume the role of the wandering seeker. Six difficult years followed during which he studied meditation and philosophy under several masters. Shakyamuni mastered and taught several meditative techniques but his dissatisfaction continued, for he found that each of these meditational practices yielded no release from the universal experience of suffering, decay, and death. Then he turned from this path to join a group of ascetics.

Siddhartha Gautama fasted, reducing his diet to the point that he was existing on a single bean a day. He gave up cleansing his body until the dirt was so thick that it would fall from his body of its own weight. He practiced holding his breath until it felt as though someone were forcing a heated sword through his skull. Other austerities were practiced at the same time, but all to no avail. In none of them did Shakyamuni find release.

He then remembered that as a child he had known a state of happiness free from sensual desires and negative or destructive thoughts. Happiness itself, he concluded, was not part of the problem facing human beings. He also began to suspect that being healthy is necessary for the successful religious quest. These two elements eventually became central to his teachings, which his followers named The Middle Way. One ought to engage in a rational lifestyle, giving the body enough to maintain its health, neither too much (his early life with his father) nor too little (his years with the ascetics). One could reject the extremes of sensual indulgence and mortification of the flesh and be healthy and happy. This became the foundation of the Buddhist religious quest. On this foundation he established his meditative practices.

According to the Buddhist records, five successive dreams informed Siddhartha Gautama that through meditation he was about to burst the bubble of ignorance and become a Buddha, that is, a being awakened to the true reality that lies beneath the eternal round of decay, suffering, and death. At the time of the full moon in May he sat down under a sacred tree facing east. There he successively entered the four stages of meditation: calming the passions and detaching his senses from sights and sounds; focusing his mind serenely, confident of success; achieving an alert, conscious mind and blissful body; and, transcending the polarities of pleasure and pain, good and bad, desire and aversion. By midnight the focal length of his mind had adjusted to the point where the entire universe appeared to him as a mirror. Toward dawn, his consciousness expanding and penetrating ever deeper, Siddhartha Gautama gained the certainty that "in me emancipated arose knowledge of my emancipation. I realized that rebirth has been destroyed, the holy life has been lived, the job has been done, there is nothing after this."[1] Ignorance about this existence and attachment to some dimension of it had been burned away. He was free at last.

The great awakening had occurred. Siddhartha Gautama's mind had been transformed and he emerged the Buddha. The Buddhist scriptures state that he remained seated beneath the sacred tree for seven weeks in a state of bliss. Following his forty-nine days of rapture Siddhartha Gautama appears to have struggled with the question of whether or not to say anything about his new and radical insight into reality. Perhaps it was the question of whether or not his experience could be cast into language, whether it might so transcend the understanding of ordinary persons as to seem bizarre, if not irrational.

Nevertheless he felt a calling in the sense that he recognized a need, the common misery and hopelessness of most people, and knew that he had the ability to meet that need. So he left his place beneath the fig tree and journeyed almost one hundred miles to Sarnath where he met the five ascetics with whom he had shared many austerities during his years of seeking. There, in a place called the Deer Park, he first presented the cornerstone—"the Four Noble Truths"—of what Europeans later would call Buddhism, or the Buddhist tradition.

Buddha's Teachings

The first of the fundamental observations declares that all of life is *dukkha*. The term literally means "a bone twisted out of its joint." Every dimension of life is saturated with pain. Most people live with the illusion that life without pain is possible, if not now, then this evening or this weekend or after school is out or after one retires. Siddhartha Gautama asserted, on the other hand, that life without pain is a contradiction in terms, that suffering is indeed a necessary aspect of all sentient experience. No person can escape suffering.

There is the pain of birth. Arthur Janov (*The Primal Scream*) was not the first person to recognize the trauma the child experiences

---

[1]Henry Clarke Warren, *Buddhism in Translations* (Cambridge, Mass.: Harvard University Press, 1896), pp. 380–81.

Todaiji Temple Buddha at Nara.

in being born. Psychotherapists have long been aware that the pain of birth can sometimes be severe enough to leave an individual listing for life like a badly launched ship. There is also the pain of growth, especially adolescence. How many are there who would like to repeat the seventh grade? There is the pain of aging, made greater by the fear of becoming increasingly dependent upon others for the most elemental personal needs. There is the fear of dying, which Swiss psychiatrist Carl Jung called the root fear in anyone more than forty years old. There is the pain of being joined to something for which one feels an aversion, perhaps even hatred: a job which fills one with boredom or anxiety, yet provides little or no sense of reward; there is the pain of an incurable disease; there is the pain of a destructive disease such as alcoholism. What is more, pain arises from being separated from what one loves: a friend, a child, a family, a place, a time.

According to the Four Noble Truths, most people suffer pain

most of the time. Only the degree of suffering changes—from low-level anxiety to grief to raw physical pain. Most people try to cope with their pain by living with the dream that soon life will become pleasurable. This, however, is a great illusion, for the pleasures of life are few, superficial, and ephemeral. They are not substantial and they do not compensate for the pain we all experience.

From a Western point of view a life in which the pleasures are mostly empty promises and the pain of living is constant might be tolerable, because it is assumed by our culture that a person lives only once. An opposing assumption, however, permeated the Indian perception: one is reborn into this life countless times. Each person is subject to the pain of birth, maturation, aging, and dying not once, but for an eternity. Thus the suffering that penetrates all dimensions of existence is a burden indeed.

What is the cause of this pain? The pain, according to Shakyamuni, has a double root: one cause is our ignorance (avidya) of the true nature of reality and the other is our attachment (tanha) to some aspect of this existence.

Avidya is an active rather than a passive characteristic of a person. It is the attribution of enduring meaning and value to that which is only momentary and ephemeral, which is characteristic of all phenomena in this life: objects, institutions, nations, languages, ideas, ideals and, of course, one's own self and that of others. We attribute reality and, therefore, some degree of ongoing significance to an institution, a program, a project, a career, a skill, a family, a child, or our own ego. Everything, however, in this life is subject to time. It begins in time. It is in a constant process of change from growth to maturation to aging, decay, and death. Because all phenomena within this existence are subject to time, they have no meaning, significance, or reality in any final or ultimate sense. We assign reality to them and in so doing we cling to them.

We are like people watching a movie, engrossed in the story. Perhaps we see a woman reading beside a fire in an upstairs room of a large old house. She is oblivious to the presence of a mentally deranged murderer who has started up the stairway. As we attribute reality to the play of shadow and light and image upon the screen, we become caught up in that which is essentially unreal. We begin gripping more tightly the arms of our seats. Our breathing becomes shorter. Perhaps the palms of our hands begin to perspire. We are attaching (tanha) ourselves to the insubstantial images and, as we do so, we become anxious (dukkha).

To be sure, life is filled with little meanings from the Buddhist point of view. Commitment to a child, a career, the furtherance of an ideal can give meaning to one's life. For a time this commitment can make one's life seem worthwhile and occasionally enjoyable. The child, however, grows up and leaves home. Age or some other condition such as a stroke forces retirement. Ideals become distorted, compromised, or otherwise defeated. If a person has attached himself to one of these transitory phenomena, that is, if in any way the child, career, or ideal has become the center of his being, he will suffer as the changes and finally the loss occur.

The core act of avidya is the attribution of reality or substantiality to our own ego. From Siddhartha Gautama's point of view we have no enduring core. Behind the "I" is nothing more than a whirl of energies, memories, thoughts, aspirations, hopes, anxieties, and fears. As the multiple images of fire on a twirling baton are perceived to be a wheel of fire, so a person perceives a substantial self behind the activities of the mind and senses. Thus the ego itself is a fiction.

The fictitious self, however, clings to itself. This momentary center of a transitory consciousness not only attaches to other phenomena, but also takes itself with utmost seriousness. This egocentric act is the underlying cause of all greed, anger, hatred, alienation, and aversion, as well as the destructive social behaviors that arise from them. Thus the act of ignorance produces clinging and from clinging arises the pain that is common to the human condition.

Although at first it appears that Siddhartha Gautama made an extremely pessimistic evaluation of the human plight, nevertheless a basic optimism pervades his message. For, although the first Noble Truth states the symptoms (all people suffer) and the second states the cause (ignorance and attachment), the third truth suggests that a way exists out of this dilemma. In other words, while the patient suffers greatly and his suffering is caused by his ignorance and attachments, the prognosis is good. The patient can recover. The fourth of the Four Noble Truths presents the prescription, the Eightfold Path, the first of what came to be a wide range of solutions to the dilemma of existence as perceived within the Buddhist tradition.

This course of treatment has eight parts, which are not successive steps but are to be carried out simultaneously. They are the belief that the Four Noble Truths are accurate and reliable statements; a total commitment of body, mind, and will to the training and discipline required to extricate oneself from the human predicament; a careful and reflective watching of what one says to others: one's words must be not only charitable but also free from egocentricity; a beneficent behavior extended universally to all living things coupled with an abstinence from alcohol and drugs, for a person must have complete control over his mind to accomplish the difficult task of redemption; a proper means of support, that is, a livelihood in which a person does not inflict pain on other people or creatures; an effort of the will which reaches deep inside oneself to draw upon all the energy a person possesses; a close attention to one's mood, emotions, and feelings, for as the *Dhammapada* puts it, "All we are is the result of what we have thought"; and the practice of meditation in which "in the fierce combustion of immediate awareness, thought itself . . . [is] annihilated" and "the mind rests."[2]

This state of enlightenment in the early or southern Buddhist traditions is called *Nirvana*. The word is an intransitive verb and means "to gutter out." That is, when enlightenment or the root religious experience occurs, ignorance and attachment are consumed and the flame of egocentricity ceases to burn. The person is free from the anxieties and fears that beset ordinary people; he is released from the eternal round of decay, suffering, and death. The passions, worries, and happenings of the world no longer threaten him, for the boundaries of the finite self have been burned away. Never again will he be reborn into *samsara*. Eternal bliss is his.

Early Western scholars thought that the term *Nirvana* implied annihilation and some concluded that the Buddhist tradition is essentially pessimistic and life-denying.[3] Subsequent study, however, has shown that the Buddhist faith clearly affirms that human

---

[2]*The Dhammapada*, trans. Irving Babbitt (New York: New Directions, 1936), p. 3.
[3]See, for example, Albert Schweitzer, *Indian Thought and Its Development* (Boston: Beacon, 1936).

beings do have a destiny that transcends this realm of suffering. The Buddhist scriptures report Siddhartha Gautama as saying, "There is, O monks, an Unborn, neither become nor created nor formed. . . . Were there not there would be no deliverance from the born, the made, the compounded."[4] This statement strongly affirms that human beings can expect deliverance from this realm of suffering because the ineffable makes it possible. The ultimate is incomprehensible, hidden, and essentially unknowable, but one can be as certain of both its existence and its beneficence as one can be certain of the existence of the wind. It offers eternal bliss, happiness, and unassailable refuge to the weary sufferer.

Furthermore, the charge that the Buddhist traditions are life-denying and escapist overlooks the long history Buddhists have had in education, medicine, and public works. Almost from their beginning Buddhists have been known for founding schools from the elementary level to great learning centers, for establishing hospitals and hospices, for providing food, medicine, and clothing for the poor, and more recently in countries from Japan to Sri Lanka for sponsoring social legislation to assist the lower classes. While they yearn for a home beyond this realm of suffering, they do not neglect those caught in the net of pain.

Buddhist Schools

Siddhartha Gautama died in 483 B.C., and within a generation different views of his teachings emerged. Today the Buddhist heritage is composed of two major schools, the Theravada and the Mahayana. The former is found in Burma, Thailand, and Sri Lanka. Until very recently it was also the religious heritage of the people of Laos and Kampuchea, but its existence in these two countries is now in doubt because of the recent wars. Its name, Theravada, which means literally "the way of the elders," implies that it embodies the Buddhist tradition in its oldest form. With qualifications this is a generally correct implication.

The Mahayana tradition, on the other hand, is located in eastern Asia: Japan, Korea, China, and Vietnam. This tradition appeared in northwestern India as late as four hundred years after Gautama's death. Adopting the name *Mahayana* (Great Raft;

4James B. Pratt, *The Pilgrimage of Buddhism* (New York: Macmillan, 1928), p. 113.

for crossing the sea of suffering), it saw itself providing a broader range of means for emancipation from samsara than the older Theravada tradition, which it denigrated by the name *Hinayana* (Little Raft). Because the name *Hinayana* is an aspersive word, one should avoid its use.

In contrast to the reserved, sober, and pragmatic tone of the South Asian Buddhist tradition, the Mahayana Buddhists show an exhuberant openness to the creative power of the imagination. They trust the validity of the religious imagination and warmly embrace a wide range of speculation about the nature of the sacred and the plight of the human condition.

While it is true that many of the Mahayana teachings are modifications and amplifications of themes already present in the Theravadin heritage, nevertheless there are important differences. The two traditions have contrasting points of view regarding the person of Siddhartha Gautama, the means by which one can be freed from samsara, the canon, the reality of the world, and the cultic ways of the *bodhisattvas*.

The Theravadin Buddhists believe Siddhartha Gautama was a superior—even a heroic—person but nevertheless only a man. Within the Mahayana communities, on the other hand, Shakya-muni is not seen as merely a human being. Rather he is under stood to have been and to be a manifestation of the Absolute. Like Docetist Christians in the West, who viewed Christ as a man in appearance only, Mahayana Buddhists see Gautama as essentially sacred. His physical body and activity such as eating and sleeping were only illusions.

In the Theravadin communities of South Asia redemption from samsara, the eternal round of rebirths in this vale of suffering, is essentially dependent upon one's own effort. At some point the individual must make the decision to enter the monastery where he will engage in a qualitative disentanglement from this life. If he perseveres, he can in time—perhaps it will require several rebirths—achieve freedom from samsara. At that moment his ignorance of and his commitment to the affairs of this life will fall away and he will be a nonreturner. Never again will he be reborn into this realm of suffering, and when he dies eternal bliss will at last be his destiny.

Mahayana Buddhists allow for redemption to occur through an individual's own effort, but self-effort is no longer necessary, for one can appeal to the Absolute for emancipation from the sufferings of life. The grace and love of the Buddha are sufficient for the redemption of people and all of creation. A person need only trust in the Absolute. In one of the large Mahayana communities even one's ability to trust is seen as a gift of the Buddha. Emancipation from samsara is not even dependent upon an individual's living an upright and honest life for, however evil a person is, the grace and love of Buddha is adequate to rescue even the meanest and foulest of men. Indeed, Shinran, an important Japanese Buddhist leader of the thirteenth century A.D., stated that if Buddha loves a good person, how much greater is his love for an evil person.

It is this teaching that has enabled Buddhist immigrants from East Asian nations to adapt a Protestant Sunday-school song to their congregations' needs in Los Angeles, San Francisco, New York, and elsewhere. They sing,

> Buddha loves me, this I know,
> For the Sutra tells me so;
> Little ones to him belong,
> They are weak but he is strong.

This is consistent with a centuries-old teaching of the Mahayana Buddhists.

The Theravadist canon is composed of *suttas* or "discourses," which rarely exceed twenty pages each. Tradition states that the southern canon was composed in the first century B.C. in Sri Lanka and in the Pali language, a descendant of the classical language of India, Sanskrit. Known as the Tripitaka (literally, three baskets), the Theravadist canon is divided into three parts: the discourses of Siddhartha Gautama, those of his disciples, and the scholastic commentaries composed by schoolmen in later centuries. This canon is limited in length; it can be bound into three volumes for a modern bookshelf.

By contrast the Mahayana canon is extensive. Parts of it are available only in Tibetan or Chinese or Sanskrit. The entire set of *sutras*, the Mahayana counterpart to the Pali word *sutta,* is not available in a single language. Most of the sutras were composed from the first through the sixth centuries A.D. There are many of them and they are very long.

Whereas the Theravadin Buddhists value the Tripitaka because of its message, many, if not the majority, of the laity in the Mahayana tradition attribute magical power to the sutras. They are the embodiment of the truth of the Absolute, but because truth, regardless of its content, is effective, it must be effective against illness, demons, traffic accidents, and so forth. Thus in China, Korea, or Japan it is not uncommon for people to carry a portion of a sutra as protection, nor is it unusual to see them hanging from rearview mirrors in automobiles. Several of the more popular sutras promote this perception by promising the reader protection and material success if he masters the message of the sutra. Those of less intellectual vigor simply resort to carrying the sutra in the pocket or purse.

This attribution of power to a sutra appears in a dramatic form in the Nichiren movement in Japan and its modern laymen's organization, Soka gakkai. Nichiren Buddhists worship the *Lotus Sutra* (*Saddharmapundarika* is the Sanskrit name) and believe that the chant *namu myoho Rengekyo* (praise to the *Lotus Sutra*) protects them from evil and gives success to their efforts.

The Theravada and Mahayana traditions also differ in their perceptions of this world. In the former heritage, the world is seen as psychologically real. The Mahayana Buddhists perceive it as illusion, although this can only be known by the person who has achieved spiritual insight, the sage. Inevitably, the responses to these different perceptions are different. The Theravadin Buddhists generally seek to transcend samsara by a psychological analysis of the world and by using the insights gained thereby to disentangle themselves from any attachment to it. On the other hand the Mahayana Buddhists want to help the world, for this tradition educates its people to the ideal of selfless effort for others and grants them recourse to transcendent sacred powers which will assist them in their efforts. In this regard a commonly-told Mahayana parable is instructive.

> Four men lost in the desert had become weak and emaciated and were slowly dying of hunger and thirst. Barely able to move, they stumbled upon a stone wall. It rose high above them. After some consideration one of them with the last bit of energy he could muster slowly climbed the wall. At the top he peered over, let out a scream of delight, leaped to the other side, and disappeared from sight. The three who remained were puzzled and looked silently at

each other. Finally after some time had passed and nothing was heard from the other side, the second person made the arduous climb with his last reserve of strength. He too looked over the top of the wall, shouted for joy, and disappeared from sight. The excruciating ascent was then made by the third man and he too with a cry of great delight leaped to the other side. Then the fourth person slowly pulled himself stone by stone up the wall. At the top at last his eyes gazed upon a cool green oasis filled with fruit and bubbling springs of water. Having momentarily refreshed himself, he climbed back down on the desert side of the wall and wandered off into the desert looking for others who were lost among the rocks, the sand, and the heat.

The first three wanderers were Theravadin monks. The fourth was a bodhisattva, a person who is emancipated from the world but elects to continue in this realm of suffering that others might be redeemed. Thus the parable makes clear the Mahayana ideal. Most Theravadin Buddhist monks and nuns see their immediate goal to be reaching Nirvana (the oasis) and exiting this life (the desert); the Mahayana Buddhists teach that it is more important to minister to the needs of others. One's own redemption cannot be fully realized until all are redeemed. The primary goal must be that of bringing mercy to those in suffering.

Mahayana Buddhists therefore have a strong sense of social obligation and doubt the value of working toward self-enlightenment alone without regard for the salvation of others. Hence the bodhisattva, the enlightened person who postpones his own complete emancipation from the world until all creatures can be saved, is the Mahayana ideal. The bodhisattva ideal stands in clear contrast with the image of the *arhat*, the individual in the Theravadin heritage who seeks his own redemption. This ideal is represented in the story by the three men who entered the oasis.

Buddhist Traditions

Mahayana Buddhists share with the Theravadin tradition reverence for Shakyamuni, but the former also affirm the existence of numerous other Buddhas and bodhisattvas (the distinction between the two is not consistently maintained) for whom there is no historical basis, but who are also said to be manifestations of the Absolute. Of the transcendental Buddhas in the Mahayana pantheon the most important among the people in East Asia is Amitabha, the Lord of the Western Paradise (O-mi-to-fo in Chinese and Amida in Japanese). His worship began in India perhaps in the second century A.D., and it was the dominant form of Buddhist devotion in China, Korea, and Japan by the middle of the thirteenth century.

Three scriptures or sutras are important to the Amitabha movement, which because of its penultimate concern for a paradise where the faithful are received after death is also called Pure Land Buddhism. These sutras are *The Sutra of Infinite Life* (*Sukhavativyuha*), *The Sutra of Amitabha* (the smaller *Sukhavativyuha*), and the *Sutra on the Meditation of the Buddha of Infinite Life* (known generally by its Japanese name *Kammuryojukyo*).

The highly imaginative *Sutra of Infinite Life* tells how the Buddha Shakyamuni, on Vultures' Peak near Rajagraha, in India, answered questions put to him by his disciple Ananda. In the discourse Shakyamuni relates how the Bodhisattva Dharmakara, deeply moved by the suffering of millions of people, determined to establish a paradise where everyone could know freedom from pain and anguish. Before he ever achieved enlightenment and became a bodhisattva he vowed that should his goal be achieved he would establish a land of bliss where anyone could enter who sincerely trusted in his mercy. His goal of bodhisattvahood was achieved and his vow was fulfilled. He became the Buddha of the Western Paradise where the faithful will be reborn in bliss, there, gradually, to achieve enlightenment.

The smaller *Sukhavativyuha*, which may be the oldest of the three sutras, is notable for its description of Amitabha's paradise, a fine example of religious fantasy. It is a place of silver, gold, coral, and crystal trees bearing a variety of gems, fragrant flowers, and luscious fruit. The trees are set in gorgeous parks and gardens where the perfumed waters run clear and cool into lakes of lotus blossoms. Beside the lakes and among the trees, where the melodic sounds of birds are heard, are magnificent palaces for the blessed. The resident will be free of every care. In the words of a famous Japanese writer, Yukio Mishima,

> If one feels like having something to eat, there automatically appears before one's eyes a seven-jeweled table on whose shining

surface rest seven-jeweled bowls heaped high with the choicest delicacies. But there is no need to pick up these viands and put them into one's mouth. All that is necessary is to look at their inviting colors and to enjoy their aroma: thereby the stomach is filled and the body nourished, while one remains oneself spiritually and physically pure. When one has thus finished one's meal without any eating, the bowls and the table are instantly wafted off.[5]

Here in vivid terms we see a very important difference between the Theravada and Mahayana traditions. In contrast to the ascetic reserve of the South Asian Buddhist tradition, the Mahayana tradition sees a positive role for the imaginative powers of the human being. The creative imagination can provide the effective bridge away from the trammels of our problem-filled lives to the Buddha. The person who would transcend the dilemma of human existence has in his imagination the means to see the Truth.

The passage just quoted from Mishima is from his short story, "The Priest of Shiga Temple and His Love," the tale of a Pure Land Buddhist priest who had achieved release from this realm of suffering through his marvelous power of religious fantasy. In both sleep and wakeful reverie he thought only of the Pure Land and its attractions. His fantasies freed him from attachment to the affairs of this world.

When the Great Priest saw the rich and noble, he smiled with compassion and wondered how it was that these people did not recognize their pleasures for the empty dreams that they were. When he noticed beautiful women, his only reaction was to be moved with pity for men who still inhabited the world of delusion and who were tossed about on the waves of carnal pleasure. . . . In his dreams he lived nightly in the Pure Land, and when he awoke he knew that to subsist in the present world was to be tied to a sad and evanescent dream.[6]

Another important bodhisattva in the Mahayana pantheon is Avalokitesvara (Kuan Yin in Chinese and Kannon in Japanese). Although she was never the center of a massive devotional

[5]Yukio Mishima, "The Priest of Shiga Temple and His Love," in *Death in Midsummer and Other Stories* (New York: New Directions, 1966), p. 60.
[6]Ibid., p. 62.

movement, Avalokitesvara's image will be found painted on wall scrolls and folding fans, incised on jade and ivory, carved in precious woods, cast in bronze, and fashioned in shining porcelain. People burn incense to her in wayside shrines and mountain grottoes or in the temples of boat dwellers and fishermen. In India Avalokitesvara is male, but in East Asia this bodhisattva became female primarily because women are more likely to be experienced as compassionate figures in Chinese culture. Like Amitabha, she has a paradise over which she rules.

The dwelling place of Avalokitesvara is Mount Potalaka, which popular Buddhist lore locates somewhere in the sea south of India. Popular Japanese Buddhism, however, places the paradise south of Tokyo near the Nachi Falls on the southern part of the Kii peninsula.

Avalokitesvara's name, which means "bearer of cries," is indicative of the role she plays in the Buddhism of the people of East Asia. She is the figure of mercy who attends to the immediate needs of those who call upon her. She will grant children to the woman who worships her. If you fall into a fire, think of Avalokitesvara and the flames will be quenched. She is said to protect the faithful, who call upon her, from thunderbolts, snakes, wild beasts, robbers, imprisonment, shipwreck, and traffic accidents. Buddhist artists suggest her merciful nature by carving her images with a multitude of arms and sometimes eleven heads. She can hear all and reach out to everyone.

Avalokitesvara is said to have been born from a ray of light emitted from the right eye of Amitabha Buddha. Her subordinate role is further indicated by the notion that she is the messenger of Amitabha. Again this theme is depicted in the common East Asian sculptures and paintings of the "Amida Trinity," which portray a large image of Amitabha flanked by two smaller images of Avalokitesvara and Mahasthamaprapta. The latter is a relatively unimportant bodhisattva, usually recognizable by the water jar in his crown. The relationship between Amitabha and Avalokitesvara might be explained in part through the hypothesis offered by some scholars, namely, that in Central Asia Amitabha originated as a sun deity and Avalokitesvara as a celestial or star deity and that both were absorbed into the pantheon by Buddhist missionaries passing through Central Asia on their way to China.

The *Surangama Sutra*, however, offers a story that is difficult to reconcile with the notion that Avalokitesvara originated from the eye of Amitabha, for it infers that at one time she was not a bodhisattva. The story opens with Avalokitesvara speaking to Siddhartha Gautama Buddha and an assembly of millions. In her discourse she tells how she achieved enlightenment many ages before through meditation on sound. According to the narrative, once enlightened she acquired two qualities—compassion and sympathy for every creature floundering in samsara's sea of suffering and the ability to transform herself into thirty-two different forms that she might be able to provide mercy in any situation. (For more information, see John Blofeld, *Bodhisattva of Compassion* [Boulder: Shambala, 1978].)

Although Amitabha and Avalokitesvara are the most important deities in the Mahayana pantheon, Maitreya is the earliest cult bodhisattva. He is called Mi-lo-fo in Chinese and Miroku in Japanese, and his devotees anticipate his imminent coming to earth. Because the Buddhist tradition has taken history more seriously than the Hindu tradition, its parent religious heritage, and because it has been willing to embrace and absorb phenomena from other religions and cultures, it might have absorbed the idea about messianic expectation from teachings contemporary in Afghanistan or Persia, through which Buddhist missionaries were traveling as they journeyed from India to China, perhaps as early as the second century B.C. Numerous statues, paintings, and texts discovered by archaeologists in Central Asia and Afghanistan testify to Maitreya's once immense popularity in that part of the world.

A central motif in the Maitreya schools of devotion is the common Buddhist notion that all phenomena within time are momentary and ephemeral. Absolutely nothing endures. Applied consistently, this principle means that not even the teachings of Siddhartha Gautama nor any form of the Buddhist tradition will endure forever. In time Buddhist teachings and practices will decline and life will become very difficult indeed for the faithful. When that occurs Maitreya will come and reestablish the form and means of the Buddhist faith. Once again meaning will exist in the midst of meaninglessness. Life and hope in the sea of suffering and death will again be possible. This recurring hope has had serious political ramifications. Many peasant revolts in East Asia have found their energy in the fevered anticipation of Maitreya's coming.

身代リ銀杏御守
金龍山淺草寺

This amulet is said to act as a substitute for the
bearer, taking any misfortune upon itself. If a person
is in an automobile accident, for example, it is
believed that the amulet will take much of the pain
and suffering into itself. It is a hollow seed of a
ginkgo tree with an image of the Buddhist deity
Kannon inside it, and is from Konryusan Sensoji, a
very popular temple of Kannon in Tokyo. The amulet
(4″ long) is mounted on an explanatory card, which is
to be discarded.

Until the rise to prominence of Amitabha and Avalokitesvara in Buddhist piety, Maitreya shared preeminence with Manjusri in the pantheon of the great bodhisattvas. Curiously he is important in several of the Mahayana scriptures, including the *Lotus Sutra*, but he appears to have been of less interest to the artists than the three other deities. When he does appear in art, he is shown with a five-pointed crown, a sword in his left hand, and a book in his right. With the sword he cuts through ignorance and with the sutra he brings enlightenment. As the patron of all knowledge, provider of insight, custodian of memory, and the patron saint of inspiration, he is the favored Buddhist deity of not only those who seek enlightenment, but also those with more pedestrian ambitions—a good education or success in examination. In the nations of East Asia which share a culture where the book is revered, teaching is the highest vocation, and success in education is celebrated, Manjusri is an object of devotion.

Buddhist Philosophy

If a person journeys to the countries of East Asia he will see the great temples and liturgies of devotion to Amitabha, Avalokitesvara, Maitreya, and Manjusri. They dominate the Buddhist landscape. Certainly there are other ways of devotion—the worship of Jizo, the protector of children in Japan, for example. But visual evidence of the great philosophical schools of Mahayana Buddhism is less easily found. They have made a significant and creative contribution to the cultures of East Asia, but they no longer attract large numbers of people or the best minds. Their temples are elegant, tucked away in serene locations; they are few, quiet, and sometimes empty.

Nevertheless these Mahayana schools, combined with the strong influence of philosophical Taoism, gave birth to the Ch'an or Zen Buddhist tradition which has given the world haiku poetry, ink painting, gardens, the tea ceremony, Noh theater, and some of the martial arts.

Zen, which is in part a spiritualized form of the Yogacara, one of the two great philosophical schools of Mahayana and the one which believes that world is only mind, was established in China in the sixth century A.D. and flourished in East Asia from the eighth to the fifteenth centuries. When it began, it bore some

A gold image of Kannon, a Buddhist deity of mercy, is inside a grotto carved in a block of wood. Attached to the block is a ball and a red tassel; the amulet is suspended from a suction cup by a red cord. The ball is a common symbol for the numinous presence, and red is the color of life and vitality. Gold is the one metal that never corrodes; thus it is beyond time, eternal. This amulet (4½″ long) can be used to protect against traffic accidents, and is from Konryusan Sensoji.

resemblance to the Theravadin tradition with its insistence upon the practice of meditation and the immediate goals of enlightenment. It, however, rejected the study of sutras, the discussion of the fine points of Buddhist philosophy, and the use of images and other objects of devotion as well as the devotional life itself. It sought to empty the mind of all ideas so that a person might awaken to the insight that all that exists is in essence the Absolute, the Buddha-mind, Mind-only, or No-mind. Once this unity of all things and all moments is central in a person's consciousness, he is able to live free of the anxieties and fears that vitiate the lives of normal people. He becomes a natural person, spontaneous and creative.

In surveying the different traditions within the Buddhist heritage the question occurs, what holds it together under a single name? What—if anything—do Buddhists have in common, or is there simply a variety of Buddhisms instead of a single heritage? Essentially, most Buddhist traditions share the following features: a belief in rebirth which is governed by one's behavior; a belief that this world is in a constant process of change and that change brings suffering; anticipation of redemption from this pain-filled existence; recognition that final liberation is dependent upon a change in consciousness (enlightenment); and a realization that to achieve release one must have faith in the teachings of Siddhartha Gautama or in the grace and mercy of a bodhisattva or Buddha or in the teaching of one's meditation instructor.

Although the Buddhist tradition has suffered grievously from Marxist revolutions in Asia during the last forty years, it is alive and showing signs of new vigor in countries that have avoided the conflict—Japan, South Korea, Taiwan, Thailand, Burma, and Sri Lanka. Moreover, Pure Land Buddhism has been carried to the East and West coasts of America by immigrants from Asia, and Zen Buddhism has made its way to America and Europe through literature, painting, and the martial arts.[7]

[7]The Buddhist Churches of America have their national headquarters at 1710 Octavia Street, San Francisco, California, 94109, and The Buddhist Society of England, 58 Eccleston Square, London, SW 1 VIPH, publishes a quarterly, *The Middle Way*. Dom Aelred Graham's *Zen Catholicism* (New York: Harcourt Brace, 1963), "suggests" that East and West may most effectively encounter each other at the spirit's center.

4

Confucianism

C. George Fry

American author Gore Vidal in a recent novel, *Creation*, narrated an imaginary "journey through that greatest of all ages, the fifth century B.C."[1] Called the Golden Age of Religious Creativity, that century produced spiritual mentors in many parts of Eurasia. In Greece this was the time of Socrates, the father of Western thought. Further east, in Israel, the fifth century was an era of reconstruction. The exiles returned from Persia to rebuild the city of Jerusalem and its temple. Legislation was given Ezra and Nehemiah, and the last prophet, Malachi, closed the writings of the Old Testament. This epoch also provided the setting for the stories of Esther and Daniel. In the Indian subcontinent the fifth century was the time of Gautama, the Buddha (c. 560–483 B.C.), and his reformation of Hinduism. To the north, in China, it was the era of "the twin philosophers," those near contemporaries, Lao-tzu (c. 604–531 B.C.) and Confucius (c. 551–479 B.C.). From the shores of the Aegean to the South China Sea it was a time of religious innovation. Only two major world faiths—Christianity and Islam —were born after this great age.

Although he was part of a constellation of spiritual genius in China at this time, Confucius remained unique, profoundly different from his contemporaries, his predecessors, or his successors. He remains unlike other religious role models in either life or

[1]Compare Karl Jaspers's reference to this same period as "the axial era" of human thought.

literature. Confucius was, like Joseph and Daniel, an advisor to kings, but he was not a visionary. He was, like Aristotle, a tutor of royalty, but he was not a scientist. He was, like David, fond of music and poetry, but he was not a warrior. He was, like Solomon, a student of wisdom, but not a theologian. He was, like Moses, a lawgiver, but not a liberator. He was, like Buddha, committed to simplicity of life, but he was not an ascetic. He was, like Socrates, an advocate of justice, but he escaped martyrdom. Like Jesus, he was a popular teacher, but he was not a savior. And although, like Muhammad, he was a statesman, Confucius was not a prophet. In that contrast one can find the key to his character, for Confucius made no claim to being a prophet; he was content to be a great teacher. His philosophy, Confucianism, is called *Ju chiao*, "the teaching of the scholar" or "the cult of the cultured." During the heyday of Nationalist China his birthday was observed as Teacher's Day. Confucius was preeminently a teacher.

Confucius did not found a nation, like Moses, or a church, like Jesus. He did not establish a school, like Plato, or a new cultural system, like Muhammad. He did not generate a theological position, like Aquinas, or a reformation, like Luther. Yet Confucius, a man with a message, became the most important influence on the earth's most populous nation, China, and a cult, Confucianism, honored his memory. His thought dominated the schools of China for almost twenty-five hundred years and his philosophy was the basis for promotion within the imperial civil service. Codified and analyzed almost beyond recognition, the teachings of Confucius came to be both a cause of stagnation and a source of periodic renewal within Chinese society. In one sense, Confucius was China, China was Confucius.

This mutual identification of Confucius and China occurred in spite of much opposition. Confucius claimed no divine revelation; he denied originality or any thought of innovation. During his lifetime Confucius was deprived of popular acclamation or any permanent position. Following his death his ideas were nearly forgotten as the result of a deliberate effort to obliterate his memory and literary legacy. Yet the power of his philosophy survived, his heritage revived, and Confucianism became the "ancient and honored way of China."

The Life of Confucius

Who was Confucius, "the sage of China"?

That question is not easy to answer.

To begin with, little reliable information is available concerning the life of this remarkable man. Even his name, Confucius, is a concoction of Western missionaries rather than his Chinese epithet. His real name was K'ung Ch'iu. The Chinese referred to him as K'ung fu-tzu, or Master K'ung, just as the disciples of Jesus referred to him as master or teacher. The term *fu-tzu* was an

This sketch is based on Ma Yuan's Confucius.

elaborate version of the Chinese word *tzu,* or "teacher" (as preserved in the title of Confucius's contemporary, Lao-tzu) and from K'ung fu-tzu the Westerners derived the Latinized name *Confucius.* This confusion concerning his real name is indicative of many problems faced by the professional historian in his attempts to reconstruct the life of this Chinese teacher.

What is more, when we talk about Confucius, we seem to be dealing in reality with three figures of the same name: the man of history, an itinerant teacher of the fifth century B.C.; the national legend, a person surrounded by folklore, civic piety, near-religious veneration; and the symbol of the sage or the scholar, the archetypal man of wisdom. It is difficult, if not impossible, to separate these three figures, yet each has his own personality and his own impact on Chinese civilization.

Around the year 551 B.C. Confucius was born in the state of Lu, in the modern province of Shantung. He was said to be the youngest of eleven children, the only son to perpetuate the family tradition. It is reported that his father was "an old soldier, tall and strong," about seventy years of age. Concerned that he did not have a living son to honor him after his death by offering sacrifice at the ancestral shrines, he married a woman who was much younger than he was. This wife, named Ching Tsai, prayed for a son. In a plea reminiscent of Hannah's prayer for a child, Ching Tsai invoked heaven. During the night she had a dream, in which a spirit said, "You shall have a son, wise beyond other men." The prophecy was to be fulfilled, although only after much tragedy. Confucius's father died during his infancy, and the boy and his mother lived in poverty, although they were of the aristocratic class. As a child Confucius had a passion for wisdom. Later Confucius informed his followers that when he was fifteen his chief ambition was the acquisition of knowledge. Although he was an intellectual, the lad did not neglect the other aspects of life. It is said that he loved to hunt, participated in gymnastics, played the flute, and did manual labor. Because he worked with his hands, many viewed him with contempt, but Confucius's answer was that work bestowed dignity.

Confucius became China's first professional teacher. At the age of fifteen he began taking tuition-paying students, and evidently he was employed by the state of Lu when he was seventeen. Two years later he married and at the age of twenty had a son. The marriage, like that of Socrates, proved to be an unhappy one, and Confucius was eventually divorced. As a result, most of his life was spent traveling without spouse or relatives. His son does not appear to have understood his father's thought or to have appreciated his principles. Further grief was occasioned by the death of his mother when he was twenty-four. It is said that Confucius mourned her for more than three years. At this time Confucius left his position with the state of Lu and wandered about China seeking a prince who would offer him employment. This period of pilgrimage through a China filled with warring principalities ended when Confucius was invited to return to Lu to serve successively as chief magistrate of the town of Chung-tu, as assistant to the state superintendent of works, and as minister of justice. According to tradition, Lu prospered so much during the administration of Confucius that the prince of Ch'i, a rival state, sent the ruler of Lu some eighty beautiful dancing girls. They were instructed to poison the mind of the prince against Confucius. They succeeded. At the age of fifty-six he went into exile once more.

For the next fourteen years Confucius roamed the land. These were tragic times for the sage. Two of his closest disciples died, as did his son. However, a surviving grandson in time continued both the family and the philosophy of Confucius. Like the wandering medieval Muslim sage, Avicenna, Confucius went from court to court seeking a patron. No prince would employ him. He was ready to pioneer new worlds of thought, but his teachings failed to win him an appointment, and many of his disciples began to forsake him.

In spite of this decade and a half of adversity, Confucius maintained his dignity and the integrity of his teaching. Kenneth Scott Latourette describes the sage in these words:

> Dignified, courteous, conscientious, high-minded, studious; modest but self-confident; a lover of antiquity, of books, of ceremonial, and of music; thoughtful, affable, but frank in rebuking what he deemed wrong in men in high and low positions; calm, serenely trustful in an overruling Providence—all these are terms which immediately come to mind as descriptive of the man.[2]

[2]Kenneth Scott Latourette, *The Chinese: Their History and Culture*, 4th ed. (New York: Macmillan, 1968), p. 102.

The integrity of the master's teaching is reflected in an outspoken conversation with Tsekung:

'What kind of a person do you think can be properly called a scholar?' Confucius replied: 'A person who shows a sense of honor in his personal conduct and who can be relied upon to carry out a diplomatic mission in a foreign country with competence and dignity can be properly called a scholar.' 'What kind of person would come next?' 'One who is known to be a good son in his family and has a reputation for humility and respect in a village.' 'What kind of a person would come next after that?' 'A person who is extremely careful of his conduct and speech and always keeps his word. That is a priggish, inferior type of person, but still he can rank below the above two types.' 'What do you think of the officials today?' 'Oh!' said Confucius, 'those rice-bags! They don't count at all.'[3]

The years of exile were painful ones for the sage. While he maintained his dignity and the integrity of his thought, his outspokenness lost him opportunities for employment in the states of North China. Although Confucius was confident that he could establish "a new Chou in the east" and bring about national revival, he was consistently denied a position. On occasion Confucius lamented that he was "like a gourd that is fit only to be hung on the wall and is never put to use." However, these years out of office were far from unproductive. He said, "I do not mind not being in office; I am concerned about being qualified for office. I do not mind that no one gives me recognition; I seek to be worthy of recognition." Yet behind the resignation, one senses much frustration.

In his old age Confucius returned to his native state of Lu and retired to private life. There, in his seventies, he died, having filled his final years with teaching and writing. It is reported that prior to his death the great sage said, "The great mountain must crumble, the strong beam must break, and the wise man wither away like a plant." Or again it is reported that he said, "No intelligent monarch arises; there is not one in the kingdom that will make me a minister. My time has come to die." Within a week

---

[3]Quoted in "Aphorisms of Confucius" (The Analects), in The Wisdom of Confucius, trans. and ed. Lin Yutang (New York: Modern Library, 1966), p. 173.

he was dead. After his death Confucius received more honor than in his life. Temples were erected in his honor. Twice a year governmental officials offered sacrifices in his name. Pilgrims visited his birthplace. Others went to T'ai Shan, the mountain near the village where he lived. But in *The Analects*, the sayings of Confucius, we find a statement that best serves as his eulogy:

> The Master said: 'The gentleman devotes his mind to attaining the Way and not to securing food. Go and till the land and you will end up being hungry, as a matter of course; study, and you will end up with the salary of an official, as a matter of course. The gentleman worries about the Way, not about poverty.[4]

The philosophy of Confucius is sometimes called the Way. Such terminology is common in the world of religion. Jesus said, "I am the way" (John 14:6). The early Christians were known as "those of the way" (Acts 24:14). Buddhism offers the Noble Eightfold Path. Shintōism, the religion of Japan, is "the way of the gods." Lao-tzu, the near contemporary of Confucius, taught Taoism, which is sometimes called the Way. Islam is a Way and the most familiar chapter of the Qur'an, surah 1, picks up the same motif:

> In the name of God, the Merciful, the Compassionate. Praise is God's; He is the Lord of all creation, the Merciful, the Compassionate. Only You do we serve; only You do we ask for aid. Guide us in the path made straight, the path for those You favor. Not [the path for those] at whom You are angry, nor the path of those You are leading astray.[5]

Confucianism is also a Way. What C. S. Lewis once suggested, Confucianism affirms: the Way is but a reflection of the *Tao* or pattern inherent in the physical and social universe. As a Way Confucianism offers an interpretation of moral reality for daily living.

The Confucian Way is best known to us through certain classic texts and certain classic teachers.

The great literary sources of Confucianism are the Five Classics and the Four Books. These volumes have been compared to the

---

[4]Confucius, *The Analects*, trans. D. C. Lau (New York: Penguin, 1979), 15.32, p. 136.
[5]Translated by James R. King.

Old and New Testaments respectively. From a survey of these works and their contents we can see that Confucianism became more than Confucius taught. As a wise teacher, he sowed seed; this bore much fruit in the reflection of others.

The Five Classics are:

1. The Canon of History *(Shu Ching)*, which is an anthology of narrative history from ancient China. This text has been compared to the historical books of the Old Testament.
2. The Canon of Poetry *(Shih Ching)*, which is an anthology of some three hundred poems from ancient China. This work reminds us of the Psalter of the Old Testament.
3. The Canon of Changes *(I Ching)*, which is a treatise on sixty-four diagrams used for divination in ancient China.
4. The Canon of Rites *(Li Chi)*, which is an anthology of cere-monial and ritual lore from ancient China, comparable in some respects to the Book of Leviticus in the Old Testament.
5. The Annals of Spring and Autumn *(Chung Chiu)*, which apparently were composed by Confucius himself, not merely collected by him as were the others. This is an anthology of the chief events in the history of the state of Lu, and it bears comparison with the Book of Chronicles in the Old Testa-ment.

The Four Books are:

1. The Book of Great Learning *(Ta Hsueh)*, a treatise on higher education, emphasizing the relationship of virtue and wis-dom.
2. The Doctrine of the Mean *(Chung Yung)*, a treatise on the Doctrine of the Golden Mean. Reminiscent of the Aristotelian ideal of moderation or the English virtue of the via media, the Golden Mean is the middle way between two extremes, the way of compromise.
3. The Analects *(Lun Yu)*, a treatise by Confucius, composed of sayings and aphorisms. Similar in format to the Book of Proverbs in the Old Testament, its function within the Confucian system is comparable to that of the Gospels of Christianity. Although at times the pithy sayings of *The*

Analects suffer from a lack of context and continuity, thus causing some puzzlement to Western readers, it is, nevertheless, in this anthology of wisdom that one feels closest to the sage himself.

4. The Works of Mencius (Meng-tzu). Mencius, as we shall see, was a major interpreter and preserver of the thought of Confucius. His relationship to Confucius was comparable of that of Paul to Jesus. For that reason some have compared his writing to the Epistles of the New Testament.[6]

Scholars continue to debate the real role of the historic Confucius in the creation of this corpus. To what extent he compiled or wrote these volumes is much disputed. How accurately they have been transmitted and still communicate his teaching is also much argued. The founder, the philosophy, and the system so fuse that any segregation of the individual, the ideology, and the institutions becomes virtually impossible.

If this is the case in the literary legacy of Confucianism, it is even more the situation when we turn to the great interpreters of the tradition.

Early Confucianism had two great interpreters and one greater defector. To these three pivotal personalities, whose thought was influential in the development of the Confucian consensus, we now turn our attention.

Mencius (whose traditional although debatable dates are 371–289 B.C.) was the first major interpreter of Confucianism. The name *Mencius* is a Latinized form of the Chinese Meng-tzu (Master Meng). In certain respects Mencius's early life resembles that of Confucius, for he was also of aristocratic origin, and he was reared by a widowed mother. Latourette observed that Mencius "seems to have owed to a wise mother even more than Confucius." Upon the death of his mother, to whom he was bound by deep psychological ties, Mencius mourned extravagently, to the point of embarrassing his disciples. Like Confucius, Mencius also led the life of an itinerant teacher, seeking—and failing to find—employment with the princes of feudal China.

---

[6]For these comparisons of the Confucian classics and the Judeo-Christian Scriptures I am indebted to Y. C. Yang, *China's Religious Heritage* (Nashville: Abingdon-Cokesbury, 1943), pp. 66–72.

In spite of these similarities, Mencius differed from his master in both personality and philosophical emphasis. Confucius advocated simplicity; Mencius lived sumptuously, allowing himself to be "wined and dined" by the powerful whenever possible. Confucius urged humility; Mencius behaved pompously. As one scholar noted, "He was probably the most erudite man of his age. He knew this, and he made the most of it."[7] For example, Mencius "believed and stated forthrightly that it was natural and proper for Brain to govern Brawn and for Brawn to support Brain."[8] A Confucian by education and inclination, Mencius added certain philosophical emphases of his own to the emerging synthesis. For one thing, Mencius stressed the natural goodness of man. To him this was the only anthropology ("doctrine of man") that was consistent with the ethical imperatives inherent in the Confucian system. Although, like Confucius, Mencius cited the importance of education and training in the nurture of character, much of this to be provided by the state, he did not hesitate to justify revolution. Violence was legitimate if the state became oppressive. Under such conditions, Mencius contended, the people had a "mandate from heaven" to overthrow the ruler. In these and in other ways Mencius altered and added to the tradition. His thoughts are best preserved in the *Meng-tzu Shu, The Book of Mencius,* believed to be autobiographical, and containing reports of key incidents of his career that are illustrative of his thought.

Hsün Tzu or Hsün K'uang (approximately 300–235 B.C.) was the second major interpreter of Confucianism. Said to have been a native of the state of Chao in the north of China, Hsün Tzu, like Mencius, believed that the science of good government should take priority in one's thinking. Like Confucius, Hsün Tzu believed in the necessity of personal morality, but this should be nurtured in the context of political responsibility and social stability. A tree, no matter how good the stock, will not flourish unless it is planted in fertile soil, fed with nutrients, treated with care, bathed with the sun, protected from storms and predators, and allowed under optimum conditions to fulfill its potential. Hsün Tzu, whose thought is preserved for us in the *Hsün Tzu,* a book of his teaching,

---

[7]Charles O. Hucker, *China's Imperial Past: An Introduction to Chinese History and Culture* (Stanford: Stanford University Press, 1975), p. 80.
   [8]Ibid.

arranged in logical and systematic order, differed from Mencius in his evaluation of human nature. Confucius had indicated that there were good and evil potentialities within human personality; Mencius had stressed the positive forces; Hsün Tzu came to emphasize the negative. While holding fast to the Confucian concern for ethics, Hsün Tzu contended that only a positive and powerful environment can guarantee the triumph of good over evil. The "uncivilized" or "barbarian" impulses within human nature must be restrained, retrained, and redeemed by a strong society. Within society, the chief "reformers" are teachers and rulers. For that reason Hsün Tzu honored schools and the state as the "civilizing" influences active on human character. Both are to be sources of discipline: in a positive way through example and education; in a negative way through legislation, regulation, and punishment. Hsün Tzu also differed from Mencius and Confucius in his attitude toward the supernatural. While the master had been modest in his comments about "invisible realities," he had encouraged his disciples to obey the religious rituals of the empire and "to honor heaven." Mencius admonished his students to do their best, to submit to "fate" or "destiny," as "heaven wills." Hsün Tzu, however, was skeptical about the existence of spirits and felt that the rites should be retained only for their social, not spiritual, benefits.

The only one of the early Confucianists to obtain a governmental position (he was a minor official in southern Shantung), Hsün Tzu was able to test his principles in practice. As a contributor to the tradition he indicated its flexibility, its capacity for various forms of elaboration, its ability to be related to various world views (both spiritual and material), and its continuing central emphasis on ethics and political science.

Mo Ti or Mo-tzu (approximately 470–391 B.C.) is called both a defector from Confucianism and an originator of a system of his own. Only a half-century removed from Confucius in time, Mo Ti found himself far in spirit from the disciples of the master who became his teachers. Independent in heart and mind, Mo Ti has come to rank with Lao-tzu and Confucius as one of the three fathers of classic Chinese philosophy. It has been said that Lao-tzu was the interpreter of nature, Confucius of man, and Mo Ti of God. His book, the *Mo-tzu*, is an anthology of his thought. Surely his disagreement with the Confucianists is in large measure joined at the issue of the supernatural. Mo Ti, like Confucius, Mencius, and Hsün Tzu, believed that man is to lead a moral life and live in an orderly society. Unlike them, Mo Ti contended that this is impossible apart from a right relationship to the supernatural. This emphasis he felt had been neglected in Confucianism, for Confucianists had placed their main concern on society (especially the state and the school, and, as we shall see later, the family) and the self. Although the Master acknowledged heaven and fulfilled the rituals, he had been silent on many spiritual matters. Mencius had indicated his priorities when he said, "The people are of the greatest importance; the gods come second; the sovereign is of lesser weight." Hsün Tzu's skepticism concerning the spirits has been discussed.

By contrast, Mo Ti felt that it is impossible to have a moral self or society without a declaration of dependence upon the supernatural. In a fashion reminiscent of Elton Trueblood's description of a "cut flower civilization," one severed from its living roots, which can flourish for a time, but will surely perish, Mo Ti called China back to its ancestral faith. Ancient China, Mo Ti affirmed, was founded on "the worship of heaven." The Supreme Being was known as T'ien, an impersonal form, and as Shang-ti, a more intimate name (the one generally agreed upon by Protestants as the word to designate the Christian God). The emperor ruled "by the mandate of heaven." T'ien (heaven) or Shang-ti (the Ruler Above) endowed government with its authority and responsibility, man with his dignity, society with its prosperity and stability, and religion and philosophy with emotional and intellectual certainty, just as surely as he provided nature with fertility of life and regularity of seasons. Shang-ti had a personal interest in man, for he was boundless love. Mo-Ti said of the Deity, "The will of God is love, love for all and without distinction." This is strangely reminiscent of John, who centuries later wrote, "Beloved, let us love one another: for love is of God; and every one that loveth is born of God, and knoweth God" (1 John 4:7). Mo Ti apparently lived by this philosophy, giving himself "from head to heel" for his neighbor. He felt that because God is love, love ought to be the basis of human relations. It is surprising to Western observers that Mo Ti's thought did not result in the development of a universal moral monotheism in China. Such did not happen, although a belief in a Supreme Being persisted. He and his followers divided into rival, often contradictory, sects—some ascetic, some sophist, some cultic. This meant that Mo Ti's criticisms came to strengthen, not to supplant, the growing Confucian synthesis.

So the Confucian Way grew—as a stream that has its origin in a mighty mountain spring waxes by working its way through rocky crevasses, all the while receiving tribute from other streams, until finally it emerges as a major river. On that river commerce of many (and often contradictory) kinds can be carried. So it has been with Confucianism, which emerged as the philosophy of China. To its values and virtues we now turn.

The Ideal Self

Confucianist thought is similar to an ellipse. One side is "the ideal self," the other is "the ideal society." These two foci form the bicameral world of Confucian philosophy.

Let us consider first the ideal self.

A. C. Bouquet, in *Comparative Religion*,[9] asks, "What sort of human being does a particular human group admire?" For the ancient Romans and Japanese, the model man was the disciplined warrior. For the classical Greeks it was the handsome and virtuous man, the one who, to use Aristotle's definition, contemplated the universe; as Xeno and the Stoics taught, he was self-controlled. The inner and outer worlds were to be ruled by reason and restraint. For the Indian saints, both Hindu and Buddhist, the ideal man was the ascetic. Through renunciation of the temptations of the flesh and the mind, the self escaped illusions and made a pilgrimage in spirit toward reality. For those in the Abrahamic tradition—Jewish, Christian, and Muslim—the ideal man is inconceivable apart from his relationship to God. All view man as the image of God or even "the shadow of God" on earth. That relationship between God and man became the crucial dimension. For the Hebrews the ideal man was the righteous man, whose "delight is in the law of the LORD" (Ps. 1:2); for the Christian the ideal man is the "saint," filled with the Spirit of Christ; for the Muslim the ideal man is the servant of God, *'abdullah,* who practices both active and passive obedience, harmonizing his will with the will of the Infinite. For the Confucianist

[9]6th ed. (Baltimore: Penguin, 1964), pp. 301–2.

the ideal man is variously called the princely man, the superior man, or the gentleman. Confucius took the term *chün-tzu*, literally, "son of a ruler," which had applied to the old warrior class, and transformed it to refer to a man of moral stature. In similar fashion he took the term *li* (ritual) and redefined it not so much as ceremony but as propriety. Tao or the Way became "the moral Way" or the ethical structure of the universe itself. A gentleman is one in harmony with the Tao, living by li. This is the model man of Confucianist thought.

It is sometimes suggested that the gentleman of the Confucianist mold is indifferent to supernatural realities. Although Confucianism did not originate as a religion in the Western sense of the word, it cannot be denied that the sage had a great respect for the Supreme Being. Confucius believed in the faithful observance of civic and religious ceremonies. The sage prayed not only in public but also in private. It is reported in *The Analects* that

> the Master was seriously ill. Tzu-lu asked permission to offer a prayer. The Master said, 'Was such a thing ever done?' Tzu-lu said, 'Yes, it was. The prayer offered was as follows: pray thus to the gods above and below.' The Master said, 'In that case, I have long been offering my prayers.'[10]

Confucius was a man of worship. Moreover, he was a man who submitted himself to the will of heaven:

> Po-nius was ill. The Master visited him and, holding his hand through the window, said, 'We are going to lose him. It must be Destiny. Why else should such a man be stricken with such a disease?[11]

History, for Confucius, was more than simply the arena of human activity. Divinity was to be recognized.

Although there is evidence to indicate that Confucius was a man of piety who kept the liturgy of his time and regarded history as under the influence of the Deity, he did not speak much on the subject of religion. His silence on theological themes causes some to regard him as an agnostic (or even an atheist). To Western *philosophes* of the eighteenth century he seemed to be a Deist like

[10]Confucius, *The Analects*, trans. D. C. Lau, 7.35, p. 91.
[11]Ibid., 6.10, p. 82.

Benjamin Franklin or Thomas Jefferson. Moreover, *The Analects* states that "the topics the Master did not speak of were prodigies, force, disorder and gods" (7.21, p. 88). Now how can we explain this seeming paradox: on the one hand Confucius regarded religious values as integral to the personality of the ideal self, but on the other hand Confucius seldom taught his followers truths concerning the supernatural?

The sage's silence on the supernatural derived from his lack of knowledge on the subject. A key virtue for the ideal man is truthfulness. When one knows not, one ought not speak. Now religious knowledge can be obtained through either revelation or tradition. Direct revelation from God (in nature, history, personality) is the source of wisdom claimed by prophets. Confucius denied having an experiential knowledge of the spiritual realm. In *The Analects* we read:

> Chi-lu asked how the spirits of the dead and the gods should be served. The Master said, 'You are not able even to serve man. How can you serve the spirits?'
> 'May I ask about death?'
> 'You do not understand even life. How can you understand death?'[12]

For his understanding of the supernatural world Confucius had to rely on tradition. His knowledge was based on human accumulation—both personal and social—not on divine donation or special revelation. On one occasion "the master said, 'I was not born with knowledge but, being fond of antiquity, I am quick to seek it'" (7.20, p. 88). Having no extraordinary religious insight, the master refused to speak extensively on that matter, for "shall I tell you what it is to know? To say you know when you know, and to say you do not when you do not, that is knowledge" (2.17, p. 65).

A mark of the gentleman is the possession of wisdom. Confucius believed that learning could be acquired from various sources, including the collective experience of the human community, or tradition. On one occasion he said, "I transmit but do not innovate; I am truthful in what I say and devoted to antiquity" (7.1, p. 86). Like the great masters of medieval Europe, Confucius

---

[12]Ibid., 11.12, p. 107.

regarded himself as a midget, able to see much because he stood on the shoulders of giants, his forebearers.

Confucius also asserted that the practice of observation—both sensory and social—is critical to the possession of wisdom. Once the Master said:

> I use my ears widely and follow what is good in what I have heard; I use my eyes widely and retain what I have seen in my mind. This constitutes a lower level of knowledge.[13]

Or, in another context, he remarked:

> Even when walking in the company of two other men, I am bound to be able to learn from them. The good points of the one I copy; the bad points of the other I correct in myself.[14]

For Confucius the mind had many doors, one being provided by the body, through sensory perception (empiricism); another being given by the soul, through the evaluation of actions by moral standards (pragmatism).

Confucius also valued the practice of interrogation, or the asking of questions, as a means of gaining wisdom. Once Confucius was inside the Grand Temple of the Duke of Chou, the founder of the state of Lu. There he asked many questions. When asked why he raised so many questions, Confucius replied, "The asking of questions is in itself the correct rite" (3.15, p. 69). For the Christian reader this is reminiscent of a scene from the childhood of Jesus: "And it came to pass, that after three days they found him in the temple, sitting in the midst of the doctors, both hearing them, and asking them questions" (Luke 2:46). Like Socrates, who invited discussion by posing questions, Confucius learned by interrogation.

Confucius further believed in the integration of wisdom, the old and the new, into a creative synthesis. Once Confucius said, "A man is worthy of being a teacher who gets to know what is new by keeping fresh in his mind what he is already familiar with" (2.11, p. 64). This is reminiscent of the saying of Jesus: "Every scribe which is instructed unto the kingdom of heaven is like unto a man

[13]Ibid., 7.28, p. 89.
[14]Ibid., 7.22, p. 88.

that is an householder, which bringeth forth out of his treasure things new and old" (Matt. 13:52).

Wisdom, for Confucius, was both practical and social. For that reason Professor Yong Choon Kim can say that Confucius "was basically a humanist and a pragmatist."[15] To Confucius, wisdom had to have consequences that were beneficial. In this respect he was like the American philosopher William James, the father of Pragmatism. Because the self, no matter how developed, lives in a network of interpersonal relationships, the consequences of wisdom that count are social. Knowledge ought to facilitate "the realm of right relationships." As a result of his reflection, Confucius felt the royal man, or the superior man, or the princely man, or the gentleman would do three things.

The ideal man orders all relationships in society according to the Law of Reciprocity. This became clear when Tzu-kung asked, "Is there a single word which can be a guide to conduct throughout one's life?" To this Confucius answered, "It is perhaps the word *shu* (reciprocity). Do not impose on others what you yourself do not desire" (15.24, p. 135). Essentially this is the Golden Rule, found almost universally in the higher religions. It is reminiscent of the Sermon on the Mount, where Jesus said, "Therefore all things whatsoever ye would that men should do to you, do ye even so to them: for this is the law and the prophets" (Matt. 7:12). Some scholars suggest that because Confucius stated the principle in a negative rather than a positive form, his version of it should be called the Silver Rule. The notion, however, of the term *shu* is that of "fellow-feeling" or "empathy" or "mutual consideration." It can be expressed positively.

The ideal man can order all relationships according to the Law of Reciprocity because he displays the Five Constant Virtues. Once Confucius was asked how one could live according to the spirit of benevolence, fulfilling the Law of Reciprocity. The master suggested that "there are five things and whoever is capable of putting them into practice in the Empire is certainly benevolent." When asked to list the five, the teacher replied: "They are respectfulness, tolerance, trustworthiness in word, quickness and generosity" (17.6, p. 144). Let us consider these Five Constant Virtues.

---

[15]Yong Choon Kim, *Oriental Thought: An Introduction to the Philosophical and Religious Thought of Asia* (Totowa, N.J.: Littlefield, 1981), p. 51.

Respectfulness is the Confucian equivalent of fulfilling the Great Law of Love as outlined by Jesus. When a lawyer asked Christ how to obtain eternal life, Jesus invited him to summarize the Law and the Prophets. The lawyer replied, in words which Christ commended, "Thou shalt love the Lord thy God with all thy heart, and with all thy soul, and with all thy strength, and with all thy mind; and thy neighbour as thyself" (Luke 10:27). Love for self, for society, and for God was the goal of the Law. For Confucius, self-love or self-respect was the first saving virtue. A man who honors himself will not dishonor another.

Tolerance or magnanimity is the Confucian equivalent of the catholic spirit. Some Western scholars have seen more in this than merely the philosophy of "live and let live." One rendered it, "Nothing human is alien to me." Another saw it in the teaching of "ecumenical community" and "global fraternity." Still another said it was the Oriental match to the Occidental injunction given by Paul, "Bear ye one another's burdens, and so fulfill the law of Christ" (Gal. 6:2). Although that evaluation may be extreme, the Confucian notion is akin to Charles Williams's emphasis on "coinherence"—the interpenetration of personality that occurs when there is charity. James called it "the royal law": "Love thy neighbor as thyself" (James 2:8).

Trustworthiness is honesty, the Confucian equivalent of the Truth Commandment, "Thou shalt not bear false witness" (Exod. 20:16). The same virtue is commended by James, who condemns "a double minded man . . . unstable in all his ways" (James 1:8). He further commented, "If any man offend not in word, the same is a perfect man" (James 3:2).

Quickness or earnestness means to be serious about doing good and is a Confucian equivalent of the biblical teaching of faith bearing good fruit. As James warned, "Faith, if it hath not works, is dead" (James 2:17). It is the opposite of such biblically condemned vices as sloth or *acedia.*

Generosity or benevolence is the Confucian equivalent of the Judeo-Christian virtue of charity. It is good will at work in the world. One can recall again the concept of wisdom, as taught by James:

But the wisdom that is from above is first pure, then peaceable, gentle, and easy to be intreated, full of mercy and good fruits,

without partiality, and without hypocrisy. And the fruit of righteousness is sown in peace of them that make peace. [James 3:17–18]

Once I was traveling on the West Coast of the United States. On
Sunday I attended an Episcopal church in a predominantly
Chinese community. To my surprise I found the children in the
church school studying the ethics of Confucius. As they worked
through the Five Constant Virtues, I asked the rector, a man in his
middle years, the rationale for this procedure. The priest replied:
"The moral law is universal, written in nature and the self. Few
have understood it better than Confucius. Virtue, as he taught it, is
a preparation for the gospel of Christ; it is also a prescription for
the good life for a man now in Christ. That is why we teach the
ethics of Confucius—both to inquirers as well as to the confirmed."

The ideal man, who lives by the Law of Reciprocity, who
embodies the Five Constant Virtues, will exhibit certain traits. One
of these is *jen*, or "humaneness," "benevolence," or "sympathy."
This is somewhat reminiscent of Albert Schweitzer's doctrine of
"the respect or reverence for all life." The superior man also
exhibits *yi*, or "righteousness" or "justice." This means not merely
"passive obedience to rules" but an "active and imaginative
obedience," seeking to make things right. Yet another mark of the
gentleman is li, which means literally "propriety" or "ceremony,"
but which in a broader context means "the regulatory principle
and law of human conduct." It is prudence, or the Golden Mean,
the avoidance of extremes, the knack for saying and doing the
right thing at the appropriate moment.[16]

The Ideal Society

Man does not exist in isolation, for he is, as Aristotle observed,
"a social creature." Thus from time immemorial thinkers have

[16]The similarities between Confucianist virtues and the ideals of the Christian humanism of an Erasmus of Rotterdam or a Philip Melanchthon are often cited by Western
observers of Chinese culture. Christian scholars have often suggested that this similarity
gives rise to a paradox: precisely because of the kinship, Confucianist philosophy can
become one of the most formidable barriers to Christianity. There is an analogy to
humanism in the West. For an Erasmus or Melanchthon, drawn into Christianity by his
concern for virtue, there is also a Thomas Jefferson or a Benjamin Franklin, indifferent to it
because he is satisfied with the ethic he possesses. Similarities can be barriers as well as
bridges.

speculated on the nature of the ideal society and we are not surprised that Confucius has a good deal to say on this topic. Confucius realized that the individual manifested and fulfilled himself through a series of social relationships, five in all, in which the Principle of Reciprocity was to apply. We will note that these Confucian natural orders differ to some extent from those familiar to us in the Christian world.

The first relationship is that of father and son. This is the role of parent, but with particular emphasis on the interaction between the male counterparts—father and son. There are some parallels here with concepts familiar to Christians. The Christian notion of God's revelation to mankind centers in the relationship of God the Father and his divine Son, the Christ. Through the Old Testament there is a running theme of father-son relationships: Adam disappointed in Cain; Abraham asked to offer up Isaac; Jacob mourning for lost Joseph; David lamenting the folly of Absalom. This is an archetypal pattern, a primordial relationship, which for Christians is anchored not merely in history but also in eternity, for it is not simply an accident of nature but a reflection of metaphysical realities. Although Confucius could not speak of the fatherhood of God as did Paul, he could contend that loyalty to one's parent extends beyond the grave.

Confucius felt that the key virtue of the father toward the son is kindness. The father has a responsibility to the child and for him. This obligation has no bounds and is to be fulfilled with grace, wisdom, and generosity. Confucius felt that the key virtue of the son toward the father is piety. At this point Confucius was building upon the social reality of the China of his day. The strongest institution was the family. Its solidarity and stability were regarded as the foundation of Chinese civilization. Our Western notion of individualism, born during the Renaissance, is quite alien to the thought of Confucius and his generation. Indeed, a son was to obey his father, without question, and respect for the parent continued even after death. Grafted onto the cult of ancestors already in existence in China, Confucianism's ethic of filial piety lasted until recent times. Sometimes expressed as ancestor worship, it resembled the cult of saints as understood in some sectors of Islam and Christianity.

The second relationship is that of husband and wife. As before, the first named is regarded as superior. Confucius taught a philosophy of male domination. While the husband was to be "righteous" to his wife, she was to be "obedient" to her husband. Lest this be thought totally Oriental, one need only recall the teaching of Paul the apostle: "Wives, submit yourselves unto your own husbands. . . . For the husband is the head of the wife. . . . Husbands, love your wives" (Eph. 5:22, 23, 25).

Today many would regard Confucius as a male chauvinist, but, in effect, he was simply reflecting the reality of Chinese society. Marriages were arranged by families, and romantic love was not part of the process. Man and woman came together as a unit to meet biological, social, and economic needs. Actually, Confucius was humanizing the marital bond by stressing that more than sex, reproduction, companionship, and economic survival were involved. By stressing justice and cooperation as suitable standards for the home, the sage tried to ameliorate existing conditions.

For many this explanation is not a justification. Critics point to the fact that while Confucius speaks of the father-son relationship, he has nothing to say about the function of the mother. For them it is below the standard of the Old Testament, where a son is warned to "forsake not the law of [his] mother" (Prov. 1:8). Furthermore, it is said that female figures are notoriously absent from the Confucianist tradition. In the Hebrew Scriptures there are matriarchs of Israel, like Sarah, Rebecca, and Rachel; the prophetesses, like Miriam; the rulers, like Deborah and Esther. Within the New Testament literature many women are mentioned, and within the Christian tradition Mary has always been assigned a place of high honor. For critics who point out such things, Confucianism is to be indicted for its negative attitude toward women.

The third relationship of which Confucius spoke was that of the elder brother and the younger. Confucius's followers extended this relationship from the nexus of the family to include other relationships as well. Yet the Confucian ideal for society is derived from the family, and it is an ideal of brotherhood.

Stories about brothers are basic to all world literature. The Bible records an account of two brothers, Cain and Abel, and the crime of fratricide. Later on there is the account of Jacob and Esau, with the younger brother defrauding the elder. The ideal in Confucianism is gentility in the elder brother and humility and respect in the younger; these virtues are often honored more in the breaking than in the keeping. What the Confucianist ethic of brotherhood involves is an extension of the principle of loyalty from the family to the rest of society.

The fourth relationship is that of friend and friend, or, sometimes, of patron and client. The virtue of the patron is human consideration; that of the junior or client is one of deference. Confucius hoped that the ethic of friendship would come to permeate even such diverse orders of society as education and business.

The fifth relationship to which Confucius called attention is that of ruler and subject, which is the basis of the state. The ruler is to be benevolent, the subjects are to be loyal. For Confucius that was a crucial relationship. Living in a time of anarchy and feudal lords, Confucius recognized the necessity of reestablishing a central authority. One critic defined his science of government as one that "combines monarchy and democracy." And indeed there is a sense of monarchy in the way Confucius advocates "law and order and . . . social stability." On the other hand, elements of democracy are clearly present, for Confucius pleads for the people's right to good government. The ruler, furthermore, must live under the Tao or moral law, and revolution was justified within Chinese thought, because an emperor who dealt unfairly with his subjects had forfeited "the mandate of heaven" and could be replaced. What Confucius attempted to do was to provide a science of government that reconciled security and liberty.

Confucianism and China

Called the School or Doctrine of the Learned, Confucianism was to have a profound effect on China. For a time the Confucian canon was destroyed, its advocates killed. But then two things happened.

The Chinese honored the individual, Confucius. Although his own descendants and disciples never ceased to worship him, in 195 B.C. the first of the Han emperors gave him that honor. Confucius successively became the Duke, Foremost Teacher, Prince, and Ultimate Sage. By the early Middle Ages Confucian temples were erected, his tomb in Shantung became a national shrine, and official worship continued until the revolution of 1911. Even the Chinese Republic declared August 27 to be his birthday and a national holiday.

The Chinese honored the ideals that we designate today as Confucianism. Not only did Confucianism take on some of the traits of a religion, but also it became the official philosophy of the Chinese empire. Civil-service examinations based on the Confucian classics were still administered in China in the early twentieth century. Seldom has a sage or a system exercised such influence over a society as Confucianism has on China. Following the revolution of 1911 many felt the old curiosity shop of Confucius should be closed. His values, however, survived. With the rise of Marxism in the 1940s, and the substitution of secular and material values, the Confucianist ethic was seriously challenged. Many feel, however, that while Confucianism may never be restored as it was known in 1911, it will survive Marxism and Maoism, for it is too deeply seated in the Chinese soul to be forgotten.

Y. C. Yang, professor of Chinese civilization at Bowdoin College, once suggested a fivefold influence of Confucianist thought on China.

Confucianism impressed on the Chinese the supreme importance of education. The pursuit of wisdom, through the study of the humanities, philosophy, and political science, was placed at the core of the curriculum.

Confucianism impressed on the Chinese the supreme importance of building character. Wisdom without consequences for the personality and for society is folly. The primary product of the school system must be a person able to function responsibly and creatively within the context of society.

Confucianism impressed on the Chinese the supreme importance of making education available to all. There ought to be education not only of the entire man but also of all men. A Chinese proverb states that "with education there is no class distinction." The ideal of a universal public education was inherent in the Confucianist philosophy.

Confucianism impressed on the Chinese the supreme importance of building a great civilization. No civilization is genuinely great unless it produces culture and persons of moral character. These are the marks of civilization that count. Without them a society is barbarian, no matter how much technology it has mastered.

Confucianism impressed on the Chinese the supreme importance of spiritual values. These are of more consequence than wealth and material achievement. Jesus asserted that to gain the world, yet lose one's soul, is to have missed the point of life, and the Confucianist legacy encouraged generations of Chinese to seek *the real* not in things but in right relationships—to self, to others, and to the Supreme Being.[17]

These values, which today are challenged not only in China but also throughout the world, are virtues suitable for all persons, regardless of color, country, or creed, for they appeal to that which is fundamentally human in us all. This was demonstrated to me recently when I attended a conference on the human future. One of the speakers, a distinguished British scholar, predicted that "the long dark night of Materialism is finally coming to an end." Then he affirmed that "there is a planetary quest today for social values—values which are personal, ethical, idealistic, and spiritual." Should his prophecy prove to be true, then the ancient heritage of Confucianism will have much to offer to the human family of the twenty-first century.

[17]Yang, *China's Religious Heritage*, pp. 100–2.

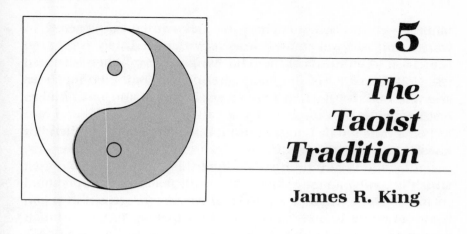

5

The Taoist Tradition

James R. King

I had my first real-life encounter with Taoism in Taiwan, in 1963, when, after much study and reading, I set off one afternoon for a Taoist temple in Tinan, for what I felt would surely be a profound spiritual experience. Unfortunately, the influence of the great classic texts which I had read so eagerly, the spirit of submission to the natural way of things, the excitement of the dynamic process of change were nowhere in evidence. Instead, grotesquely dressed priests moved about the temple area; the air was hideous with the noise of gongs and drums and shrill wind instruments; and the faithful, instead of meditating on unity and diversity or entering into "the flow," were tossing joss sticks into a huge kettle above a fire that flared up brilliantly but not very spiritually each time some magical offering was hurled into it. It was my disillusionment that was profound.

Several years later, in my home workshop in the American Midwest, I was struggling one day with the difficult art of brass-carving, a process supposedly carried out with a blunt, triangular tool called a burin, which one pushes through the brass to engrave the desired line. For two weeks I pushed and struggled with the metal, an inch an hour, leaving a jagged edge and thoroughly exhausting my arm and my patience. Then suddenly, one day when I was close to giving up, the brass seemed to turn to butter, the burin moved easily and effectively through it; the cut was smooth and deep; I could work for several hours and feel no weariness. What had happened was that arm, hand, fingers, tool, metal, angle of attack, pressure had all fused; I had come upon the natural way of carrying out a process, and when I discovered it I could stop struggling and work effortlessly. Later, I read in Chuang-tzu the words of the Wheelwright P'ien: "When I chisel a wheel, if the blows of the mallet are too gentle, the chisel slides and won't hold. But if they're too hard, it bites in and won't budge. Not too gentle, not too hard—you can get it into your hand and feel it in your mind. You can't put it into words, and yet there's a knack to it somehow."[1]

And at the very time I was writing this essay, I found myself struggling with an extremely difficult problem in interpersonal relations. There was a part of me that wanted to lash out in anger, to do anything I could to control the situation, to get as much from it as I could. But the Taoist texts I was rereading—Lao-tzu's *Tao te Ching* and the *Essays of Chuang-tzu*—were eloquent in warning me to go easy, to lie back, not to push anything, to let the process work itself out by itself. Quiet passivity, I was being told, would in the long run serve me better than angry action—as indeed it did.

These three incidents tell us a good deal about the religion that we are dealing with. They also suggest why Taoism is so different from the other great religions we are discussing, and why Taoism is both so hard and so easy to talk about. Taoism can be said to enter into every phase of Chinese culture. It is, says Mai-Mai Sze, "the basic Chinese belief in an order and harmony in nature"[2] and, according to Lewis Hodous, it represents "the emotional, spontaneous, imaginative side of Chinese life."[3] At a rather lofty level, it determines the subject matter and the style of countless Chinese paintings; at the popular level, it is a bizarre religion of magic or pseudo-magic, gods and goddesses, cultic rituals, and extravagant claims to healing, alchemy, and prophecy. At a philosophical or psychological level, Taoism speaks a truth that most human beings have at one time or another encountered— the idea that there is a natural way of carrying out any process or activity that ultimately is more effective than learned, artificial, or manipulative ways; a teacher can point a student to it, but words

[1]*The Complete Works of Chuang-Tzu*, trans. Burton Watson (New York: Columbia University Press, 1968), pp. 152–53.
[2]Mai-Mai Sze, *The Tao of Painting* (New York: Pantheon, 1963), p. 3.
[3]*The Great Religions of the Modern World*, ed. Edward J. Jurji (Princeton: Princeton University Press, 1946), p. 2.

are only pointers, and one must come to the process himself, by working with the material patiently and sensitively. John Evelyn's comment about a carpenter—he handles a saw like the saw itself would like to be handled—is richly Taoist. There is a Tao of tools and crafts, just as there is a Tao of sex, of athletics, of teaching.

The third example, relating to my problem in interpersonal relations, may seem primarily psychological rather than religious, except that insofar as I was being torn between two opposing patterns of activity, I was being impelled to make a critical choice, a commitment to one strategy or the other. For many centuries, activism, manipulation, anger, control, the drive for mastery have been the characteristic Western approach to problems, and in being encouraged to choose the quieter, more passive, more acquiescent approach which Taoism teaches I was being invited to a reorientation, a conversion of sorts. I was being pressed to make a new and different kind of commitment, to perform an act of faith in a way that was somewhat strange to me. This was an essentially religious process.

The same problem occurs constantly within the larger framework of the Christian church, for on the one hand, there are those who argue for social action, and on the other, those who argue that religion is a private affair. The question is where does power lie, and unfortunately there is little to indicate that either the activists or the quietists have their hands on very much of it. Taoism, however, is clearly on the side of those who hold back from very strong action so that God's spirit will have a chance to operate in a given situation. Such a position, however, must not be dismissed as mere ineffectual idealism; Taoists come through as hard-nosed, practical people who simply happen to have concluded that going with the flow of things puts more effective power in their hands than bucking the current.

It is suggestive and significant that I should have experienced more of the Tao in the American Midwest than in China, and particularly significant when the question of definitions of Taoism and the Tao come up. For one of the most striking emphases of the Taoist tradition is that one cannot convey the essence of it in words. Definitions, then, really do not define; they indicate or point. They say, "Yes, that power, that harmony which you are feeling is what is meant by Tao." The definition, then, is really a label for the experience, a means of identifying it, nothing more.

To know the definition is of little help if the experience is what one craves. A Christian could say no more—or no less—about his experience of Christ; a Muslim would make a similar assertion about his experience of the Qur'an.

Basically, as Arthur Waley suggests, that set of experiences to which the word *Tao* refers has to do with one's experience of a "road, path, way . . . method, principle, doctrine."[4] Again, one can point to Christ's statement that he is "the way" and to the Islamic concept of the *sunnah* or orthodox path and to the *tariq* or particular method used by a school of mystics to achieve enlightenment. A scientist could understand Waley's statement that Tao refers to "the way the Universe works" (p. 30) and Sze's comment that Tao is the law of nature, "a sort of divine legislation that regulated the pattern in the heavens and its own counterpart on earth" (p. 3). All of this can be referred to my own experience of deciding to face a certain situation in a passive, gentle, rather than a hostile and aggressive manner. The content of that act was the faith that the universe responds more readily to quietude than to violence.

For Taoists, this road, path, or method has certain very specific qualities, so that "being a Taoist" is certainly not a matter of assenting to certain dogmas, or even of getting somewhere, but of being "in the way." Even the longest journey, as Chuang-tzu puts it, begins when one takes the first step. Thus the qualities of the process function as a definition, and what stands out in all definitions is the quality of the Tao as the enormous, vital, creative power of the universe. As Chuang-tzu says, "Emptiness, stillness, limpidity, silence, inaction—these are the level of heaven and earth, the substance of the Way and its Virtue. Therefore the emperor, the king, the sage rest in them" (p. 142), and Chung-yuan Chang takes an even more dynamic view when he observes that "the value of Tao lies in its power to reconcile opposites . . . in order to achieve a balanced way of living." Chang's assertion that Tao is "the unification of infinite possibility and potentiality"[5] reminds us of Dante's description of God: "Where power and will are one." Waley asserts that Tao is "the Way of the Vital Spirit," and Hodous calls it "universal energy." Sze speaks of it as "the Primal

---

[4]Arthur Waley, *The Way and Its Power* (London: Allen and Unwin, 1956), p. 30.
[5]Chung-yuan Chang, *Creativity and Taoism* (New York: Julian, 1963), p. 5.

Unity and Source, the Cosmic Mother, and Dark and Mysterious, the Unfathomable, the Formless Form, the Infinite and Ineffable Principle of Life" (p. 15). Little wonder, then, that in translations of the Gospel of John into Chinese, the word *logos* is rendered Tao, since both terms point to the force that created the world and continues to sustain it.[6]

The idea of Tao as original power, vitality, and energy may seem to clash with the view that the Tao is in some sense feminine in nature, representing the passive element in creation, "the still pool," valleys rather than hills, that which is shaped rather than that which shapes. Once again, however, it must be asserted that the Taoist sees real power lying in stillness and the cultivation of stillness, and that there is nothing "unpowerful" about the maternal matrix out of which all life emerges, "that which was the beginning of all things under heaven" (Waley, p. 206). Clearly Taoists are strong individuals who employ quietness and passivity to achieve important ends, but this does not mean that they are hypocrites who simply feign nonaction to hide what they are doing. Nothing is being feigned. Taoism, however, does represent a contrast with Zen Buddhism (to which it has so many parallels), which, although it asserts the importance of meditation, also employs violence, both physical and psychological, to gain its ends.

Still other definitions stress the idea that the Tao represents or makes possible real achievement: Tao is the fulfillment of what one wishes, the something through which things are done. And others imply a link between the Tao and ultimate reality. Tao is, as Herrlee Creel suggests, "not merely a substance and a thing. It is the only substance and the only thing, for it is the totality of all things whatsoever."[7] Huston Smith's definition—Tao is "the Way of Ultimate reality," so overwhelming in its intense reality that mortal man could not stand to see it—is perhaps too abstract to

---

[6]For a discussion of Tao as Logos, see Herrlee Creel, *What Is Taoism and Other Studies in Chinese Culture* (Chicago: University of Chicago Press, 1970), pp. 29–30, to which is added an account of objections to this translation by S. Julien, who argues that typically Tao implies something that is devoid of action, thought, or desire. It might further be argued, in support of Creel, that the Tao brings salvation in the sense that it makes possible freedom from distress or perturbation, opening the way to harmony between nature and the world of man. Admittedly, this may not be salvation in the full sense of that word as it is used by Christians.

[7]Creel, *What Is Taoism*, p. 2.

be helpful, although it points, interestingly, to Moses' experience on Sinai.[8]

Such a wealth of definitions—definitions that imply such a wide variety of understandings and emphases—reflects the ambiguity and the complexity of our topic as well as its extraordinary simplicity. These contradictory characteristics are reflected also in the history of Taoism, a history that is filled with uncertainties and puzzles, marked by huge gaps, and yet is, by comparison with the history of Islam, Buddhism, Christianity, or Hinduism very simple indeed.

The legendary founder of Taoism, founder in the sense that he is the one who is alleged to have put together or written down the first major text, the *Tao te Ching*, was Lao-tzu, "the Old Fellow," who was born, according to tradition, in 604 B.C. However, not only the date of his birth is open to question; his very existence is by no means certain. If there was indeed such a person, he seems to have been the curator of the imperial archives, and he began, at one point, to question the validity of any sort of government and, indeed, the value of knowledge itself. According to one legend, Confucius himself visited Lao-tzu during this difficult period.[9] Eventually, the story goes, Lao-tzu resigned his official post and went into seclusion, although even in his isolated retreat he found himself so constantly beseiged by visitors that he headed off toward the west in an oxcart and was never heard of again. The gatekeeper at a border crossing, however, was so intrigued by Lao-tzu's philosophy of life that he refused to let him pass until he had stopped long enough to write down his moral views, the book now known as *Tao te Ching, The Way and Its Power*.[10] In any case, we can assume that the author of this fascinating book was himself an intriguing and baffling personality, odd, starry-eyed in one sense, yet enormously practical and earthy in other ways. Smith's suggestion that he was a kind of Chinese Abraham Lincoln may not be far from the mark, although there were elements in him, too, of the Sufi mystics

[8]Huston Smith, *The Religions of Man* (New York: Harper and Row, 1958), p. 195.

[9]There is an interesting imaginary account of this conversation in Herryman Maurer's novel about Lao-tzu, *The Old Fellow* (New York: John Day, 1943).

[10]For a discussion of modern views of dating, see Chang, *Creativity and Taoism*, p. 29. Some modern scholars tend to see it as much later than the traditional date in the seventh century B.C.

of Islam, the Indian fakirs, and the Hasidic teachers of Russian Judaism.

We must also remember that many important thinkers and religious and philosophical movements preceded Lao-tzu, and that to them he was surely indebted. Again, it is not easy to talk about possible influences without having a clearer idea as to when Lao-tzu lived, but it is clear that the very concept of Taoism is far older than Lao-tzu himself, it being, from the very beginning, an essential feature of Chinese culture. *The Book of Changes (I Ching)*, usually dated around 1150 B.C. (early Chou period), was a major part of the stream of ideas flowing in Lao-tzu's thought, for it forcefully presented life as an unceasing flux, with man at his best somehow involved in the flow. The *I Ching* offered an analysis of some sixty-four life situations, along with suggestions about how to behave in each, thus contributing what is a very important theme in Lao-tzu and in the thought of his successor Chuang-tzu, the idea of caring for life, reflecting upon experience, giving thought to one's stance and one's options. A later school of moralists, the so-called Hedonists, made its contribution by focusing attention on the needs and pleasures of the living rather than on the problems of the dead, and this idea too comes across in the text of the *Tao te Ching*, whether it preceded or followed the work of the philosophers of happiness. The Hedonists also taught that rulers were most effective when they allowed their subjects maximum freedom to lead their own lives—another important theme in Lao-tzu. Finally, yet another group, the Quietists, sought freedom from external impressions so as to free their minds from perturbations, seeking to achieve truth, happiness, and power by getting back to the essential roots of the personality.[11] They believed that by eliminating all negative feelings from the mind—anger, hatred, meanness—they could encourage operations of the vital life forces.

Many of these ideas, and still others which tend to gather around the great theme of "caring for life" were presented, a few centuries after Lao-tzu, by Chuang-tzu (369–286 B.C.), whose essays have been frequently translated and widely reprinted. Their anecdotal style and homely, vivid ideas make them one of the most popular of all Chinese texts. Basically, Chuang-tzu

---

[11]Waley, *The Way and Its Power*, p. 45.

The Chinese symbol for Yin and Yang, the
negative and positive elements of experience.

stressed his vision of the eternal flux of things, seeing Tao as change, as process, as the eternal alteration between states of being and nonbeing. Thus, in his work, the famous symbols of Yin and Yang, the negative and positive elements of experience, are often linked, reality being the endless play of all the dualities of life—light and dark, night and day, activity and passivity. The Chinese symbol for Yin and Yang has become as universally recognized a symbol of Taoism as has the cross for Christianity.

Chuang-tzu also stressed the relativity of all things, the impossibility of our ever possessing any absolute truth to which to refer in defending our own positions. The righteous Po Yi died of starvation at the top of a mountain rather than rule unjustly; Robber Chih died in search of gain atop another summit. "The two of them died different deaths," observes Chuang-tzu, "but in destroying their lives and blighting their inborn nature they were equal. Why then must we say that Po Yi was right and Robber Chih wrong?"

> Everyone in the world risks his life for something. If he risks it for benevolence and righteousness, then custom names him a gentleman; if he risks it for goods and wealth, then custom names him a petty man. The risking is the same, and yet we have a gentleman here, a petty man there.[12]

Much the same point is made by many Taoists who discuss the impossibility of asserting that a stick is long or short. Such

---

[12]*The Complete Works of Chuang-Tzu,* p. 102.

qualities gain meaning only in relation to events in which other, similar qualities are to be found.

Another important theme in Chuang-tzu has to do with the importance of sensing the flow of life or experience rather than struggling against it. This idea is well illustrated by the famous story of Cook Ting, who knew how to care for life—and for his meat cleaver:

> A good cook changes his knife once a year—because he cuts. A mediocre cook changes his knife once a month—because he hacks. I've had this knife of mine for nineteen years and I've cut up thousands of oxen with it, and yet the blade is as good as though it had just come from the grindstone. There are spaces between the joints, and the blade of the knife has really no thickness. If you insert what has no thickness into such spaces, then there's plenty of room—more than enough for the blade to play about it. That's why after nineteen years the blade of my knife is still as good as when it first came from the grindstone.[13]

Chuang-tzu's eloquent efforts at simplification, his conviction that the primitive, the natural, the unhurried were superior to what civilization had to offer remind us of such Western primitivists as Rousseau and Thoreau. And the efforts of the Chinese thinker, like those of his French and American counterparts, represent a commitment to a certain view of life, to a certain mode of behavior, that is essentially religious.

On the other hand, Chuang-tzu's insistence that morality must be natural, unforced, certainly clashes with the Christian view of man. "My definition of expertness has nothing to do with benevolence or righteousness," he says,

> it means following the true form of your inborn nature, that is all. When I speak of good hearing, I do not mean listening to others; I mean simply listening to yourself. When I speak of good eyesight, I do not mean looking at others; I mean simply looking at yourself. He who does not look at himself but looks at others, is getting what other men have got and failing to get what he himself has got. He finds joy in what brings joy to other men, but finds no joy in what brings joy to himself. . . .[14]

[13]Ibid., p. 51.
[14]Ibid., p. 103.

And then, it does not matter, says Chuang-tzu, whether he is Robber Chih or Po Yi: he is equally deluded.

But nowhere is Chuang-tzu's stress on the importance of natural rather than artificial behavior stronger than in the famous incident of his refusal to weep upon the death of his wife—instead pounding on a tub and singing. This is going too far, a friend complained, and Chuang-tzu responded:

> You're wrong. When she first died, do you think I didn't grieve like anyone else? But I looked back to her beginning and the time before she was born. Not only the time before she was born, but the time before she had a body. Not only the time before she had a body, but the time before she had a spirit. In the midst of the jumble of wonder and mystery a change took place and she had a spirit. Another change and she had a body. Another change and she was born. Now there's been another change and she's dead. It's just like the progression of the four seasons, spring, summer, fall, winter.
>
> Now she's going to lie down peacefully in a vast room. If I were to follow after her bawling and sobbing, it would show that I don't understand anything about fate. So I stopped.[15]

Clearly, Chuang-tzu was a worthy successor to Lao-tzu, a man of simple, direct, unshakable faith in the natural way, eloquent, direct, and witty in his writing; balanced, realistic, hopeful in his view of man.

After the death of Chuang-tzu, in the second and third centuries before Christ, Taoism became impregnated with elements of magic and alchemy, as well as with various efforts to master the body and to delay bodily decay and death. A text of some importance from this period was *The Secret of the Golden Flower*, also known as *The Art of Prolonging Human Life*. It deals, from a spiritual point of view, with various physiological and psychological issues and touches on various matters pertaining to alchemy, the ancient attempt to turn baser metals into gold. The significance of this for Taoism Carl Jung, who wrote a commentary on it, explains eloquently:

> The symbolism [of the Golden Flower] refers to a sort of alchemical process of refining and ennobling; darkness gives birth to light; out

[15]Ibid., p. 192.

of the "lead of the water-region" grows the noble gold; what is unconscious becomes conscious in the form of a process of life and growth. . . . In this way the union of consciousness and life takes place.[16]

There also developed at this time a school of immortality which was concerned, as Creel has noted, with the "perpetuation of the physical body" and perhaps also with the theme of resurrection. Drops, herbs, yoga-like physical exercises, breath control, magic talismans, dietary restrictions all were seen as ways to avoid death and/or hell and to achieve a life of beatitude beyond this present one.

There has been much scholarly discussion about where these ideas came from, for they seem to stand in such striking contrast to all that is implied in the Taoist doctrine of Wu Wei, the teaching about quietude. One way of bringing these two diverse viewpoints together has been to suggest that those who are weak or gentle are often less prone to physical death than are more aggressive persons. Creel has advanced the theory that Lao-tzu and Chuang-tzu, the most accessible classical sources on Taoism, never did give more than a partial picture of the whole of this religion, and that in its popular forms, Taoism may always—or for a long period—have embraced teachings about immortality. Such a view is helpful, although it further confuses our thinking about what the essence of this complex system really is.

The fact remains, however, that by the first century of the Christian era, Taoism was dominated by popular cults, by alchemy, and by innumerable forms of magic. Magic practices centered especially on the development of charms which could, when worn or swallowed, protect the user from all kinds of harm, or confer immortality. Other charms, as John B. Noss has indicated, made possible shape-shifting, or transportation through space, or walking on water. One magic seal was said to ward off dangerous beasts and protected animals or stores of food. Geomancers (prophets who read "earth signs") practiced the arts of *Feng-shan* (ceremonies linked with a sacred mountain that assured immortality) and *Feng-shui* (the art of locating and orienting buildings in

---

[16]*The Secret of the Golden Flower*, trans. Richard Wilhelm, commentary by Carl Jung, rev. ed. (New York: Harcourt Brace, 1962), p. 102.

order to expose the structures and their residents to the most positive natural currents).[17] The cults, which featured sorcerers and sorceresses who offered advice about the future, required enormous offerings from the devout. Through them, a wide range of deities were worshiped with songs and dances, as well as with prayers and animal sacrifices, and claims regarding the healing of certain illnesses were made.

Finally, in the second century A.D., partly as a result of the influence of Buddhism, Taoism began to take on the characteristics of traditional religious groups: Lao-tzu was made a god and around him there developed a whole set of gods and goddesses, including divinities of heaven, sun and moon, the Great Bear, as well as various minor gods assigned to important parts of the household and the fields, such as the doors and the soil. The celebrated "eight immortals" were borrowed from popular tradition and may perhaps originally have been humans who were thought to have gained immortality by asceticism.[18] Also, at this time, various festivals were formalized, for the intermingling of gods and men at common meals, the remembering of ancestors, and the making of the seasons.

During this stage of Taoism, concepts of heaven and hell as places of reward and punishment were elaborated, and a priestly class developed, headed by a papal figure called the Celestial Teacher. The "popes" in this dynasty, who belonged to the family of Chang, were able to establish themselves so powerfully in Szechuan province[19] that they levied taxes and carried out a number of reforms. Their dynasty lasted on the mainland until 1927, when they were unseated by the Communists, and presently continues in Taiwan. So important are the Celestial Masters in the history of Taoism that Michael Strickmann has proposed using the word *Taoist* only in referring to

> those who recognize the historical position of Chang Tao-ling, who worship the pure emanations of the Tao rather than the vulgar

[17]See John B. Noss, *Man's Religions*, 3d ed. (New York: Macmillan, 1963), p. 363, and John Michell, *The Earth Spirit* (New York: Avon, 1975), pp. 11–12.

[18]Noss, *Man's Religions*, p. 366.

[19]Jurji, *Great Religions*, p. 32.

gods of the people at large, and . . . who safe-guard and perpetuate their own lore and practice through esoteric rites of transmission.[20]

According to Strickmann, "the social history of Taoism" begins
with the founding of the way of the Celestial Master in the second
century A.D.

It was during this period, too, that certain "sacred books" were
canonized, among them the celebrated *T'ai p'ing Ching*, a religious
book that teaches a doctrine of salvation.[21] This text touches on
various moral virtues and vices, such as the sin of accumulating
Tao and keeping it for oneself; gathering riches without helping
the poor; refusing to study the Tao, even when one is aware
of it; living in idleness when one has the strength to work;
drinking alcohol; and practicing female infanticide. The *T'ai
p'ing Ching* also touches on the role of princes and how they can
comply with the will of heaven, and it provides prescriptions
for long life, stressing the importance of equity, "the duty
to give everyone the place that suits him in the hierarchy of
beings."[22]

Despite the objections of Strickmann, just quoted, most writers
on Taoism have indeed assumed the existence of a philosophical dimension to this religion, and although we must admit
that anyone who has spent a good deal of time on Taiwan or in
Hong Kong would be likely to be most impressed by the "popular" manifestations of Taoism, the fact is that most Western
readers encounter this religion through texts with a decidedly
moral and philosophical cast. So it seems important that
we devote some time, now, to a survey of the principal ideas
and concepts that Taoism has—if not given birth to—at least
nourished.

I attempt this with full knowledge of the fact that one of
the principal tenets of Taoism is the impossibility of talking
about it. The very first chapter of the *Tao te Ching* makes
this point:

[20]*Facets of Taoism: Essays in Chinese Religion*, ed. Holmes Welch and Anna Seidel (New
Haven: Yale University Press, 1979), p. 165.
[21]Ibid., p. 24.
[22]Ibid., p. 45.

The Way that can be told is not an Unvarying Way;
The names that can be named are not unvarying names.
It is from the Nameless that Heaven and Earth sprang;
The named is but the mother that rears the ten thousand
    creatures, each after its kind.[23]

Elsewhere, Lao-tzu observes that "the force of words is soon spent" (p. 147).

On this point of "teaching without words," Taoism may have been influenced by Zen Buddhism. Chang tells a story that is apropos, about the day when the celebrated teacher Fu-hsi was discovered at court

> wearing a monk's robe, a Taoist hat, and the shoes of a common laborer. The Emperor, seeing him, asked, "Is that a Buddhist costume you are wearing?" Fu-hsi pointed to his Taoist hat. The emperor asked, "Are you a Taoist?" Fu-shi pointed to his laborer's shoes. "Are you a common man?" asked the Emperor. Fu-hsi pointed to his fine Buddhist robes.[24]

And on the same point Chuang-tzu has this to say:

> The Great Way is not named; Great Discriminations are not spoken; Great Benevolence is not benevolent; Great Modesty is not humble; Great Daring does not attack. If the Way is made clear, it is not the Way.[25]

This refusal to try to put into words or define has psychological as well as philosophical overtones; philosophically, the typical ideas of Taoism cannot be expressed because they are not really ideas at all but rather psychological stances, ways that one "positions" oneself vis-à-vis the world and the powers in it. Thus Lao-tzu defines three stances that one might assume after hearing about the Tao: a man of the highest abilities will put it into practice; a man of middling abilities may feel anxious about it; a man of few abilities laughs at it.[26] Elsewhere Lao-tzu

---

[23]Waley, *The Way and Its Power*, p. 141.

[24]Chang, *Creativity and Taoism*, p. 45.

[25]*The Complete Works of Chuang-Tzu*, p. 44.

[26]Waley, *The Way and Its Power*, p. 193; Christ's parable of the soils may come to mind here.

describes how the sage "works on" the myriad creatures of the world:

> He rears them but does not lay claim to them,
> Controls them but does not lean upon them,
> Achieves his aim but does not call attention to what he does.[27]

This is parenting that involves complete acceptance of the fact that one's children are their own people; it means teaching with the goal of making one's pupils independent of oneself; it suggests complete respect for the integrity of another person, no matter how dependent that person is upon you; it requires eschewing all forms of manipulation:

> He that works through violence may get his way;
> But only what stays in its place
> Can endure.[28]

Equally eloquent on the problem of stance is a passage from Chuang-tzu's chapter on perfect happiness: is there such a thing, the moralist wonders, or isn't there?

> Is there some way to keep yourself alive or isn't there? What to do, what to rely on, what to avoid, what to stick by, what to follow, what to leave alone, what to find happiness in, what to hate?[29]

Quite characteristically the issues are left as questions; answers, assertions would be inappropriate.

In part, what lies behind all of these careful accounts of stance is the simple refusal to act aggressively or to try to impose one's will on a situation. As Smith has observed, "The Taoists rejected all forms of self-assertiveness and competition. The world is full of people who are determined to be somebody or give trouble. They want to get ahead, to stand out. Taoism has little use for such ambition."[30] Lao-tzu affirms this, observing that the sage stays out

[27]Ibid., p. 143.
[28]Ibid., p. 184.
[29]*The Complete Works of Chuang-Tzu*, p. 190.
[30]Smith, *The Religions of Man*, p. 207.

of the race, refusing to become involved in whatever competitive struggle *(agon)* a particular culture devises for itself, cultivating instead a "subtle, abstruse, mysterious, penetrating . . . watchful . . . ceremonious . . . yielding . . . blank . . . receptive stance."[31] Like water, the sage

> Puts himself in the background; but is always to the fore,
> Remains outside but is always there.[32]

Moreover, the sage realizes that one must know when to stop in time so as not to push a person or an issue too far: if you bend the bow, it will snap, says Lao-tzu; if you stand on tiptoe, you will fall; if you boast about your work, you will succeed in nothing (p. 173). Or, as Chuang-tzu puts it, "Do not deviate from your orders; do not press for completion." A good completion, he observes, may take a long time, but a bad completion cannot be changed later (p. 61). Conversely, "who stops in time nothing can harm," and the person who is content with what he has achieves a certain measure of security against disaster. To have pity on one's enemy, not to press the attack, not to push him into a corner is to assure that one himself will not be destroyed.

Also influencing the typical Taoist stance is a strong sense of the relativity of all things. The central symbol of Taoism, the circle of interpenetrating light and dark, suggests that reality emerges through the interaction of all the polarities that enter into our experience, and that reality cannot be defined, ever, except in terms of such interactions and relativities. The only Absolute is that which gave birth to the Yin and the Yang.[33] This has important implications for morality, for as Creel observes, "'Right' and 'wrong' are just words which we may apply to the same thing, depending upon which partial viewpoint we see it from. For each individual there is a different 'true' and a different 'false.' From the transcendent standpoint of the tao all such things are irrelevant."[34] Lao-tzu puts this well when he observes that

[31]Waley, *The Way and Its Power*, p. 160.
[32]Ibid., p. 150.
[33]See Sze, *The Tao of Painting*, p. 37, and Creel, *What Is Taoism*, p. 27.
[34]Creel, *What Is Taoism*, p. 3.

Long and short test one another
High and low determine one another.
Pitch and mode give harmony to one another;
Front and back give sequence to one another.

Or that

He whose braveness lies in daring, slays.
He whose braveness lives in not daring, gives life.
Of these two, either may be profitable or unprofitable.[35]

Also involved in the development of a stance, a way of looking at life, is the problem of constantly acquiring or maintaining a fresh and original point of view. Lao-tzu apparently, like the Sufis of Islam, was well known in his own day for the odd but curiously relevant positions he took on various issues, and Chuang-tzu is today enjoyed especially for the "off-beat" quality of his thinking. Thus, in one story he talks about the approach of two thieves to their trade and shows how one, who was successful, brought unusual insights to his work:

If one is to guard and take precautions against thieves who rifle trunks, ransack bags, and break open boxes, then he must bind with cords and ropes and make fast with locks and hasps. This the ordinary world calls wisdom. But if a great thief comes along, he will shoulder the boxes, hoist up the trunks, sling the bags over his back, and dash off, only worrying that the cords and ropes, the locks and hasps are not fastened tightly enough. In that case, the man who earlier was called wise was in fact only piling up goods for the benefit of a great thief.[36]

And in another—perhaps his most famous—he describes a form of confusion that could prove very productive:

Once Chuang Chou dreamt he was a butterfly, a butterfly flitting and fluttering about, happy with himself and doing as he pleased. He didn't know he was Chuang Chou. Suddenly he woke up and there he was, solid and unmistakable Chuang Chou. But he didn't know if he was Chuang Chou who had

[35]Waley, *The Way and Its Power*, pp. 143, 233; also see pp. 51–53.
[36]*The Complete Works of Chuang-Tzu*, p. 107.

dreamt he was a butterfly, or a butterfly dreaming he was Chuang Chou. . . .[37]

In our own day, this way of thinking which is so typical of Lao-tzu and Chuang-tzu has come to be known as new think or lateral thinking. The technique of this mode of creative thinking and problem solving is to question all assumptions, particularly one's assumptions about the kind of answer that one is seeking, and most certainly the method that one is employing. New think refuses to go at a problem stubbornly from the same old angle and prefers to come at it from the side, in some unusual way. Its results are always surprising and can often prove surprisingly relevant. There is much of the spirit of new think in the great Taoist thinkers.[38]

So important is this question of stance, so numerous the efforts of Taoists to describe the appropriate stance for any situation, that one is tempted to suggest that achieving whatever stance is appropriate to, productive, or harmonious with whatever situation one is facing is the key to Taoism. Yet the "Western mind" tends to reject the stance of passivity which Taoists so often recommend, failing to grasp the real power which such passivity enables a believer to bring to a situation, not noticing the productive interplay of two kinds of power which can be exploited. This insight is expressed in many ways in Taoist literature, but it finds its most striking expression in Taoist landscape painting, which characteristically includes enormous amounts of open space—sky, water, or earth. "In the handling of vast space," writes Sze, the ink paintings of the Southern Sung painters "are some of the greatest expressions of the human spirit" (p. 95). Space is seen as liberating the spectator from the bonds of earth, revealing the sublimity of the cosmos, suggesting the contrast between the eternity of space and the time boundedness of the world, and through stillness and silence suggesting mystery.

Other common images of emptiness are the well, the pool, any kind of vessel out of which something can emerge. Emptiness is pregnant with possibilities, for it is the space between the spokes

[37]Ibid., p. 49.
[38]See the volume by Edward DeBono, *New Think: The Use of Lateral Thinking in the Generation of New Ideas* (New York: Avon, 1967).

of the wheel, as Lao-tzu observes, that turns them into a useful wheel (p. 155). The useless tree is far safer than the tree that can be turned into useful wood, and besides, it offers richer possibilities. As Chuang-tzu observes,

> Now you have this big tree, and you're distressed because it's useless. Why don't you plant it in Not-Even-Anything Village, or the field of Broad-and-Boundless, relax and do nothing by its side, or lie down for a free and easy sleep under it? Axes will never shorten its life, nothing can ever harm it. If there's no use for it, how can it come to grief or pain?[39]

Elsewhere, Chuang-tzu observes, in his very earthy way, that "in the Chieh sacrifice, oxen with white foreheads, pigs with turned-up snouts, and men with piles cannot be offered to the river" (p. 65). Truly, the Tao is appropriately designated the Great Void, for in it reside all things.

The question of dynamic passivity raises, in turn, questions about the Taoist view of power and the meaning of Te, which embodies some of the central ideas of Taoism. Waley defines Te as "the stock of credit (or the deficit) that at any given moment a man has at the bank of fortune" (p. 31) and as "a latent power, a 'virtue' inherent in something" (p. 32). For Smith, Te means "the power that holds society together" (p. 201); for Hodous, the "activity" in which Tao, universal energy, resides.

Finally, a word about the Taoistic teaching on the ideal man, on humanity at its highest manifestation, for Taoism, like every great religion, every great cultural epoch has such a vision. From a variety of texts, we learn that the figure of whom we are speaking is one who takes great care about his stance, about positioning himself:

> Puts himself in the background; but is always to the fore.
> Remains outside; but is always there.
> Is it not just because he does not strive for any personal end
> That all his personal ends are fulfilled?[40]

---

[39]*The Complete Works of Chuang-Tzu*, p. 35.
[40]Waley, *The Way and Its Power*, p. 150.

He does not attempt to dominate or control, of course (Waley, p. 143), and approaches whatever situation he is in noncompetitively (p. 157). Lao-tzu describes himself as one who "droops and drifts" as though he belongs nowhere (p. 168), and of course the element of passivity is constantly stressed. This kind of quietude leads, as we have already noted, to freedom from fear of death ("When a man leaves his burden of anxiety and fear behind him he attains an inner serenity and reaches a higher and more integrated level of consciousness," Chang, p. 239), so that he can affirm with Lao-tzu that "when one dies, one is not lost" (Waley, p. 184), and that concern with life after death is a game "that nature did not intend us to play." Elsewhere, Lao-tzu describes the ideal man as "subtle, abstruse, mysterious, penetrating, Too deep to be understood" (p. 160) and as one who can live "in a world of free identity" without having to impose his story, his myth, his scenario, on events around him, free of any self-conscious ego (Chang, p. 39). And from Chuang-tzu we have a moving account of "The True Man of Ancient Times" which sums up much of what others have said:

> What do I mean by a True Man? The True Man of ancient times did not rebel against want, did not grow proud in plenty, and did not plan his affairs. A man like this could commit an error and not regret it, could meet with success and not make a show. A man like this could climb the high places and not be frightened, could enter the water and not get wet, could enter the fire and not get burned. His knowledge was able to climb all the way up to the Way like this.
>
> The True Man of ancient times slept without dreaming and woke without care; he ate without savoring and his breath came from deep inside. The True Man breathes with his heels; the mass of men breathe with their throats. Crushed and bound down, they gasp out their words as though they were retching. Deep in their passions and desires, they are shallow in the working of Heaven.
>
> The True Man of ancient times knew nothing of loving life, knew nothing of hating death. He emerged without delight; he went back in without a fuss. He came briskly, he went briskly, and that was all. He didn't forget where he began; he didn't try to find out where he would end. He received something and took pleasure in it; he forgot about it and handed it back again. This is what I call not using the

mind to repel the Way, not using man to help out Heaven. This is what I call the True Man.[41]

We have observed already that it is possible to divide Taoism into philosophical and religious or popular elements. It is evident, too, that Taoism, like every other great religion, can be divided into elements that have to do with the outer world—with rituals, cults, hierarchies, forms of worship, social action (the exoteric dimension) and elements that relate to the inner life—prayer, meditation, the cultivation of quietude (the esoteric or hidden dimension). Creel distinguishes helpfully between purposive and contemplative Taoism and argues that originally this religion was essentially mystical, contemplative, and meditative; that applications of the insights of the religion to external problems came later. Others, as we have seen, take an opposing view, to argue that only organized, hierarchial Taoism deserves the name.

Whatever the truth of the matter may be, it does seem important at this point to indicate certain elements in Taoism which do have a meditative or esoteric cast, which suggest that there are indeed ties between Taoism and mysticism, that in this great religious tradition subjective, intuitive elements are important. We note, for example, that within the Taoist tradition considerable attention is paid to such meditative devices as the maintenance of certain postures and to specific breathing techniques—as in Yoga, Zen, and Sufism (see Chang, p. 129). Much importance is given, also, to the elimination of destructive emotions from the personality—anger, anxiety, and joy even, so that one can reach what Smith calls "the serene and immovable source" of one's life. The cares of the world are to be eliminated, as are all accumulations of "dust" from the soul, so that a sense of harmony with and awareness of all living things is gained. A poem by Wang Wei expresses this sense of cleansing the heart so that one can enjoy the simple beauty all around:

Since the days of my middle life
I was deeply devoted to Tao.
Recently I came to live
In the mountain of Chung-nan.

[41]*The Complete Works of Chuang-Tzu*, pp. 77–78.

Oftentimes—with joy in my heart—
Alone, I roam here and there.
It is a wonderful thing
That I am aware of myself.
When the streamlet ends my trip
I settle down and catch
The moment of rising mists.
Now and then I meet
A furrowed dweller of the woods.
We chat and laugh;
Never do we want to go home.[42]

In recent years we have seen a rash of books applying Taoist principles of harmony and simplicity to a wide range of current problems. Fritjof Capra, in *The Tao of Physics* (1977), discusses recent advances in modern physics which lead to a picture of material reality that is just as transient and uncertain as the world viewed in terms of the Tao. Jean S. Bolen, in *The Tao of Psychology* (1979), treats the phenomenon of synchronicity—the unexpected and fortuitous coming-together of highly diverse events—as a manifestation of the Tao, the flowing together of all things. And Ralph G. H. Siu, *The Tao of Science* (1958), discusses current problems in the conduct of scientific research by modern executives. He stresses the need to encourage new and changing concepts, the importance of universals and broad general ideas, and the importance of "sage-knowledge" as well as rational knowledge.

The harmony-simplicity theme is most apparent to laymen, however, when they begin to develop some knowledge and love of Taoist painting. It is not too much to say that all of the great classical landscape painters and all of the great classical landscapes—the most common genre in Chinese painting— reflect to a profound degree the Taoist feeling for the mystical harmony between man and nature, a harmony of spiritual, nonmaterial quality. This harmony has to do with both the painter's own development (and his approach to his art) and the subjects he chooses to paint—tiny man living in a state of complete harmony with the natural world around him.[43] The

---

[42]Quoted in Chang, *Creativity and Taoism*, pp. 177–78.
[43]Sze, *The Tao of Painting*, p. 33.

Painting by Chang Feng,
landscape (hanging scroll).

painter functions through the power of the spirit to reveal the spiritual dimension of life. How different this is from the situation in the Christian world where, as Alan Watts points out, a Christian art has not evolved at all; "that is to say, it thinks of religious art in terms of liturgical art—painting, literature, and music having formally religious subject matter. There is no conception yet of painting a landscape, a group of flowers, a portrait, a street scene, in a Christian and incarnational way."[44] By contrast, as Chang observes, Taoist painting is "the spontaneous reflection from one's inner reality, unbound by arbitrary rules from without and undistorted by confusion and limitations from within" (p. 203).

The central spiritual concepts behind Chinese painting, the means by which the inner harmony of the subject matter was achieved, are Ch'i, the vital force behind all life (Sze, p. 34) and Yin and Yang, already discussed, the positive and negative elements of life which, according to Taoist doctrine, are in constant interplay. Ch'i has been compared to the Greek concept of *pneuma*, to the Latin *spiritus*, and most significantly to the Hebrew *ruah*, as it is used in Genesis 1:27, where God is described as breathing into man the breath of life.[45] The painter attempted to achieve a sense of this spirit by harmonizing the impressions received by his eye and his mind and it was felt that even though he could not see the entire universe, he could express the harmonious wholeness of things if he succeeded in conveying Ch'i.

Similarly, Chinese painters attempted to convey the concepts of Yin and Yang by depicting the constant process of change through which nature is always passing. Thus, favorite topics for painting were dragons, which, by their link with sky, rivers, sea, and rain could symbolize the ceaseless movement of nature, in both its beneficent and its ferocious aspects; and the four seasons, themselves products of the ceaseless flow of all things. Wind becomes in Chinese painting a symbol of both divine favor and divine wrath, and calligraphy ("beautiful writing") could also express in an effective way the power that ebbs and flows through life. And by catching a flower or a plant in a certain stage of maturing—growth, bloom, decay—it was possible in yet another way to suggest the great processes of change in which all of life and spirit were involved.

[44]Alan Watts, *Behold the Spirit* (New York: Random, 1972), p. 113.
[45]Sze, *The Tao of Painting*, pp. 52–53.

But content and symbolism alone were not enough: the expression of the Tao through painting also was a matter of style, style that was fresh, nervous, free, unhampered by constrictions of any kind. In achieving "style," a number of factors were involved, the most important being the brush which the master used. The master painter carefully selected the bristles for his brush, bound them just so, and in using it, treated his brush with the utmost care and respect. It was, as Sze has observed, "the painter's or the scholar's chief means of individual expression," an almost organic part of his fingers, which in turn were under the control of his mind and spirit. Great care was also taken in the manufacture of the ink, which was molded into sticks and dried, awaiting use. Paper came in many varieties—smooth, round, thick, thin—and in a wide range of tints and materials, including silk. Skill, spiritual insight, quietude, subject matter, instruments, and media—these were what enabled the painter to embody in his work "the fullest possible experience . . . of total harmony" (Sze, p. 79).

The contemplative, quietist strain in Taoism has also had an important influence on Chinese theory of government. The spirit of passivity which is so central to this religion, the non-involvement in human affairs which it encourages, the sense which it imparts of moving with the flow of things—these have clearly, over the years, influenced thought in China about government and thought where China has been an influence. At the philosophical level we can cite the general Taoist view that the concerns of the civil state are not particularly "real," (e.g., what, indeed, does the phrase *the public good* mean?), and how can the state judge between—much less come to terms with— all the conflicting interests within its borders. For another thing, the state's chief weapon has always been war, and all war-like processes clearly conflict with the Taoist view that by softness, subtlety, and yielding what is hard and aggressive can be overcome:

> The man of highest 'power' does not reveal himself as a
>   possessor of 'power';
> Therefore he keeps his 'power.' . . .
> The man of highest 'power' neither acts nor is there any
>   who so regards him . . .

It is best to leave the fish down in his pool;
Best to leave the State's sharpest weapons where none can
    see them.[46]

Consequently, Taoists advocated the separation of the ruler
from the day-to-day processes of government, the emperor exert-
ing simply a general influence on the overall direction of affairs, as
a kind of "majestic arbiter"[47] who refuses to tamper:

Can your mind penetrate every corner of the land, but you
    yourself never interfere?
Rear them, then, feed them,
Rear them, but do not lay claim to them.
Control them, but never lean upon them;
Be chief among them, but do not manage them.[48]

This also, of course, frees the people from harassment by their
rulers, although it offers little relief when it is the imperial
underlings who are doing the harassing. Lao-tzu also appears to
feel that it is beneficial for the people to feel that things happen
of their own accord (Waley, p. 164) and indeed this makes sense:
they can neither blame the government nor come to depend
upon it; instead, they develop an awareness of how events flow
and how, by fitting into this flow, they can render their own
lives harmonious and reasonably complete. As Chuang-tzu observes, "When I talk about having no feelings, I mean that a man
doesn't allow likes or dislikes to get in and do him harm. He
just lets things be the way they are and doesn't try to help life
along."[49]

A statement by Shen Pu-hai, who was a Chinese prime minister
in the fourth century B.C., summarizes much Taoist thinking about
government, and, indeed, much Taoist thinking about experience
in general:

[46]Waley, *The Way and Its Power*, pp. 189, 187.
[47]Creel, *What Is Taoism*, p. 98.
[48]Waley, *The Way and Its Power*, p. 153.
[49]In Siu, *The Tao of Science*, "The Median Way" and "The Philosopher-Executive," there
are interesting suggestions about executive and corporate behavior that makes use of
Taoist principles.

Worship of the Earth God is an example of
popular Taoist practice in Taiwan.

[The ruler is like] a mirror, [which merely] reflects the light [that
comes to it, itself] doing nothing, and yet [because of its mere
presence], beauty and ugliness present themselves [to view]. [He is
like] a scale, [which merely] establishes equilibrium, [itself] doing
nothing, yet [the mere fact that it remains in balance causes]
lightness and heaviness to discover themselves. [The ruler's] method is [that of] complete acquiescence. [He merges his] personal
[concerns] with the public [weal, so that as an individual] he does
not act. He does not act, yet [as a result of his nonaction] the world
[brings] itself [to a state of] complete [order].[50]

We know that philosophical Taoism is flourishing in the West
today, but we are less well informed about the position of popular
Taoism—the various cults devoted to immortality that are contemporary in the Orient. We do know, however, that the government of Communist China has taken steps to stamp out the more
superstitious element of the religions within its borders, even
though it is officially dedicated to the promotion of religious
freedom. A Bureau of Religious Affairs, established in 1950, has
devoted itself to retraining religious leaders along lines more

[50]Quoted by Creel, *What Is Taoism*, p. 64.

appropriate for a communist state, and has confiscated religious property and cut off gifts to religious institutions. By the 1960s, the great religions of China had been "deinstitutionalized and declericalized." However, this process was carried out by permission rather than by force, and efforts were made to make Taoist practices—when they were not superstitious—fit into and contribute to national goals. By 1978, the government of the People's Republic of China appeared to be taking a more open view of religion.[51]

It is in Hong Kong and Taiwan—sites peripheral to the Chinese mainland—that popular Taoism is most lived at the present time. In Taiwan some two thousand Taoist temples serve the people, and in Hong Kong, Taoist temples and shrines are constantly visited, a local god of particular importance being T'ien Hon, the protector of seafearing folk.

[51]See Frederick M. Kaplan and Julian M. Sobin, *Encyclopedia of China Today*, rev., 3d ed. (New York: Harper, 1981).

6

The Shintō Tradition

Eugene R. Swanger

Before the arrival of the Christian faith in Japan, two religious traditions had been institutionalized there—Shintōism and Buddhism. The Shintō tradition, indigenous to Japan, is prehistoric in origin. The Buddhist tradition, on the other hand, arrived relatively late, that is, in the sixth century A.D., after one thousand years of evolution on the Asian mainland.

It is characteristic of the Japanese religious situation that there has been relatively little conflict between the two traditions. Indeed, the themes and motifs of the two have become so inextricably entwined in the minds of the Japanese people that it is difficult to tell where one ends and the other begins. This facile blending of Shintō and Buddhist beliefs reflects the eclecticism that is characteristic of Japanese thought, for the Japanese have never held that the acceptance of one set of religious beliefs might preclude adherence to another.

The general absence of tension between the two is certainly not due to any intrinsic harmony between these ways of belief. Indeed, in some crucial areas one can hardly imagine two more different religious patterns. For example, the Shintō tradition is characterized by a joyful acceptance of the natural world and a deep abiding gratitude for its bounty and beauty, coupled with a horror of disease and death. Consequently a Shintō priest could not be present at a sickbed or a funeral, nor could diseased persons enter a shrine compound. In contrast, the Buddhists have dwelt on the sorrows of the earthly condition. They regard the

139

pleasures of this existence as transitory and delusive and there-fore reject them. They offer release from the eternal round of decay and death by retirement from the world and a modification of human consciousness through meditation.

The extreme simplicity of the Shintō tradition is one of the reasons for the absence of conflict with the antithetical Buddhist heritage. The indigenous Japanese tradition had no metaphysical, speculative, or ethical structures of thought. It had no sophisticat-ed liturgy or priestly hierarchy, no founder, no saints or martyrs. It was without written scriptures and the exegetical discussions that always accompany them. It had no painting or sculpture. To a significant degree it was the lack of these characteristics that enabled it to adapt to the challenges that the Buddhist tradition presented.

In time, however, the Shintō heritage adopted and adapted selected Buddhist characteristics. Over the centuries a priestly hierarchy was created; the oral tradition was written down—in Chinese at first because there was no Japanese writing. Shintō painting and sculpture slowly developed. Shrines were organized into associations. Liturgical rites and vestments became more elaborate and sophisticated. But the theological and philosophi-cal development of Shintō has remained modest. In marked contrast to the Buddhist tradition, which has extensive theological and philosophical teachings, the Shintō intellectual leaders have not responded in like manner. Thus the Shintō tradition has existed down through the centuries without religious doctrine, that is, without systematic statements of belief to be taught to each succeeding generation. The indigenous Japanese religious heri-tage and its sentiments, which enrich and give meaning to the totality of Japanese life, were shaped and nourished in the mountain, farming, and fishing villages of the countryside where the rituals, festivals, shrines, and sacred objects symbolized the eternal's continual intercourse with village life. Growing up in this village context one learns gradually through a long experien-tial process, which is largely unconscious and is analogous to the way in which a person's feelings toward his family might develop as he grows up in his home. As one Shintō theologian stated, "In Japan Shintō is caught, not taught."[1]

---

[1]Sokyo Ono, *Shintō: The Kami Way* (Tokyo: Charles E. Tuttle, 1962), pp. 6–12.

The Basic Concepts in the Shintō Tradition

Because the Shintō tradition has little doctrinal structure, it is more profitable to examine the symbols that constitute the essence of the heritage, for it is the symbols that are prehistoric and that remain important to the Japanese people. In this essay we will examine two kinds of symbols—those of space, the shrine complex, and those of time, the festival.

Both symbols can be understood in terms of a relationship between the sacred and the profane. By "profane" is meant all of the qualities and events in life that drain life of its joy and verve: disease, accidents, wounds, bleeding, death, failures, weakness, fear, anxiety, foul-smelling substances, and unseemly noise. In contrast the sacred is that which gives and sustains life. It is the source of all power, fecundity, abundance, joy, love, and peace. The Shintō tradition is immediately concerned with overcoming the former, which it calls pollution, and sustaining the latter, the source of which it calls Kami.

The word *Kami* has often been translated into English as "god" or "deity." Because such translations carry with them Western notions that are foreign to the Japanese, the term *Kami*, which is both the singular and the plural form, will be retained throughout this chapter.

As there is no adequate translation of the word *Kami*, so there is no definition or concept of the term that is generally acceptable. In fact the Japanese people have been quite content to practice their native faith for countless centuries without any formal definition of this important term.[2]

It is generally accepted by Shintō theologians, however, that the term *Kami* is derived from the words *ka*, which means that which is hidden, mysterious, and invisible, and *mi*, which implies something visible and tangible. Literally then, "Kami" means "a manifestation of the hidden." But as a definition it must be taken with a good deal of freedom.[3]

According to the sacred scriptures of Shintō, the *Kojiki* and the *Nihon Shoki*, the Kami have created all, the seen and the unseen. Everyone and everything is of the Kami and, being Kami-born,

[2]H. Byron Earhart, *Religion in the Japanese Experience: Sources and Interpretations* (Encino, Calif.: Dickenson, 1973), p. 10.

[3]Jean Herbert, *Shintō* (London: Allen and Unwin, 1967), pp. 23–24.

everyone and everything has the Kami nature. But in some persons and some things there is a clearer and more perceptible manifestation of Kami than in others. The number of manifestations is countless. Kami can be revealed in a mountain, an unusual rock, a towering tree, an awe-inspiring waterfall, an aromatic plant, a fox, a bird, a leaf, a peach, or a person of extraordinary accomplishment.

From the viewpoint of the Shintō theologians, when a person points to Kami it does not imply any specific kind of existence that is different from any other existence. The term signifies the way in which something exists rather than an existence itself. That is, if a Japanese experiences a sense of numinosity in the presence of a particular mountain and utters "Kami," the term refers to the content of the experience itself and is not an ontological statement about the mountain.

Again, from the viewpoint of more reflective Japanese, certain objects, such as a rock of unusual shape, refract an otherwise unseen or unperceived dimension of the way existence exists. The rock is no longer perceived as being simply a rock, but it is distinguished from other objects because it reflects more clearly a deeper essence. It is not a supernatural being from a supernatural world, but an inchoate presence, sensed but not seen, presenting itself in the natural world. Yet it is actually a natural presence because it is natural for the source of life to be present within life. It is simply manifesting its authentic nature. The Kami of the rock is not an eternal being from an eternal world. Rather the Kami of the rock is something in time presenting itself as though on a timeless plane.

On the other hand, less reflective and more literal-minded Japanese do not appear to know about or make such careful qualifications. As in most religious traditions, there is a gap between the reflections of the trained mind of the Shintō leader and the untutored viewpoint of the lay person. Probably for most Japanese people the word *Kami* means an unseen presence from another realm manifesting itself in an external object. It is something from the eternal revealing its presence in an object in the temporal realm.

Although a person's first experience with Shintō might cause him to think that the tradition is polytheistic, that is, that the Japanese believe there are many different Kami, a closer examination indicates that there is also a sense that behind the multiple manifestations of Kami there is a single life force. In other words, among the Japanese there appears to be a strongly felt subconscious intuition that beneath the many appearances there is a unified center.

This sense that Kami is the invisible root of the visible world has fostered and sustained the notion that all of nature is infused with the eternal, and that there is a strong continuity between the temporal and the eternal, nature and human beings, history and mythology, which makes a clear distinction between them naïve, if not impossible, from the Japanese point of view. A Japanese scholar has said that because of this immanentist position a Japanese person will "refuse to treat natural objects purely as instruments, and he [will feel] that contact with nature involves latently religious meaning."[4]

This was brought home to me quite clearly one day when after a class a discussion occurred about an American who was playing for a Japanese professional baseball team and had lost his temper. In anger he had hurled his bat to the ground, an act that—because it is unacceptable in Japan—had attracted some attention in the Japanese press. One Japanese student, who had argued that the American's behavior was disrespectful to the umpire, concluded, "and besides the bat and the ground are alive."

The Shintō tradition has shown no interest in personal salvation, nor has it asked questions about the transcendental significance of life. Rather it has an explicit emphasis upon everyday life and its concerns. Its energies therefore are directed to the ritual maintenance of the normal, commonplace realities. Within Shintō the accent has always been on the sustenance and enrichment of life here and now: the fertility and abundance of the crops, the birth of children, protection from storm, fire, and disease, safety in travel, and more recently success in examinations and prosperity in business. Thus Shintō, which sees the world permeated with numerous manifestations of the sacred, is very much a religion of daily life.

Moreover, with its strong orientation toward having a safe,

[4]Iwao Munakata, "Ambivalent Effects of Modernization on Traditional Folk Religion of Japan," *Japanese Journal of Religious Studies* 3 (June-September 1976), nos. 2–3, pp. 108–9.

prosperous, and happy existence in this world, this tradition has given little attention to the nature of life after death. The other world is not clearly conceived and people seem not to have concerned themselves with its nature. It is generally believed that even the deceased are primarily attached to this life and that the high point of the year for the dead is the festival when they visit the living.[5]

So strong was the interest in the maintenance of this life that, when the Buddhists began arriving in Japan in the sixth century, responsibility for serving at funerals and memorial services was given to the Buddhist priests. Today this practice continues. Most Japanese, who visit the Shintō shrine on the great festival days, will summon the Buddhist priest if a death occurs in the family.

The Symbolism of Shrines

Let us now examine the shrine as a central symbol of the Shintō faith. There are approximately one hundred thousand shrines in Japan, which vary in size from several thousand acres to minor shrines as small as beehives. Many shrines, although certainly not all, are located at places where manifestations of the Kami are said to have occurred. A manifestation can happen via a dream, a vision, or most often through a subtle sense of beauty or serenity that evokes an awareness of Kami in this place.

In earliest times no buildings were erected at the sacred sites. A grove of trees, a stone, a shrub, or a place that offered a striking view of a mountain would be fenced and marked as a sacred area. Through the centuries buildings have been erected on nearly all of the ancient sacred sites.

A distinguishing feature of Shintō shrines is the presence of the *torii*, a gate composed of two vertical posts joined at the top by two horizontal beams. The earliest torii were constructed of unpainted tree trunks, but today bronze and ferro-concrete are also used and the majority are painted bright red or orange. They will vary in height from ten to fifty feet with the pillars of the large ones having diameters of four feet. The more important shrines have three torii. The first one marks the entrance onto the sacred

[5]Ibid., pp. 110–11.

The Great Torii at Meiji Shrine, Tokyo, during New Year's festival.

ground. The other two mark the progression to the most sacred spot on the holy ground, the *honden*, where the Kami resides.

The shapes of the torii vary considerably, and actually there are more than twenty styles, each of which denotes a different family of shrines.

Draped from the lower horizontal beam of the torii is a heavy rope of large diameter in the middle and tapering to reduced diameters at both ends. Called *shimenawa*, these ropes sometimes have a circumference of six feet at the center. Woven of rice straw by members of the parish, they sometimes weigh more than a ton.

After walking under the first torii, a visitor can expect to cross a small stream, which is understood to be a barrier to the profane. By walking across it the visitor leaves behind a portion of whatever within himself might have been undesirable. He is therefore better prepared to enter the increasingly sacred region of the shrine complex. Many of the bridges have high arches in imitation of the rainbow and some bridges are so steep that they are difficult to cross. Consequently, less demanding bridges are sometimes constructed nearby.

In addition to the torii and the bridge there are fences to protect the sacred areas of the shrine from the profane. The great shrine at Ise has four fences; most of the other well-known shrines have two to three. Of course, because of a lack of space, neighborhood shrines usually will have only one.

The approach to the most sacred area in the shrine complex ought not be straight. Somewhere after passing under the first torii the visitor will find a bend in the pathway *(sandō)*. The visitor cannot walk straight toward the sanctuary for three reasons:

A neighborhood shrine.

religious, aesthetic, and ethical. In reality, however, from the Japanese point of view, these cannot be separated. A bend in the pathway is one more way of marking a change toward the increasingly ontically-charged region in the shrine complex. Second, it is aesthetically satisfying to make a turn in the path and have the eye greeted, or perhaps surprised, by a new view. Third, indirection has high ethical value in Japan. Being indirect in asking a question, making a request, or approaching the Kami is understood to be much more respectful than being direct. The latter is perceived by the Japanese people as an act of impertinence.

Somewhere along the sandō the visitor will come to a small structure at the side of the path. Open on all sides, the building covers an oblong stone basin in which fresh water is running. Here the worshiper will rinse his mouth and wash his hands before proceeding further. Again impurities are washed away and the visitor is prepared to proceed further.

At the center of the shrine are the religious buildings, one in front of the other: the honden, or Holy of Holies, where the Kami resides; the *heiden*, a hall in which the rites are performed by the officiating clergy; and the *haiden*, where the worshipers can assemble for rites and prayers. Many of the more important shrines, such as the imperial shrine at Ise, have no haiden, the worship being performed in the open after the ancient custom.

In marked contrast to the great cathedrals of the West, Shintō shrine buildings are constructed on a small scale. The one-story structures are built of wood and pampa grass instead of stone and tile, and many are dismantled and completely rebuilt after a specific number of years—twenty in the case of Ise Shrine, which appears to represent the purest expression of pre-Buddhist, pre-Chinese expression of Japanese religious architecture. Accordingly, we shall look at the Ise Shrine more closely.

The archaic buildings, which resemble the dwellings of South Sea islanders, are made of *hinoki*, Japanese cypress, and are left unfinished. No nails or metal fasteners are used. Instead all pieces are cut to a close tolerance and interlock to give a tight and sturdy fit. The roofs of each of the buildings are covered with a kind of reed-like material called *kaya*, which is related to the pampa grasses of the Philippines and Southeast Asia. A striking feature of the roofs are the *chigi*, peculiar crossed beams that rise from the gables at both ends and the even stranger cigar-shaped logs *(katsuogi)*, about five feet long, which lie horizontally along the ridge of the roof and perpendicular to the ridge line itself. The chigi at Ise Shrine are cut vertically at the top ends because the Kami enshrined is Amaterasu, the female Kami of the sun. If the Kami of a shrine is male, the top ends of the chigi are cut horizontally. The number of katsuogi on the roof usually indicates the rank of the Kami. The higher the rank, the more katsuogi a shrine is entitled to have.[6]

The most important building of the shrine complex is the honden. Because the Kami is within, no lay person is allowed to look into it. Many are kept always closed except for a visit by the high priest of the shrine once during the year. In addition, within the honden there is often a still more sacred place, a cabinet or *sanctum sanctorum*, which contains the object, *mitama-shiro* (literally: divine soul-body), in which the Kami is present. In nearly all shrines the cabinet is never opened.

According to Shintō priests, the mitama-shiro contains a *goshintai* (literally: revered sacred substance). The mitama-shiro can be a sword or a mirror or more often a natural object. There are several important shrines which are without a honden. In these cases the haiden faces a mountain, a woods, or a waterfall, or another natural geographical feature that is the mitama-shiro. That is, the Kami is felt to be present in the mountain, the trees, or the cascading water. Because of the need for concealment and hiddenness to protect the sacred from the erosion of the profane, the view of the mitama-shiro will be obscured with a wood lattice grill at the back of the heiden.

In not a few shrines the priests no longer know what the mitama-shiro is and they are reluctant to discuss it. It has been wrapped in a number of precious cloths and placed inside of several boxes. Over the passage of generations, when the most recent outer covering began to show signs of age, a new outer covering was added. Again because of the deep respect felt for the *Mysterium*, that hidden spring of life, no one will commit the sacrilege of removing the many protective layers.

When the mitama-shiro must be removed from the honden at the time of its reconstruction, a ceremony called *sengu*, which

[6]Herbert, *Shintō*, pp. 107–14.

evokes a deep sense of awe and reverence, is conducted. The priests, who must be near the Kami, wear white cloth over their faces and hold green *sakaki* branches in their mouths so their breath will not profane it. Three silk veils encircle the palanquin in which the Kami is carried in the transfer procession. Sometimes a shimenawa, the sacred straw rope, will surround the entire procession and will move with it as it processes to a neighboring shrine where the Kami will be housed temporarily until the new quarters are erected. Usually the transfer ceremony is carried out in the middle of the night when all lights have been extinguished, sometimes within a radius of half a mile. Occasions when all automobile lights in an entire region had to be turned off are known.[7]

The Symbolism of Space

In all of these architectural devices and religious practices associated with the shrine complex—three torii, the bridged stream, the indirect approach, the closed honden with the sealed cabinet inside, the sengu ceremony—themes fundamental to Japanese culture in general and the Shintō tradition in particular are embodied.

First there is the fundamental Shintō notion that in seclusion and darkness there is life-giving power. The mysterious center of existence is hidden and beyond the ability of people to perceive or understand except in a dim, vague, and inchoate way. Its presence can be sensed but not seen, perceived but not directly. A person can approach the Mysterium, but only with discretion and never completely. Even as the Kami is revealed, it remains concealed. And in the concealment the power of life gestates until it burst forth and gives new life to all of nature, including the people of the community.

This theme of a spirit coming out of a dark, enclosed space to be a blessing to people is a fundamental one in Japanese culture and is well illustrated in Japanese folk tales and children's stories. A popular children's story is that of a little boy who is born out of a peach and brings new vitality and health to an elderly couple.

[7]Ibid., pp. 117–25.

Another is that of a little girl who is discovered inside a bamboo tree by an old woodcutter and brings joy and prosperity to him and his wife. A religious tale, which has now become little more than a story to entertain children, tells of a one-inch boy who arrives at a city in an enclosed boat (ancient boats of Northeast Asia were sometimes completely enclosed) and rescues a princess by blinding some demons with his sword. The same theme appears again in the story of a little girl who is discovered inside a melon and brings security to an elderly couple by weaving for them.[8]

There is also the story of Urashima Taro, a fisherman, who is taken to the palace beneath the ocean or across the ocean (the versions differ), the home of the Kami of the sea. The fisherman forgets about time and enjoys the raptures of the monarch's daughter's companionship. When he decides to visit his home, the princess gives him a small box, which he must never open if he is to return safely to the palace. When he returns home he discovers that several centuries have elapsed during his absence. In order to comprehend the mystery of what has occurred he opens the box. A purple vapor (a symbol in Japanese stories of a numinous presence) issues from it and instantly the fisherman dies, an old man who has lived for more than three hundred years![9] The blessings of an endless life or at least a very long life were his as long as the mysterious numen was kept in a sealed space. This is a fundamental theme in Shintō architecture.

Other elements of the shrine complex symbolize events told in Shintō mythology, which is recorded in the *Kojiki* and the *Nihon Shoki*. Both documents were written in Chinese in the eighth century A.D. and are believed to be the result of a long tradition of oral transmission by a guild of reciters, who memorized the words originally uttered by shaman-priestesses in a state of Kami-possession. The *Kojiki* is believed to reflect a Southeast Asian Melanesian origin, whereas the oral tradition of the *Nihon Shoki* is

---

[8]*Folktales of Japan*, ed. Keigo Seki, trans. Robert J. Adams, Folktales of the World Series (Chicago: University of Chicago Press, 1963), pp. 40–42, 90–92; Kunio Yanagita, *Japanese Folk Tales*, trans. Fanny Hagin Mayer (Taipei: Orient Culture Service, 1972), pp. 82–83.

[9]Edgerton Ryerson, *The Netsuki of Japan* (New York: Castle Books, 1958), p. 45.

thought to have begun in central Asia, the place of origin of Japan's imperial clan.[10]

Stories of creation start both narratives, which are somewhat parallel. The *Kojiki* tells us simply that the Kami appeared in the high plain of heaven when heaven and earth began. Two Kami, Izanagi and Izanami, who are both brother and sister and husband and wife, came down from the high plains to the sea by crossing the rainbow (this is why the rainbow-shaped bridges are part of the shrine compound). By stirring the ocean with a jeweled spear they created the islands of Japan. Next they created Amaterasu, the sun Kami, later to become the paramount Kami in the great family of Kami, and the moon Kami. Next Izanagi and Izanami produced the turbulent Kami, Susunoo, who behaved so outrageously that he finally was banished to the underworld, but not before Amaterasu was offended by a series of vulgar and obscene acts which Susunoo committed against her. So she fled into a cave and closed herself in. The result was terrifying both in heaven and on earth: "Then Takama-no-para [the sky or heaven] was completely dark, and the Central Land of Reed Plains was entirely dark. Because of this, constant night reigned . . . and all manner of calamities arose."[11]

To entice Amaterasu from the cave other Kami pulled up a sakaki tree by its roots and covered its branches with a string of five hundred jewels, a mirror, and strips of white and blue cloth. The sakaki tree was placed before the cave and Ame-no-uzume, a strong and stout female Kami of the heavens, wearing a headdress of sakaki leaves, began a dance on an inverted tub. Then "before the heavenly rock-cave door, [she] stamped resoundingly upon it. Then she became divinely possessed, exposed her breasts, and pushed her skirt band down to her genitals. Then Takama-no-para shook as the eight-hundred myriad Kami laughed at once."[12]

The cacophony included the crowing of a rooster. Intrigued by the sound and merriment outside her cave, Amaterasu opened the entrance to her cave to see what was happening. The mirror

---

[10]*Kojiki*, trans. Donald L. Phillipi (Tokyo: University of Tokyo; and Princeton: Princeton University Press, 1969); *Nihongi*, trans. W. G. Aston (London: Allen and Unwin, 1956). Note that the *Nihongi* is also known as the *Nihon Shoki*, the latter name being more common among contemporary Japanese.

[11]*Kojiki*, p. 81.

[12]Ibid., p. 84.

was thrust before her face and the brilliant light startled her, for she had expected to see only darkness. A Kami took her by the hand and drew her out and another one took a shimenawa and hung it behind her, saying that the sun Kami must never again withdraw into the cave.

Divine illumination was thus restored to heaven and earth and, because of the shimenawa, the terrible ordeal through which the world had gone would never reoccur. The abundant and fertile vitality of nature with its cycles of days and nights, summers and winters was forever assured.

The word *torii* literally means "a bird perch" and is associated with the rooster, who helped entice the sun from the cave. Thus the torii also is a symbol of that sacred moment when the sun Kami's return made life possible once again.

In this way the shimenawa and the torii became symbols of trust and hope in the ongoing prosperity given to people through the creative energies of the sacred. The Japanese people therefore associate both symbols with long life, strength, progeny, plenty, and purity. These are the basic concerns of the indigenous religion of Japan and through its associations with these concerns as well as through its central role in the mythology, the shimenawa has become the chief symbol of the Shintō tradition. In other words, it is to the Shintō faith what the cross is to the Christian faith.

The other symbols in the shrine are worth comment. The indirect approach of the sandō was discussed earlier. Certain vigorous trees such as the pine, oak, and ash have played key roles in the religious traditions of Altaic, European, and other peoples, but the sakaki tree is exclusive to the Japanese heritage. It is understood to possess an unusual amount of Kami power and for that reason it not only is planted in the shrine compound and used by the priests in the religious rites, but also is used to ensure the safe delivery of babies, to maintain a happy marriage, to prevent diseases, and, if placed at the corner of fields, to ensure a bumper crop.

Water as a religious symbol is found in all religious traditions and is commonly used to symbolize new life, growth, vitality, health, and cleanliness. The use of the color red or red-orange by many Shintō shrines was adopted from the Chinese and has virtually the same meanings associated with it as water.

Finally, the construction of a shrine with such skill that it requires no metal fasteners to hold it together is unique to the Japanese. Whether it is a small sacred charm or a shrine building, the object has greater life-giving or ontic power if it is skillfully made. The Japanese call the extremely skillful act of the crafts-man *itobori. Ito* means "one knife without stopping" and *bori* is the verb *to carve*. The mental concentration and effort required to cut a piece of wood into a beautiful object in a single movement of the knife is held to be as efficacious as a prayer or other religious rite. Thus the beautifully cut, planed, mitered, and meticulously fitted woods of the shrine are in themselves powerful and therefore meaningful religious symbols.

The carpenters who reconstruct the great shrine at Ise and other shrines are *itobori no meijin* ("notable persons of great skill") and construct only shrines. They will not construct houses and build cabinets for everyday needs, even though they could increase their income by doing so. If a shrine carpenter were to make something for ordinary use, he would be a *kegare daiku*, a "not purified carpenter," one who no longer had the "power" to construct a shrine.

The Symbolism of Time: Rites and Festivals

Within the shrine one can expect to see two kinds of religious rites: those with the basic intent of cleansing the person of the various pollutions he might have wittingly or unwittingly ac-quired and those with the purpose of summoning, receiving, and sending the Kami back to the other plane or the other world in which they dwell. The first type of rite is called purification or *harai* and the second is the festival or *matsuri*.

As I noted earlier, Kami are offended by the pollutions that people usually acquire naturally through activities of daily life such as sexual acts, birth, death, and contact with dirty things and loud noises. Acts of self-centeredness also are considered pollutants, but the Shintō tradition gives less attention to prob-lems arising from the human will than do the religious traditions that have their origin in western Asia.

Purification rites exist for individuals and groups of laymen, for the shrine complex, and for the priests. Ordinary purification is performed by the individual worshiper rinsing out the mouth and pouring water over the hands. More formal purification is performed by the priest praying for the Kami to cleanse the worshipers and then waving a cluster of sakaki branches or a wand with strips of white paper attached before them. Often this second act is accompanied by lightly sprinkling the people with salt water.

Before festivals the shrines are purified by a thorough cleaning of the precincts and all religious objects in the complex. Then branches of bamboo and sakaki together with shimenawa are hung throughout the shrine to complete the purification process.

The priest also purifies himself in preparation for serving at a festival. For a stated number of days beforehand he must avoid pollution. This is done through isolation in a particular part of his house where he cooks his meager food over a separate fire. This practice, however, is disappearing and in many areas of modern Japan the purification is confined to a mere abstinence from meat and strong-smelling vegetables. Some priests stand beneath a waterfall or pour buckets of cold water over themselves, often for several hours. When shrines are located beside the ocean, ritual washing in the sea by priests is not uncommon.[13]

The matsuri or the religious drama for summoning, receiving, and placating, requesting favors of the Kami, and then sending them back to their own world at the end of the ceremony is the second type of rite to be seen in the shrines. The word *matsuri* is translated into English as "festival," but in Japanese at its deepest level it means "to live in an attitude of constant prayer and obedience to the will of the Kami."[14] The matsuri then is a special time of prayer and obedience.

Essentially there are three kinds of matsuri: those intended to give new life to the people and their village, those intended to revitalize the agricultural and fishing cycles, and those connected with local traditions—perhaps to commemorate the lifting of a plague from the city many centuries ago, or to honor the memory of a great warrior or scholar.[15]

Of the first type is the New Year's Festival, Oshogatsu, the most significant and joyous of the national matsuri. Until 1872, when

---

[13]Herbert, *Shintō*, pp. 170–71.

[14]Ibid., p. 168.

[15]The internationally famous Gion Matsuri, held in Kyoto every July, celebrates the end of a severe plague more than a thousand years ago.

Japan adopted the Western calendar, the Japanese observed the lunar calendar and celebrated the beginning of the new year in late January or February when the plum blossoms appear, marking the first sign of spring. In some regions of Japan the lunar calendar was still observed as late as 1960. Today, throughout Japan, Oshogatsu starts on the evening of December 31 and continues until January 15 with minor religious rites occurring on the seventh, twelfth, and fifteenth of the month.

Preparations begin the day after Christmas, which is observed in Japan since the American occupation as a commercial holiday, with the cleaning of the houses, which symbolizes the eradication of all past evil, sickness, accidents, failures, bad luck, and unhappiness. While the women are busy scrubbing and preparing the festival foods, the men are occupied with making repairs to the roof and sliding doors, cleaning the grounds outside the house, and acquiring an "honest purse," which means settling all debts.[16]

Unless debts are squared, the new year cannot be faced with equanimity, and one's reputation is bound to suffer. It is better to begin the new year as a pauper, since the Kami can restore one's prosperity. But if a person begins the New Year "dishonestly," that is, with debts, then he will sink deeper into the abyss during the coming year. Debts, from the Shintō perspective, diminish the person's existence. They are a form of weakness and are therefore profane.

On December 31 pine and sakaki branches are placed over the entrance and at other places in the house. In many, but not all, regions of Japan a well-formed pine bough, sometimes a section of three or five years' growth from the top of a tree, becomes the center of the home's decorations. Often it is placed beside or tied to the center post or main pillar in the central living room of the house. If it is a country home, pine branches are also hung over the doorways to sheds, the privy, and the well. Also shimenawa with pieces of white paper, ferns, pine branches, and an orange attached are hung throughout the house, including above the gate or front door. When used in the home the shimenawa is understood to be a barrier against pollutants such as disease, death,

---

[16]U. A. Casal, *The Five Sacred Festivals of Ancient Japan* (Tokyo: Sophia University, 1967), pp. 1–35.

sterility, unhappiness, and bad luck. Profane qualities are less able to enter a home protected by the shimenawa.

Several of these symbols derive their meaning and therefore their power from homophonic reasoning, a process that is common in folk cultures. Thus, for example, the orange, which is the color and shape of the sun, a preeminent source of life, is called *daidai* in Japanese. This word is related to another word pronounced the same way but written differently, which means "from generation to generation." Through its appearance and sound of its name the orange is intended to extend the life and vitality of the family through the guarantee of descendants.

The term *sakaki* is related to the word *sakaeru*, "to prosper." Prosperity for the family can be encouraged by decorating the house with the green branches of the sakaki tree. The white paper is called *hanshi*, but the more common word for paper is kami. In Japanese it is written differently from the word for the sacred presence, but pronounced the same way. So paper has the power of making the Kami present in the home. But this paper is white and as such it carries the additional connotation of purity. It therefore can overcome pollution by purifying the impure. For example, the warriors of old Japan carried hanshi to wipe the blood off their swords in the event they wounded or killed someone. Blood is a pollutant and the hanshi, because of its homophonic relationship with the sacred and its white color, could restore ontic purity to the sword. If a person must give someone currency or coins, they should be wrapped in hanshi because the act of exchanging money historically was understood among the old warrior class to be a profane act.[17] The negative attitude toward trade is a Confucian notion, but the means of counteracting the pollution comes from the Shintō heritage.

On the night of December 31 the last preparations are made. *Mochi*, cakes made from pounded rice, are placed along with candles in the *tokonoma*, a small alcove in the main room of the house where flowers are kept and a picture or calligraphy scroll

[17]Bernard Bernier, *Breaking the Cosmic Circle: Religion in a Japanese Village* (Ithaca: Cornell University Press, 1975), pp. 52–53. By the law of similarity, like is so closely associated with like that they ultimately become the same. Nevertheless, because these objects are not thought of as coercive or automatically effective, they cannot be called magical in the sense in which the word was used by early Western anthropologists or the Protestant reformers before them.

This is a small (3″ × 4″) papier-mâché dog from Suitengu Shrine in Tokyo. Usually a mother-to-be will receive one of these from her mother to enable her to have a safe and easy birth. Because dogs give birth easily and without pain, it is believed that this amulet can communicate the same ability to the new mother. Placed beside the child's bed it will enable him or her to be healthy and grow strong.

hangs. The mochi are offerings to the ancestors, who are understood to return from the other world for the festival. Here we see an ancient and central theme of the Shintō tradition.

The founders of family lines and their descendants are regarded as continuing members of the household and are believed to have an ongoing interest in the continued welfare of each person in the family. Although they have died, they are no longer regarded as being polluted, for after a time they are purified of the contamination of death and they become Kami. Indeed, a notable Japanese scholar, Kunio Yanagita, makes the point that the Kami worshiped during the Oshogatsu is the founder of the family.[18]

As late as the beginning of the twentieth century it was customary for the family to keep an all-night vigil with the ancestors on the night of December 31. This custom, although less common now, can still be observed.

Traditionally the Japanese people returned to the homestead for the New Year's festival. All the families of the lineage group would travel by train and bus to the village of the main family. There they would worship the ancestral Kami at the family shrine.

[18]Kunio Yanagita, *About Our Ancestors*, trans. Fanny Hagin Mayer (Tokyo: Japan Society for the Promotion of Science, 1970), pp. 50–51.

Today it has become more popular to go to one of the great shrines such as Meiji or Ise.

On January 1 exchanges of greetings occur between family members, between households in a village or neighborhood, and between friends. Considerable drinking often occurs at this time.

January 2 is used to prepare for the rituals at the shrine which will be held on January 3 and 4. In many villages and neighborhoods throughout Japan the most important ritual involves the shooting of arrows.[19]

From the time they agree to perform until they do perform, the archers must take steps to achieve and maintain freedom from pollution. In their homes they must sleep on rough straw mats beneath the Kami shelf, the spot in the house where symbols from the village shrine are kept. They must avoid sexual relations and any contact with postpubertal women, sources of pollution, as noted earlier, being sexual relations and menstrual blood. Because all of the people in the village or neighborhood can be sources of pollution, the archers must limit their social contacts as much as possible before the rite.

On the morning of January 4, the archers, bow carriers, arrow pickers, and village officials walk from the shrine to the shooting ground on a path made of sand from the sea. Because of the sand's association with the ocean, a source of abundance, and with the purifying qualities of both water and salt, it is a natural symbol of ontic power.

After six archers have shot several rounds of arrows, children from all of the households rush to tear apart the target and take a piece of it home, where in February it will be placed above the door to keep evil out of the house, thus insuring health, safety, and prosperity during the coming year. In major shrines arrows are given away to a person from each household. These will be used as household amulets during the coming year.

Again we see an example of homophonic reasoning. The word for arrows is *hamaya*. The purpose of the arrow is to chase away

[19]Lewis Bush, *New Japanalia: Past and Present* (Tokyo: Japan Times, 1977), pp. 43–44. From prehistoric times the arrow appears to have been thought of as primarily "an instrument which magically joins two worlds." In eastern Asia the arrow's use as a weapon was secondary to its religious use in ancient times. See Carmen Blacker, *The Catalpa Bow* (London: Allen and Unwin, 1975), p. 107.

evil *(ya)* and misfortune *(ma)* in order to obtain happiness *(ha)*. So the word literally means "happiness-evil-chase away."

The Oshogatsu is officially ended with a sacred fire ritual at the shrine in which all of the objects that protected homes and persons during the past year are respectfully burned, their ontic power having been exhausted during the preceding twelve months. Again, the fundamental Shintō theme of maintaining the life powers and processes of everyday life and avoiding or limiting those elements which drain life of its joy and verve are seen.

In October 1983, when I was in Japan on sabbatical leave, I received a telephone call from a person who knew of me and my interests through a mutual acquaintance. She invited me for dinner and asked that I come early to meet her priest. I accepted Mrs. Suzuki's offer (not her real name) and asked if I could bring my son, who is studying in a Japanese university. She agreed.

Mrs. Suzuki met Peter and me at the subway station and escorted us through a very attractive neighborhood to the home of her priest. As we entered a modern and very small house, we were asked to go upstairs and wait. At the top of the stairs we found a single room with tatami mats on the floor. An altar filled one end of the room. High above the center of the altar was the name of a Shintō qua Buddhist deity, Dakiniten, inscribed on a wooden board partially covered with folded white paper. Before the altar and on it were great pyramids of offerings: oranges, grapefruit, melons, bottles of wine, cans of tea, and bags of rice.

After waiting a short time the priest, attired in a white cassock, entered the room, knelt before us, and began to recite his story. Until three years ago he had been a successful owner and operator of a hotel and cabaret. But a series of reverses forced him into bankruptcy. At the time he was fifty-six years old, a widower with eight thousand yen in his possession (approximately forty dollars). While he was sliding into financial ruin, his eighty-year-old mother began to have a series of dreams in which Dakiniten, who is nearly always depicted riding a white fox, came to her and announced that he was the cause of her son's severe trouble. Dakiniten was allowing this to happen, according to the recitation, to shake her son loose from his fascination with money and the good life and to call him into the deity's service. Furthermore

Dakiniten stated to her in her dream that henceforth she would be his oracle.

At this point in the narration the priest's octogenarian mother (I will call her Mrs. Yamaguchi, although this is not her real name) entered the room with a tray of sweets and a pot of hot green tea. Seated on the tatami mats around a low black lacquered table, we became acquainted and shared a little of our backgrounds. Without any explanation she put on a white surplice and with her son moved to a table before the altar and began chanting an invocatory prayer to Dakiniten. She then picked up three *hashi* (chopsticks) which had been tied together at the top and bound with strips of white cotton sheeting. Holding the tripod at its apex, her right arm began to shake in palsied fashion. On the table in front of her was a board filled with characters of the *hiragana* syllabary (one of the three Japanese writing systems). As her arm vibrated jerkily at the elbow, the feet of the tripod would strike different syllables on the board and, as this occurred, Mrs. Yamaguchi would sound the syllable struck. The sounds formed words and the words sentences. Dakiniten was speaking through Mrs. Yamaguchi. He wanted to know why we had come. Mrs. Suzuki invited us. Did we have any questions? No, we had no questions. Oh, but you must have some questions. Is there nothing that worries you? Don't you have any problems? Feeling drawn into a situation not of my own choosing and being completely incredulous, I could ask no questions. Still the insistent request. Finally, Peter asked if he would be able to return to Japan after he completes his studies. The jumping, shaking motions and the slow monotonic intonation of the syllables continued. Dakiniten said Peter would be returning.

Mrs. Yamaguchi then removed from a cabinet a small *ofuda* (a board about ten inches long with the name of the deity and his temple, Toyokawa Inari, inscribed on it).[20] She placed it on the table in front of her and began tapping it with the hashi as she chanted a scripture. She was instilling the spirit of Dakiniten into the ofuda. When she finished she carefully handed it to me with

[20]Jean Herbert, *Shintō: At the Fountain-head of Japan* (London: Allen and Unwin, 1967), pp. 508–9. Toyokawa Inari, which originated as a Zen temple, is today a blend of Buddhist and Shintō devotion. According to Herbert, in about "eighty or even ninety-nine percent of the cases" Inari shrines have originated with the dream of someone in which Inari, the fox Kami, comes to the dreamer.

an imperative; I was to put the ofuda on a high place in my home and offer Dakiniten tea and rice each morning. In return he would protect me and my home.

We adjourned to the table at the other end of the room. Mrs. Yamaguchi explained that she was now eighty-three years old and did not expect to live much longer. Her son, who had no theological training, was preparing to increase his priestly power by undergoing austerities (ryo). He had given up smoking, was confined to the house most of the time, and spent much time chanting scriptures. The mother and son had gathered a congregation of a dozen or so members, who came to Mrs. Yamaguchi for Dakiniten's advice and counsel on a variety of issues, especially questions about finding a marriage partner, admission into college and graduate school, difficulties involving their children, and marital problems. Mrs. Yamaguchi explained that she and her son are looking for a Shintō shrine that will accept them (the great majority have no resident priest). When they find one, her son will be the priest and she will serve as the oracle. When she dies, she said, she expects to be enshrined and her son will be her oracle.

After about two hours of conversation the son, who had been downstairs for more than one hour, came back up. He told his mother he had some questions to ask of Dakiniten. Both put on their white ritual vestments, knelt on the tatami before the altar, and said the prayers of invocation. Then the fifty-nine-year-old son asked, "May I go out this evening? If so, when should I come back?" The white fox deity spoke through the shaking arm. "Yes, you may go out this evening [the man had not been out in nearly three weeks]. You should return by ten o'clock."

After the man left tea was again served. Clean cups were removed from a cabinet, but there were five more cups than necessary. "No," it was explained, "like Mrs. Yamaguchi, Dakiniten also has guests this afternoon and he and his fellow deities wish to join us." Two neighbor ladies, who had recently joined us, nodded in solemn agreement. Mrs. Yamaguchi took Dakiniten's cup in her left hand and with another set of hashi, again bound into a tripod, whipped the tea into a froth. As she did so, she laughed quietly and said, "He really likes this tea." The two recent arrivals softly "aahed" in appreciation. My skepticism deepened.

I felt I had caught a fleeting glimpse of old Japan when female shamans made the important decisions. For in ancient times women, known for their keen intuitive powers and thought to be close to the numen, would be held in seclusion and consulted by the elders of the village or clan about the important decisions of daily life. These women were the decision makers for the community, for they were believed to speak for the deity.

In Mrs. Yamaguchi I was witnessing a vestigal remnant of a prehistoric tradition. Much as a storm can wash away a more recent topsoil to reveal an almost timeless bedrock, the financial disaster, which had stripped this couple of their security, had been met by an oneiric vision. It had converted a tragedy into a promise. It lifted an old woman from isolation into a position of attention; she was now consulted and listened to by about a dozen people in the neighborhood and it provided a small income. As we were about to leave, it was quietly suggested by Mrs. Suzuki that I should leave a gift of five thousand yen (roughly twenty-five dollars) for the ofuda from Toyokawa Inari Temple in Nagoya. I placed the contribution in an envelope Mrs. Suzuki handed me.

Today the Shintō tradition remains a vital and active force in Japanese culture. When the matsuri occur, the shrines fill to capacity. Indeed, since the early 1950s the more popular shrines have been reporting annual increases in the number of people coming to the shrine on a day-to-day basis to offer petitions to the Kami. In the spring of 1981 a Japanese newspaper reported that the age group visiting the shrine most often in response to personal problems is young adults, those between the ages of eighteen to twenty-two. Thus while some customs have been eroding, the commitment of the Japanese people to their indigenous heritage remains strong.

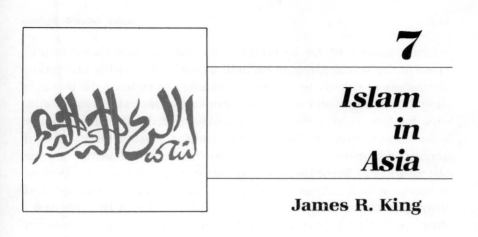

7

Islam in Asia

James R. King

Although Islam had its historical origin in Southwest Asia, on the Arabian Peninsula to be exact, it was, from its earliest days in the seventh century A.D., an aggressive, proselytizing religion which moved vigorously out of its original home northward into "Greater Syria," westward across North Africa into Spain, and eastward into Iraq, Persia, and India. Today the role of Islam in the national life of Pakistan, Iran, and Indonesia makes it one of the major religions of Asia, and it continues to be an important force in modern secular Turkey, in the Soviet Union, in the Philippines, and even in Communist China. In fact, a recent study edited by Richard V. Weekes, *Muslim Peoples*, examines more than a dozen Muslim groups on the Indian subcontinent, nearly as many in Southeast Asia and the Philippines, and eight groups in Iran. Such abundance of material forces us here to be highly selective.

My approach here is historical, for the highly specific nature of the topic dictates that we concentrate not on the nature of Islam as a coherent religious system but on the particular ways Islam has influenced and been influenced by events in Asia. What interests us here is a series of fascinating Asian variations on a Middle Eastern religion: an intensely philosophic Islam which has had great influence on the politics of South Asia; an Indonesian Islam which is very much of a social and cultural phenomenon; and an Islam which has managed to retain its identity in a Chinese culture which is foreign—even hostile—to it. A historical approach enables us to chronicle these transformations and to keep track of the essential nature of the faith within all of them.

163

Islam claims to be the oldest, indeed the original, religion, asserting as its central idea the oneness of God and the obligation of all men to submit to his will. It traces its origins back through Isma'il (Ishmael) and Ibrahim (Abraham, the first monotheist) back to Adam. Muslims recognize the prophetic role of many figures mentioned in the Bible, including Musa (Moses), Daoud (David), Ayyub (Job), and Isa (Jesus), and they identify as the historical founder of their faith Muhammad, the last and greatest of the prophets, whose role was to correct the errors that had crept into God's message to man across the centuries. Muhammad lived between A.D. 570 and 632, at first in Mecca and later in Medina (originally Yathrib, later Medina al-Nabi, "the City of the Prophet"), and his work consisted of transmitting to man the word of God as embodied in the Qur'an, laying the foundations of Islamic law and morality, establishing the essential rituals of the faith, converting much of the Arabian Peninsula to his religion, and inspiring in his followers a profound sense of loyalty and community. Islam puts great stress on the transcendence, the power, and the omniscience of Allah (God); identifies submission to God as the primary act of faith that man must perform; demands that all accept Muhammad as the final prophet of God; and envisions a coming day of judgment when the righteous will be rewarded and sinners punished.[1]

Following Muhammad's somewhat unexpected death in 632, his successors, the so-called Rightly-Guided Caliphs, embarked on a series of military conquests which led to the establishment of the Umayyad Empire in Syria in the seventh century and the flowering of the Abbasid Empire, with Baghdad its capital, between 749 and 1258. At a very early stage in Islamic history, profound differences developed about the nature and identity of the leaders of the community and the question of esoteric or "hidden" elements in Islamic theology. These differences, institutionalized in the Sunnite and Shi'ite branches of the new faith, were given a legendary or mythic framework in stories about 'Ali, the son-in-law of the Prophet, and 'Ali's two sons Husayn and Hasan. The stories of these early leaders and of the tragic deaths of two of them continue to embody issues of great importance for

[1]For a summary of the basic concepts of Islam, refer to C. George Fry and James R. King, *Islam: A Survey of the Muslim Faith*, rev. ed. (Grand Rapids: Baker, 1982), pp. 57–93.

Muslims today, not only in the Middle East but also all the way across Asia.[2]

During the Umayyad period Arab armies reached India, and during the Middle Ages Muslims were to be found even in faraway Chinese cities living peacefully and profitably in their own quarters. In fact, when Ibn Batuta, the celebrated "traveler of Islam," made his twenty-year journey to China and back, in the fourteenth century, he found hospitable Muslims at every stage of his way. At what was perhaps the lowest point of his long journey, when he was penniless in a hostile section of India and dying of thirst and exhaustion, a black Muslim greeted him with the familiar "Peace be upon you" and carried him, on his back, to the nearest village, where help was available. Later, on the east coast of India, Malabar, Ibn Batuta enjoyed Muslim hospitality, and during a stay on the Maldive Islands in the Indian Ocean, he served as Muslim *cadi* or judge. He disliked the Chinese he met, when he traveled in their country, but in Qanjanfu he found the Muslim quarter and felt at home immediately: "When I met Muslims in China," he observes, "I always felt just as though I were meeting my own faith and kin."[3] Throughout the centuries, Ibn Batuta's experience of Muslim fellowship has been shared by millions of Muslims from all over Asia, especially as they gather every year for the pilgrimage rituals in Mecca.

Islam in India

The arrival of the first Muslims in India is to some extent a matter of legend: some Arab soldiers from the period of Uthman, the third caliph, are said to have reached South Asia, and there are stories about some of Muhammad's "companions" dying there. Muslim armies arrived in force in 711–12, building cities and mosques in the extreme western part of the subcontinent—in the

---

[2]The Sunnites (from Arabic *sunnah*, straight path) are the orthodox Muslims, constituting about three-fourths of the entire body of the faithful. They regard Muhammad as the final prophet and the Qur'an as available to and understandable by all. They tend to be open to discussion of religious issues with people of other faiths. The Shi'ites or followers of the party (*shi'a*) of 'Ali have established a priestly hierarchy between man and God, envision a series of *imams* or divinely appointed successors to the prophet throughout history, and stress the esoteric or secret meanings of the Qur'an.

[3]Ibn Batuta, *Travels in Asia and Africa*, trans. and selected by H. A. R. Gibb (London: Routledge and Kegan Paul, 1929), p. 222.

province of Sind—thereby establishing an avenue by which Indian science passed westward to Persia and Iraq. Three centuries
later, under Mahmoud of Ghaznia (Afghanistan) there was another
important Muslim invasion of India, and it was at this time that
the Islamicization of Northwest India began. Muslim scholars
undertook the study of Hinduism, and Lahore (now a major city of
Pakistan—formerly West Pakistan) became an important intellectual center.

Under the Ghorids at the end of the twelfth century, Islam
expanded south and east and began to exert considerable influence in important urban centers. Many Hindus found Islamic law
and the Islamic stress on equality (Muslims abhorred the caste
system) very attractive, and in this period of comparative peace
and good feeling Delhi became a magnificent city and the seat of
independent Muslim rulers who attracted to their courts wealth
and artists, scholars, and other celebrities. Also at this time we
find the beginnings of a long-standing conflict in the history of
Indian Islam—the conflict between the conservative *ulema* (the
learned men or religious scholars) and the sultans. But during the
medieval period, at least, all Muslim rulers in India accepted
dinpanahi, the responsibility of the king to protect Islam, exalt the
Prophet, and root out the enemies of the faith. As a result, in the
thirteenth century, Islam was established as a great cultural force
in its own right in India.[4]

During this period many Sufi or mystical orders developed in
India, the most famous being the Chisti order, with its great stress
on the experience of divine love.[5] In many Indian communities,
the headquarters of the local Sufi brotherhood served also as a
center of social life, with the result that the influence of these
groups pervaded every aspect of Indian experience. A more
worldly and wealthier order is the Suhrawardi, and on the
highways of India dervishes *(qalandars)* wandered, many of whom
used various types of stimulants and intoxicants to reach the

---

[4]Annamarie Schimmel, *Islam in the Indian Subcontinent* (Leiden: Brill, 1980), has been an
invaluable source. For her comments on dinpanahi, see pp. 13–14.

[5]Sufism (from Arabic *suf,* wool, referring to the heavy cloaks worn by the Sufis) is the
Islamic form of mysticism, the attempt to achieve union with the Divine through music, the
dance, self-discipline, and sometimes drugs. The movement began to take shape in
the nineteenth century A.D. and today there are Sufi orders all the way across the Muslim
world from Morocco to India. See Fry and King, *Islam,* pp. 120–28.

mystical state. By 1400 the Sufi orders had grown so prominent and influential that there was a strong reaction from Hinduism, the development of the so-called *bhakti* movement,[6] although in the eyes of many a genuine rapprochement between the two great faiths seemed possible and desirable. In fact, one of the Shi'ite sects of Northwest India identified 'Ali as the tenth avatar of Vishnu,[7] and at this time many brahmins recited the mystical verses of Jalal al-Din al-Rumi, the great Turkish mystic.

This was a time of many flourishing, independent Muslim states as well as the rise of such urban centers as Delhi, Agra, Bijapur (a beautiful city crowded with artists and religious), and Gujarat (a popular point of embarkation among pilgrims headed for the Middle East). The ruler of Gujarat in the mid-fifteenth century was the legendary Muhammad Shah, a huge but profoundly cultured individual, liberal in his religious views, sympathetic with the Sufi mystics. His equally cultured son was a lover of music and a master of both the Qur'an and Shari'ah law.

The high point of Muslim India was the period of the Great Moguls, who were of Turkish origin (i.e., from Turkish-speaking tribes of Central Asia), and of their kingdom Delhi was the chief city. Babur was the first sultan of this dynasty, assuming power in 1526, a talented ruler and also a profound mystic. His celebrated son Humayun, and Humayun's son, Akbar, religious devotee and empire-builder, sought through their activities to combine the highest ideals of Islam and Hinduism. Both nurtured the *din-i-ilahi* movement,[8] and they also made much use of the symbolism of light, so characteristic of Zoroastrianism. Some Muslim theologians felt, however, that Akbar had created a cult with himself at the center; many found his activities heretical; it is indeed true that this ruler moved away from orthodox Islam toward a universal religion that would embrace all men.

Under Akbar's grandson, Shah Jahan, both Shi'ite Islam and Sufism flourished, and at the same time the study of the natural sciences was encouraged. Shah Jahan is best known as the builder of the Taj Mahal (1643), a mausoleum for his dead wife—by

[6]See chapter 2 on Hinduism, pp. 47–61.

[7]Hindus believe that the god Vishnu has been reincarnated constantly throughout history and indeed that one of these avatars or incarnations was Jesus Christ. Thus Hinduism is able to absorb into itself important figures from many world religions.

[8]See Schimmel, *Islam in the Indian Subcontinent*, p. 82.

The tomb of Humayun (1508–1556), the second Mughul emperor of
India, in Delhi.

common consent the most beautiful building ever constructed, anywhere in the world. Aurangzeb, sterner and more
orthodox, suppressed some of the more colorful aspects of court
life and encouraged a profound strain of asceticism in his
people. When Aurangzeb died in 1707 the Mogul Empire disinte-
grated.

The Taj Mahal, Agra, is an example of Islamic influence in
India.

Many destructive forces were at work in India after Aurangzeb's death—massacres of Muslims occurred; Delhi was virtually ruined; many Muslims actually considered suicide by immolation, Hindu-style. As a result of all of these sufferings there developed a keen interest in *marthiya*, the dirge-like poetry celebrating the martyrdom of Husayn, the son of 'Ali and one of the principal saints of the Shi'ite faith. Gradually, however, Muslim theologians worked through the problems of this difficult period and rival sects began to meet in a spirit of reconciliation. The greatest theologian of this period was Shah Wali-ullah ("the friend of God"), who lived from 1703 to 1762. He took a prominent place in the process of calling Muslims to loyalty to their common inheritance in Shari'ah law and in the traditions of the Prophet. He was also an important writer on mysticism, concerned about reconciling apparent differences among the important mystical schools.[9]

At the beginning of the eighteenth century, Indian Muslims embarked on a long quest for rediscovery of their identity and for the revival of their faith. At this time Muslims on the subcontinent were experiencing more and more interference with their law code at the hands of the British and were suffering economic hardship as the British seized the lands of the wealthy and uprooted peasants from their farm plots. It is not surprising, then, to find many eloquent Muslim leaders calling for *jihad* (holy war) against the British. One such group took the name *Wahhabi*, because its ideas about strict morality and religious revival paralleled those of the famous eighteenth century revival movement in Arabia. Another militant group went under the name *Jama'at i-Mujahadin* or Freedom Fighters; still other Indians simply abandoned India for good and settled in Mecca. All of this unrest came to a head in May 1857, in an abortive protest against British rule (the Sepoy Rebellion) which the British quickly put down and for which they blamed the Muslims. This unsuccessful revolt led to a profound crisis within the Muslim community in India over which way to turn, the ulema arguing for a return to tradition and another large group urging study of Western ways, the adoption of Western ideas (Darwinism in particular), and the

[9]On Shah Wali-ullah, see *Sources of the Indian Tradition*, ed. W. T. DeBary, 2 vols. (New York: Columbia University Press, 1958), vol. 1, pp. 448–54.

full exploitation of educational opportunities made available by the British.

Among the more important Muslim leaders of this critical period was Sir Sayyid Ahmed Khan (1817–1898), who actually began his working life in British service. However, Khan never allowed his profound respect for British ways to lessen his support for the cause of Indian nationalism and Muslim revival. He examined very carefully the roots of the 1857 rebellion (which he had opposed) and tried to convince his British masters that the Muslims of India were not solely to blame, for it was not they alone who sought independence. Throughout his life he urged closer ties between the Muslims and the British (even urging Muslims to attend British schools), and for this he was often vilified by fellow Indians. Sir Sayyid's greatest work, in the eyes of many, was establishment of the liberal Anglo-Oriental College at Aligarh, which was supported by the British and bitterly opposed by many Indian Muslims even though it was founded on Muslim ideas. Eventually this institution became a favorite avenue by which the Muslim middle classes entered the professions, and it was out of the Aligarh school that the Aligarh movement came, which promoted the continuing Anglicizing of India.

Wilfred Cantwell Smith has suggested that Sir Sayyid promoted "an Islam thoroughly compatible with progress,"[10] including a continuing attack on traditional religious authority, a rejection of traditional Muslim law, and the questioning of any ideas not based on the Qur'an or on carefully documented *hadith*. Much in Islam that smacked of the supernatural he rejected, and his effort to "demythologize" the Qur'an (Smith, p. 195) led him to interpret the *jinn* or evil spirits of the Qur'an as "savage tribes" and the angels as "moral support." He also sought to overthrow the institution of *purdah* (the veiling and seclusion of women) and the old conception of jihad that called for aggressive conversion of non-Muslim peoples. He was among the first Muslim leaders to advocate the education of women. The following statement, which suggests how intense was his effort to bring Islam into conformity with modern thought, may help to explain why so many of the conservative religious authorities condemned him as a pure rationalist:

[10]See Wilfred Cantwell Smith, *Modern Islam in India: A Social Analysis* (London, 1946), p. 15.

The Qur'ān does not prove that the earth is stationary, nor does it prove that the earth is in motion. Similarly it can not be proved from the Qur'ān that the sun is in motion, nor can it be proved from it that the sun is stationary. The Holy Qur'ān was not concerned with these problems of astronomy; because the progress in human knowledge was to decide such matters itself. The Qur'ān had a much higher and a far nobler purpose in view. It would have been tantamount to confusing the simple Bedouins by speaking to them about such matters and to throwing into perplexity even the learned, whose knowledge and experience had not yet made the necessary progress, by discussing such problems. The real purpose of a religion is to improve morality; by raising such questions that purpose would have been jeopardized. In spite of all this I am fully convinced that the Work of God and the Word of God can never be antagonistic to each other; we may, through the fault of our knowledge, sometimes make mistakes in understanding the meaning of the Word.[11]

Sir Sayyid's *Essays on the Life of Mohammad,* a "smashing attack on reliance on ancient authority" (Smith, p. 12), was part of a growing literature on the Prophet in the nineteenth century which attributed to him whatever virtues the biographer approved of. The loving spirit of Muhammad, his heroism, his sinlessness—these are among the qualities of the Prophet which Sir Sayyid picks out for repeated praise. Out of this same tradition came Syed Ameer 'Ali, whose major work, *The Spirit of Islam* (1891, 1922, and still in print), was an effort to respond to criticisms of Muhammad made by various missionaries in India. Its liberalism and its enthusiasm again come through in the following characteristic passages.

On the Prophet's childhood:

We can almost see the lad with his deep wistful eyes, earnest and thoughtful, looking, as it were, into futurity, moving about in the humble unpretentious household of his uncle, or going often into the desert to gaze upon the beauteous face of nature; sweet and gentle of disposition, painfully sensitive to human suffering, this pure-hearted child of the desert was the beloved of his small circle, and there ever existed the warmest attachment between uncle and

[11]This passage, from Khan's *Akhari Madamin,* is to be found in DeBary, *Sources,* vol. 2, p. 192.

nephew. "The angels of God had opened out his heart, and filled it with light."

On his relations with Christians:

It was about this time that the Prophet granted to the monks of the monastery of St. Catherine, near Mount Sinai, and to all Christians, a Charter which has been justly designated as one of the noblest monuments of enlightened tolerance that the history of the world can produce. This remarkable document, which has been faithfully preserved by the annalists of Islam, displays a marvellous breadth of view and liberality of conception. By it the Prophet secured to the Christians privileges and immunities which they did not possess even under sovereigns of their own creed; and declared that any Moslem violating and abusing what was therein ordered, should be regarded as a violater of God's testament, a transgressor of His commandments, and a slighter of His faith. He undertook himself, and enjoined on his followers, to protect the Christians, to defend their churches, the residences of their priests, and to guard them from all injuries.

On his humanitarianism:

Do the preachings of this desert-born Prophet, addressing a larger world and a more advanced humanity, in the nobility of their love, in their strivings and yearnings for the true, the pure, and the holy, fall short of the warnings of Isaiah or "the tender appeals of Jesus?"

The poor and the orphan, the humble dweller of the earth "with his mouth in the dust," the unfortunate being bereft in early life of parental care, are ever the objects of his tenderest solicitude. Ever and again he announces that the path which leads to God is the helping of the orphan, the relieving of the poor, and the ransoming of the captive. His pity and love were not confined to his fellow-beings, the brute creation shared with them his sympathy and tenderness.[12]

The *Spirit of Islam* is an important early example of what was to become increasingly common in twentieth-century India—works by Muslims who were well acquainted with liberal Western

[12]See Syed Ameer 'Ali, *The Spirit of Islam* (London: Chatto and Windus, 1964), pp. 10, 84, 157.

thought and tried to find in Islam qualities that would appeal to advanced modern thinkers. Like 'Ali, they see Islam as a great civilizing force, in the vanguard of progress, tolerant of diversity, welcoming to its heart people of all races. But, as Smith has observed,

> this Islam makes no demands. It distributes pride and contentment gratis: it incites to satisfaction, not to activity, certainly not to change. Muhammad is admirable; Islam is admirable; Muslims are fine people.
>   Religion seems to be but the feeling of satisfaction that accompanies the bourgeois life.[13]

Still other Islamic movements in India at the end of the nineteenth century were advocating a return to tradition or, indeed, seeing in tradition the only hope for Islam. Such movements, of course, rejected the rational approach to the Qur'an, all forms of feminism, and the kind of Western education that had come to be associated with Aligarh College. One of the most influential of these conservative movements was the *ahl-i-hadith*, "the people of the tradition," which would have nothing to do with the concept of *ijma* (a legal tool in which law was seen as based, in part, on the consensus of the community); advocates of this position insisted instead that the Qur'an is the only guide to life and morality. Members of this group turned their back on all innovation (much of which in India was the result of Hindu influence) and also on the veneration of saints. Islam . . . imam . . . ihsan (Submission . . . the prayer leader . . . sincerity in worship) was the oft-repeated motto of this group.

In 1906 the Muslim League was formed to advance the cause of Islam in India, and although it was often pro-British, its purpose, ultimately, was to do whatever could be done to promote the well-being of Muslims in India and the development of their self-consciousness. As a result of the work of the league—along with several more definitely anti-British movements—Muslims won the right to hold separate elections in their own areas. An especially important influence at this time was Mohandas K. Gandhi (1869–1948), the most famous Indian of the twentieth

---

[13]Smith, *Modern Islam in India*, p. 87.

century, who struggled against the British dominance of his country for several decades. His teachings against violence had particular meaning for Indian Muslims who were compelled to fight against Turkish Muslims in World War I. The Muslim League was also interested in expanding educational opportunities for women and in insuring that all those who wanted literature about Islam had it. One sees in both of these emphases the influence of Christian missions.

One of the early leaders of the Muslim League was Muhammad 'Ali (1879–1930), who was important because of his power as a speaker to engage the masses in the cause of Islam in post-World-War-I India. An unusual situation had arisen during this war, the pitting of Turkish Muslim troops fighting for Germany against Indian Muslim troops fighting for the British. At the end of the war, with the defeat of the Germans and the Turks, Muslims in India experienced further distress over the dismemberment of the Ottoman Empire and the elimination of the office of *caliph*—the successor of the Prophet and the leader of the faithful who embodied in his person both civil and spiritual authority. Indian Muslims, who had long suffered a loss of liberty and the lack of authoritative leadership, had grown accustomed to looking at the Turkish sultan as their caliph, even praying for him in their mosques on Friday, and it was they, encouraged by Muhammad 'Ali, who supported the so-called Khalifite movement, aimed at the reestablishment of this office. So powerful was this movement as a force for self-identity that even Gandhi, although a Hindu, supported it, and it led to a certain amount of cooperation between Muslims and Hindus. 'Ali spent some time in British jails for attempting to persuade Indian Muslim troops not to fight in World War I, and the movement died, at least for the time, when the Turkish Republic was founded, in the 1920s.[14]

At the end of the First World War there emerged the greatest Muslim thinker of India in the twentieth century and the only such figure to gain international recognition. Sir Muhammad Iqbal (1873–1938), who came from a distinguished Indian family, was British-educated, a lawyer, a poet who glorified Islam, and eventually a major modern religious thinker. All his life he fought capitalism and colonialism, racial injustice and inequality, and all

[14]For the Khalifite movement see DeBary, *Sources*, vol. 2, pp. 216–29.

forms of quietism and passivity in the face of evil. In Islam he
found what he felt was a cure for the sufferings of mankind,
especially in Islamic teachings on the cultivation of the self in the
light of God's truth. These teachings, he felt, could rid the self of its
evil tendencies and help it become part of the large community of
mankind. Iqbal asserted that many thinkers had reached the
Truth in many times and places, but that in some special way
Muhammad had grasped its essence, particularly in his teachings
about love, by which the self can achieve its destiny and find
enlightenment. Love, Iqbal felt, is not limited by reason or intellect
and is thus a force available to everyone. This conclusion led him,
in his celebrated poem *The Mysteries of Selflessness*, to an affir-
mation of the responsibility of the Muslim community to enhance
the lives of men and women of all times and places:

A common aim shared by the multitude
Is unity which, when it is mature,
Forms the Community; the many live
Only by virtue of the single bond.
The Muslim's unity from natural faith
Derives, and this the Prophet taught to us,
So that we lit a lantern on Truth's way.
This pearl was fished from his unfathomed sea,
And of his bounty we are one in soul.
Let not this unity go from our hands,
And we endure to all eternity. . . .

Our Essence is not bound to any Place;
The vigour of our wine is not contained
In any bowl; Chinese and Indian
Alike the sherd that constitutes our jar,
Turkish and Syrian alike the clay
Forming our body; neither is our heart
Of India, or Syria, or Rum,
Nor any fatherland do we profess
Except Islam.[15]

It was in 1928 that Iqbal presented his views on the relationship
between modern thought and Islam and his sense of how modern
man might achieve his destiny—in his *Six Lectures on the Recon-*

[15]Sir Muhammad Iqbal, *The Mysteries of Selflessness*, trans. A. J. Arberry (London: John
Murray, 1953), pp. 20, 29.

struction of Religious Thought in Islam. Here Iqbal revealed his familiarity with such important European thinkers as Nietzsche, Bergson, and Darwin and attempted to harmonize many of their teachings with Islam. The following passage will suggest something of the worldliness of his thought:

> Thus, wholly overshadowed by the results of his intellectual activity, the modern man has ceased to live soulfully, i.e., from within. In the domain of thought he is living in open conflict with himself; and in the domain of economic and political life he is living in open conflict with others. He finds himself unable to control his ruthless egoism and his infinite gold-hunger which is gradually killing all higher striving in him and bringing him nothing but life-weariness. Absorbed in the "fact," that is to say, the optically present source of sensation, he is entirely cut off from the unplumbed depths of his own being. In the wake of his systematic materialism has at last come that paralysis of energy which Huxley apprehended and deplored. The condition of things in the East is no better. The technique of medieval mysticism by which religious life, in its higher manifestations, developed itself both in the East and in the West has now practically failed. And in the Muslim East it has, perhaps, done far greater havoc than anywhere else. Far from reintegrating the forces of the average man's inner life, and thus preparing him for participation in the march of history, it has taught him a false renunciation and made him perfectly contented with his ignorance and spiritual thralldom. No wonder then that the modern Muslim in Turkey, Egypt, and Persia is led to seek fresh sources of energy in the creation of new loyalties, such as patriotism and nationalism which Nietzsche described as "sickness and unreason," and "the strongest force against culture." Disappointed of a purely religious method of spiritual renewal which alone brings us into touch with the everlasting fountain of life and power by expanding our thought and emotion, the modern Muslim fondly hopes to unlock fresh sources of energy by narrowing down his thought and emotion. Modern atheistic socialism, which possesses all the fervor of a new religion, has a broader outlook; but having received its philosophical basis from the Hegelians of the left wing, it rises in revolt against the very source which could have given it strength and purpose. Both nationalism and atheistic socialism, at least in the present state of human adjustments, must draw upon the psychological forces of hate, suspicion, and resentment which tend to impoverish the soul of man and close up his hidden sources of spiritual energy. Neither the technique of medieval

mysticism nor nationalism nor atheistic socialism can cure the ills
of a despairing humanity. Surely the present moment is one of
great crisis in the history of modern culture. The modern world
stands in need of biological renewal. And religion, which in its
higher manifestations is neither dogma, nor priesthood, nor ritual,
can alone ethically prepare the modern man for the burden of the
great responsibility which the advancement of modern science
necessarily involves, and restore to him that attitude of faith which
makes him capable of winning a personality here and retaining it
hereafter. It is only by rising to a fresh vision of his origin and
future, his whence and whither, that man will eventually triumph
over a society motivated by an inhuman competition, and a civilization which has lost its spiritual unity by its inner conflict of religious and political values.[16]

Thus, like his Greek contemporary Nikos Kazantzakis, Iqbal took
as his great theme the nature and the nurture of the ideal man,
the human being moving into a new, future order. And, like
Kazantzakis, he discusses how mankind must struggle to release
this ideal form within them. Iqbal's view, that modern man, like
Adam, is a coworker with God in bringing about a new order, was
far from orthodox Islam, although Iqbal of course found much in
the Qur'an to support his views.

It was Iqbal, too, who in 1930, at a time of social breakdown in
India and increasingly strong anti-British feeling, first mentioned
the possibility of a Muslim nation on the subcontinent. In his
address to the All-India Muslim League in December of that year,
he made the following observations:

The principle of European democracy cannot be applied to India
without recognizing the fact of communal groups. The Muslim
demand for the creation of a Muslim India within India is,
therefore, perfectly justified. The resolution of the All-Parties Muslim Conference at Delhi, is, to my mind, wholly inspired by this
noble ideal of a harmonious whole which, instead of stifling the
respective individualities of its component wholes, affords them
chances of fully working out the possibilities that may be latent in
them. And I have no doubt that this House will emphatically
endorse the Muslim demands embodied in this resolution. Person-

[16]Sir Muhammad Iqbal, *The Reconstruction of Religious Thought in Islam* (London:
Oxford University Press, 1934), pp. 187–89.

ally, I would go further than the demands embodied in it. *I would like to see the Punjab, North-West Frontier Province, Sind and Baluchistan amalgamated into a single State. Self-government within the British empire or without the British empire, the formation of a consolidated North-West Indian Muslim State appears to me to be the final destiny of the Muslims, at least of North-West India.*[17]

All these classes of Muslims in India shared these feelings, of course, and the power of the Muslim League grew so strong within the next decade and a half that in the 1946 elections its members won all the parliamentary seats reserved for Muslims.

Partition became a reality on August 14, 1947, with the creation of the new state of East Pakistan and West Pakistan, two "wings" of the same country separated by hundreds of miles.[18] Partition led to the exodus of millions of Hindus from the new nation and of as many Muslims from India, especially Bharat. Thousands of refugees were created; there was much bloodshed; and tensions mounted, both between India and Pakistan and between the two sections of Pakistan. A new government had to be created out of the bitter disagreements between the conservative ulema and the liberal reformers; a new capital, Islamabad, had to be planned and constructed; stances had to be developed vis-à-vis the other world powers; and the problems of thirty to forty million Muslims who chose to remain in India had to be faced.

At the time of partition, Pakistan had a population of approximately one hundred million, not at all evenly divided between the two "wings." East Pakistan, with 55 percent of the population and 15 percent of the territory, was seriously overpopulated, the "people-problem" being exacerbated by the poverty of the area and its proneness to natural disasters, especially flooding and storms. In the years following partition, it became increasingly apparent that this area had less in common with West Pakistan than was thought: the orientation of East Pakistan was toward Southeast Asia, not toward the Middle East, and the principal

---

[17]Quoted in DeBary, *Sources*, vol. 2, p. 205. Italics his.

[18]Other important contributors to the founding of Pakistan were Rahmat 'Ali, who was of special influence on Indian Muslim students studying in Great Britian and whose propaganda seems to have been a major factor in persuading the Muslim League to call for a separate state; Muhammad 'Ali Jinnah, a skilled political leader of great integrity, known today as "the father of Pakistan"; and Liaquat 'Ali Khan, who actually shaped the government of the new nation, once it had been created.

language of the region was Bengali, an Indian language, whereas in West Pakistan, Urdu (a combination of Arabic and Hindustani) was spoken. The problem of this diversity was finally resolved in 1971, when the nation of Bangladesh was formed out of East Pakistan. However, Bangladesh has not proved to be a viable entity either, being one of the world's most impoverished nations.

Efforts to draft a constitution for Pakistan began in 1947, and the first such document was adopted in 1956. An important influence on this document was a series of recommendations drafted early in 1951 by the ulema of Pakistan. At this time the theologians called for a state over which Allah was to be the ultimate authority; the legal system was to be grounded in the Qur'an. The state was not to be based upon geographical, racial, or linguistic concepts, but upon Islamic ideals, and a principal duty of the civil authority was to be the promoting of Islamic culture. Citizens were to have all the normal rights conferred on Muslims everywhere; non-Muslims were to have freedom of religion and worship but were forbidden to propagate ideologies contrary to Islam. The first constitution, based on these and similar principles, was adopted in 1956. It was supplanted by a second constitution in 1962, following which there was a long period of civil unrest and martial law. A third constitution was adopted in 1973.[19]

Pakistan today is about 97 percent Muslim, mostly Sunnite, with some Shi'ite groups and a number of powerful Sufi orders. Although there has been some combining in India of Islam with local Hindu customs, the cultural life of Islamic India (and now the life of Pakistan) has been determined by Islam. The center of life in every village is the mosque, invariably built of local materials and often of very distinctive design. As in Sunnite countries, the imam is simply the prayer leader, and he has no special qualifications. The theological experts are *mullahs*, and Sufi *sheikhs (pirs)* are also very influential. Muslims set themselves apart from Hindus by dress and (in the case of males) by beards; every boy bears some form of the name *Muhammad*, and the status of women tends to be low: while polygamy is declining,

---

[19]For a statement from Islamic leaders of Pakistan about what they envisioned by way of a new constitution, see DeBary, *Sources*, vol. 2, pp. 309–11.

An Indian Muslim.

purdah is still practiced and it influences even the form of the typical Muslim house. Kinship is the basis of society and there is still a preference for marriage to one's father's brother's daughter.

The influence of Islam can be observed, too, in the various practices that accompany every stage of life—from birthing rites to naming, circumcision, marriage, and death. Thus, for example, Muslims in South Asia bury, whereas Hindus cremate, their dead. The year is dotted with religious holidays, and Ramadan and Muharram (the tenth month of the Muslim year, when passion plays are staged honoring 'Ali and Husayn) are especially important. Many observers have noted how moving is the sight of pilgrims, garlanded with bright flowers, embarking for Mecca from the great ports of the subcontinent. And as in North Africa saints' tombs are everywhere, visited with special devotion by women. Saint veneration, says Annamarie Schimmel, "is still a living part of popular Islam in Indo-Pakistan."[20]

[20]See Schimmell, *Islam in the Indian Subcontinent*, p. 138.

Islam in Indonesia

The name *Indonesia* evokes many images in the Western mind—Java coffee, Borneo headhunters, romantic Bali, All-Asia Games in the gigantic Sukarno Stadium in Djakarta, beautiful batik designs, shadow-play puppets on sticks, ristaffel, aromatic spices. Indonesia itself, one of the most populous countries of Asia and the most intensely Muslim of all countries outside the Middle East, is composed of some three thousand islands, large and small, that stretch across the Pacific for a distance equal to that across the United States or from London to Montreal. Of these islands, the best known are Sumatra, Borneo (now Kalimantan), Java, the Celebes (now Sulawesi), Bali, Flores, and Timor. The peculiar geography of the region has encouraged many residents of the archipelago to become sea-traders, and the climate of the region has made rice the dominant crop. This is an intensely peasant, intensely rural culture, despite the density of the population in the great cities of the nation.

During the European Middle Ages, the area known today as Indonesia was largely Buddhist and Hindu, and both religions had developed over many years highly sophisticated traditions. From the fifteenth century on, however, Islam has been the dominant religious force, one reason being that the stress of Islam on equality appeared to many Indonesian traders to be a way of breaking the hated Hindu caste system which made impossible their entry, no matter how wealthy they became, into the upper classes.[21] But as Islamic influence grew, many cultured Hindus left the main islands of Sumatra and Java for Bali, and it has been suggested that this is one reason why the arts—music, dance, and painting—have flourished so bountifully there.

In the sixteenth century, the Portuguese controlled the entire island kingdom, but by the seventeenth century the Dutch (who arrived in 1596) had become the dominant force, driven particularly by the profits to be had from spices from the Island of Molucca. Later, the Dutch shifted their attention to Java, where the agricultural practices they developed formed the basis for many a Dutch fortune. (It has been estimated that at this time one in every six Dutchmen depended on Indonesia for his income.) By the end of the nineteenth century, Indonesian resentment of the

[21]See Reba Lewis, *Indonesia: Troubled Paradise* (New York: David McKay, 1963), p. 115.

Dutch was growing strong and the Dutch were forced to respond by improving the living standard of the islanders. From 1900 on, moreover, forces of nationalism were beginning to be felt: local and district councils were formed with native representation; legal reforms of various kinds were encouraged; and a series of organizations was established to promote Indonesian—especially Javanese—culture. Among the forces pushing reform were Marxist influences, various other revival movements throughout Asia, and the teachings of a number of Muslim reformers from the Middle East, most notably Muhammad Abdouh.[22] In 1911 a very important organization, the Muhammadiyah, was founded for the purpose of spreading Islam and improving conditions among Indonesia's poor—both in the country and the cities. As in India, inspiration and models for the activities of the Muhammadiyah were provided by Christian missionaries.

Sukarno, who was eventually to become the first president of the modern nation, appeared on the scene around 1925 as an organizer of various nationalistic groups striving for the expulsion of the Dutch. The cause of nationalism was also aided by the invasion of the islands by Japan during World War II, and indeed the Japanese, although they treated the Indonesians harshly, did much to build up the administration of the islands and the army. In 1945 independence was declared, although the Dutch did not accept the inevitable until 1949, and disputes with the Dutch continued for another decade. For the Dutch, departure from Indonesia was a traumatic event: many Dutch families had lived in the area for generations and many of the Dutch had Indonesian wives or husbands. However, this event does not seem to have been quite the wrenching experience for the Dutch that the departure from Algeria in 1962 was for many French.

During Sukarno's presidency Indonesia tilted sharply to the left, and although lip service was paid to Islam, it was clear that the new regime saw the principal values of religion to be the stabilizing and unifying elements they could bring to a nation's culture. A great deal of public building went on at this time, with

[22]Muhammad Abdouh (1849–1905), journalist, theologian, preacher to the masses, promoted the revival of Arabic in the Middle East, urged Muslim peoples to recover their rights, and sought to free Islam from the dominance of the West. Because he did know the modern world so well, and valued the positive elements it had to contribute, many of the ulema severely criticized his teachings.

obvious propaganda value, and a highlight was the celebrated Bandung Conference, April 1955, in which the nations of the Third World met to devise a strategy for dealing with the continuing domination of the world by the superpowers. From this conference Sukarno of Indonesia and Gamal Abdel Nasser of Egypt emerged as important leaders. Sukarno's tenure was also marked by disputes over western New Guinea and Malaysia and disagreements with India, and economic problems continued to plague the nation (rubber, oil, and tin constitute the basis of Indonesia's economy). Sukarno seized foreign industrial holdings in his country, pulled his country out of the United Nations, managed to have himself cut off from funds that the World Bank might have made available, and found himself increasingly isolated from the world, except for the Communist-bloc nations of East Asia. In 1966 Sukarno was driven from office, the Communist party was banned, and Indonesia returned to the United Nations. A more moderate course was undertaken by General Suharto, as he began to rebuild his country on a base more acceptable to most of its citizens.

This much background has been necessary if we are even to begin to understand the role of Islam in Indonesia—yesterday and today. To put it as succinctly as possible, in Indonesia as in South Asia, Islam was an important force in organizing a sense of nationhood that led to the expulsion, at some point in the twentieth century, of foreign colonial powers. However, in Indonesia, Islam seems to have been a cultural force primarily, determining affiliations, customs, and attitudes and dominating a certain class—the merchants and professionals. It does not seem to have had the intense philosophical and theological focus that it has had in Pakistan, so that instead of providing us with a rich array of stimulating texts or a series of varied and exotic customs, Islam remains a pervasive but hard-to-identify cultural phenomenon—a phenomenon that presents us with a definition or understanding of religion that is quite different from those we are accustomed to. Indeed, it is rather like the meaning of the term *Christian* in Lebanon: a certain political and family affiliation and a tendency to practice one set of customs rather than another.

When Islam came to the archipelago in the fifteenth and the sixteenth centuries, the new faith was imposed on very ancient Buddhist and Hindu traditions. Islam did not bring a new civilization to Indonesia, Clifford Geertz observes; rather it "appropriated one."[23] Indeed, Islam has never dominated the islands that make up this nation, and Islamic law does not appear to have enjoyed in Indonesia the importance it has had in Pakistan. And while nine out of ten Indonesians are Muslims, their degree of commitment to their faith (as a religious institution) varies widely. This fact may be explained, in part, by the wide variety of influences that have been at work on Islam in Indonesia.

Because many of the earliest missionaries were traders and commercial venturers, Islam became firmly entrenched in the Indonesian middle class, especially among those who traded internally. (The Portuguese and the Dutch eventually gained control of international trade.) This fact has helped to determine, as it did in the Middle East as well, much of Islam's flavor in the area. In the nineteenth century, Indonesian Islam was touched by currents of the Wahhabi movement from Arabia (a summons to a puritanical lifestyle and to strict adherence to Islam in its purest forms), and, as has already been noted, by the teachings of the Egyptian reformer, Muhammad Abdouh. Moreover, as Geertz has noted, throughout the nineteenth century an increasing number of Indonesian holy men made the pilgrimage to Mecca, and many of them on return founded schools of religious learning. These learned men (Arabic, *ulema;* Javanese, *kijaji*) thus contributed to the development of the Scripturalist movement in Indonesia, reflecting the profound commitment of Islam everywhere to the written word, and helped to make Islam in Indonesia a bookish, intellectual kind of thing, lacking the ecstatic dimension so common in Islam elsewhere. (It is interesting to note that in Indonesia, as in the Middle East, the memorizing of texts is the principal form that education takes.) The schools founded by the kijaji eventually became an important source of anti-Indian, anti-British, and anti-Dutch activity, and many of the products of these institutions helped to provide the power base that Sukarno needed for his rise to power. (It is significant that Indonesians tended to associate Christianity with the hated Dutch; Islam, with nationalism.) All those who had been to such schools and indeed, as Geertz points out, all those who sympathized with the aims of such schools, were regarded as members of the *santri* community,

[23]Clifford Geertz, *Islam Observed* (New Haven: Yale University Press, 1968), p. 11.

which in turn had close ties with the "internal marketing system" of bazaars. Thus again the links between Islam, education, and commerce in Indonesia are reinforced. And because Marxism was seen by many as a force of liberation, and as a way of improving the lot of the common people, its influence, too, was increasingly felt.

During World War II, the Japanese operated through various Muslim organizations in Indonesia to make the changes in the country that they saw necessary (creating the necessary bureaucratic infrastructure, for example), and as a result Muslims gained important roles in the postwar development of the country. It must also be noted that Muslims played an important role in the fall of Sukarno, since, as has already been suggested, his religious position was lukewarm and ambivalent. The celebrated Five Principles announced by Sukarno, which he used in justifying his stand against making Indonesia a Muslim state, included the assumption that Indonesians should believe in God (any god) and that Muslims and Christians were to practice their religion in a civilized manner and with mutual respect. Such a position did not win the approval of the traditional Muslim faithful.

The present position of women in Indonesia can also be seen as a result of the influence of Islam. The constitution of 1945 granted women equal rights with men and made the status of women in Indonesia the highest in the Muslim world. For example, Indonesian women do not cover their faces (except when they are Arabs living in Indonesia) or follow other strict rules of behavior imposed on them elsewhere in the Muslim world. However, the constitution of 1945 did not prohibit polygamy, and this continues to be a source of annoyance for educated Indonesian women.[24]

Many observers have suggested that the great diversity of Muslim practice in Indonesia can be traced in part to the enormous spread of the country, to the fact that some of the islands are quite isolated, and to the great ethnic and linguistic variety of the nation. One of Indonesia's proud mottoes, Unity in Diversity, is an attempt to make the best of this situation. However, Geertz, a highly sophisticated observer of things anthropological,

[24]For the remarkable story of what one Indonesian woman, living at the beginning of the twentieth century, was able to achieve in developing a sense of identity among Indonesian women, see Raden Ddjiing Kartini, *Letters from a Javanese Princess*, trans. A. L. Symmers (New York: A. A. Knopf, 1920).

has suggested that Islam in Indonesia today is not only multi-voiced and syncretistic but also highly malleable and increasingly tentative and faltering. Pure Islam is not to be found here, Geertz suggests, but rather Muslim believers whose doubts are increasing and who are finding it harder and harder to bridge the gap between the pronouncements of Qur'an and what they actually think.[25] A vague "Koranic moralism" is the rule in Indonesia, Geertz observes, which makes us think of the situation of much of Christianity in Europe and America.

Islam in China

Here we are on a very different ground: we know far less about Islam in China than we do about Islam in South Asia or Indonesia, and a good deal of the early material is actually legend of highly dubious quality. Moreover, Muslims in China have always been very much a minority group, out of touch with the main stream of Islam because of distance, and exercising very little influence on Chinese history (except in one province for a comparatively brief time), their own customs profoundly colored by the Chinese culture all about them. They have had to work at preserving a modicum of their faith rather than (as in Pakistan) serving as major spokespersons to the world of that faith. Also it must be noted that Muslims elsewhere do not have a high opinion of Chinese Muslims. Edgar Snow quotes a Pakistani on this question: "The only thing Muslim about them is that they don't eat pork!" This estimate is unfair, but it does suggest a widely held attitude.[26]

Pre-Islamic contacts between China and Arabia are very much a matter of legend, although apparently traders did make some contacts. One early story has Sa'ad Abu Wakkas, Muhammad's maternal uncle, making two or three visits to China, the first in 611, bearing his nephew's portrait, and later dying and being buried in Khanfu (Canton). Resting on more certain ground is the story of the visit to China in 651 of an embassy sent by Uthman, the third caliph. The Arabs visiting the emperor refused to make the appropriate kowtows and were almost executed for their

[25]Geertz, *Islam Observed,* pp. 107–17.
[26]Edgar Snow, *Red China: The Other Side of the River* (New York: Random, 1962), pp. 558–59.

arrogance, until someone suggested that their strange behavior might be due to differing customs in their own land. There were hostile contacts in the eighth century—the Arabs inflicted an important defeat on the Chinese at the celebrated Battle of Talas in 751, and Arab and Persian forces plundered Khanfu in 758. During the Abbasid period (749–1258), however, there was a large Arab colony at Khanfu with a functioning imam. Muslims in China at this time definitely regarded themselves as foreigners and returned to the Middle East whenever their business in China declined. Later, when the Mongols (Yüan) subdued China, Muslims were put in places of power and thus grew to be thoroughly disliked by the Chinese. At this time, Muslims entered Yunnan province, in the southwest, where they became a dominant force. Marco Polo noted many "Saracens" in this area, offspring of the soldiers of Genghis Khan.

Muslims were safest and most successful when they lived unobtrusively and adopted traditional features of Chinese culture. Intermarriage occurred and some Chinese were converted, and during the Yüan period many Muslims living in China made that subtle shift which turned them into Chinese Muslims.[27] And although these Chinese Muslims were exhibiting fewer and fewer Arab traits, they continued to maintain sharp distinctions in dress and appearance (the men wore beards, for example) from the Chinese. More and more common becomes the distinction between the *Hui* (Chinese Muslims) and *Han* (the Chinese name for themselves), and even today this term is retained, although its origin is uncertain.[28] As more and more of the Hui saw the eventual end of Yüan domination, they actively sought friendship with the Chinese, adopting more Chinese customs and even abandoning their Arabic names for Chinese names. Nevertheless, the period of the Ming dynasty (1368–1644) was a true golden age for Muslims in China—they held important positions in the government and the army, enjoyed toleration, and were secure as businessmen.

Under the Ch'ing dynasty (1644–1911) things at first went well for Chinese Muslims, especially during the reign of the very able

[27]Raphael Israeli, *Muslims in China: A Study in Cultural Confrontation* (London: Curzon, 1980), p. 82.

[28]Marshall Broomhall, *Islam in China: A Neglected Problem* (New York: Paragon Book Reprint Corp., 1966), pp. 167–77.

Yung Chêng, who warned the Muslims against misbehavior (im-morality, disquiet, rebellion) but in general sought to protect them. Increasingly, however, the Ch'ing emperors were forced to choose between Hui and Han subjects and Muslims knew a great deal of unhappiness during this period, which they expressed in acts of rebellion. The causes of the unrest—and bloodshed—were many: social conditions were deteriorating; police work was being taken over by various local forces; the government was no longer able to protect Muslims, who seemed to be locked in constant conflict with their neighbors. In order to secure or maintain the rights of these Muslims, many secret societies sprang up, often with Shi'ite affiliations and strong messianic tendencies. These moves were met by government efforts to force sinicization and cultural assimilation, and brutal treatment was often meted out when these efforts did not succeed.

Muslim responses included both a series of militant rebellions and a variety of efforts to revive the faith in China. Efforts to revive or renew Islam took many forms: books about Islam and about the Prophet were written in Chinese and published; various schemes of Muslim education were designed; and there were continuing calls for Muslims to return to the true faith and true ritual. During an extended period of time in the eighteenth and nineteenth centuries a movement rather vaguely known as the New Sect flourished. What one learns about this religious body differs from source to source and observer to observer, but it seems safe to say that it was revivalist, utopian (offering the promise of a better society), and even millenarian in the sense that it envisioned an imminent coming of the forces of Allah to the earth. Traditionally-oriented Chinese Muslims chose to fight the New Sect or at least remain silent about it, but it seems to have stirred the imagina-tions of many. Some scholars have linked it to certain Sufi orders of Central Asia, and indeed the stress on magic and saint worship and the concern of this movement with hidden knowledge does present parallels to Middle Eastern or Central Asian Sufism and Shi'ism. The power of the movement was often seen as a serious threat to the government.[29]

The first important Muslim rebellion occurred in the northwest part of China between 1781 and 1785; it was severely repressed.

[29]See Israeli, *Muslims in China*, pp. 155–80.

Another rebellion broke out in 1826; but the most important uprising began in 1855, the so-called Yunnan or Panthay Rebellion, led by Tu Wen Hsui, who founded a Muslim state in Yunnan province in 1856 and is still today a great hero among Chinese Muslims. This rebellion, which lasted for eighteen years, has been described as "a desperate attempt by Chinese Muslims to assert their religious and cultural identity by disengaging themselves from the psychological, and sometimes physical oppression of a greater Chinese order."[30] In 1864 Yakub Bey, a militant writer on Islam, emerged from his post as a minor official and quickly established himself as the military leader of the rebellious Muslims, a military leader with the dream of a great Central Asian empire that would defeat and suppress the Chinese and establish a new Muslim empire in East Asia. Yakub Bey quickly established his authority in parts of the West and secured recognition from Britain, Russia, and the Turks. The Chinese saw him as a real threat—how could China become Muslim?—but Yakub's sudden death in 1877 enabled the authorities to recover Chinese Turkestan.

The Ch'ing period ended in 1911 with the founding of the Chinese Republic and the start of the so-called Nationalist era. As early as the 1930s the rising Chinese Communist party, bent on challenging the leadership of Chiang Kai-shek, found in the Chinese Muslims an unhappy minority group which offered them important contacts (through Islam) with other Third-World nations. According to Snow, the Communists regarded Muslims as an essentially ethnic (i.e., Central Asian) group that happened also to be Muslim. They distinguished the *Hui-Min* (Good Muslims), seen primarily as an ethnic group, from the *Hui-Chiao* (Bandit Muslims), who attempted to practice their religion seriously. Perhaps erroneously the Communists tended to see the Hui-Min as atheists who had not formally renounced their faith and who did not eat pork. In any case, the Muslims of China live primarily in the Hui Autonomous Region of Nighsia and in Sinkiang Uighur Autonomous Region and together, in these two areas, they are thought to number about eight million. There may be seven million additional Muslims elsewhere in China.

In the 1930s, during his first visit to China, Snow, an American

[30]Ibid., p. 4.

journalist, discovered two Muslim training regiments and found that the Communists actually hoped to field a Muhammadan Red Army, in hopes of creating a united Han-Hui front. The Chinese to whom Snow talked (among whom were Muslims) insisted that they enjoyed freedom of worship. Snow suspected, however, that many were worried about Chinese plans for them. Snow also reported a great deal of work by the Communists in Muslim villages and the general feeling that Islam and Communism were not incompatible.[31] More recent observers have reported no real change in the official position of the Communist party in China that religion is a form of superstition; however, a certain willingness to take seriously—at an intellectual level—the world's great religions has been reported, and along with it, a granting of freedom of worship to adherents of the world's major religions. Indeed, in the constitution of the People's Republic of China there is a provision for freedom of religion and efforts have been made to punish government officials who violate this freedom. Bob Whyte has reported that in 1977 Islamic and Buddhist associations had "re-emerged" along with Protestant and Catholic societies. Whyte also felt that a certain "space" for religious worship was being delimited in China, including the right to public worship and the right to publish some religious literature—such as the Bible and the Qur'an. The authorities may even be willing to grant the right to train clergy. Evidently the outlook is better for the major religions than for various folk traditions—the Taoist, for example.[32]

What about the nature of Islam in China? Again, we must assert that its character is determined to a considerable degree by its isolation from the rest of the Muslim world—and by the fact that Muslims in China constitute a minority within a country that has a very old and distinctive culture base—to which Muslims must somehow relate. Over the centuries there have been sporadic contacts with Muslims in South Asia and Afghanistan, occasional visits from Persian, Indian, and Turkish Muslims, and very little contact with Islam in Indonesia. However, numbers of Chinese Muslims have made the pilgrimage to Mecca and Medina and

[31]Edgar Snow, *Red Star over China* (New York: Grove, 1973), pp. 312–16.

[32]See Bob Whyte, "The Future of Religion in China," *Religion in Communist Lands*, vol. 8, Spring 1980, pp. 4–10.

there appears to exist among Chinese Muslims an eschatological hope that at the end of the world a worldwide communion of Muslims will be realized. Of this hope, the Ka'aba in Mecca is the great operative symbol. Apparently the Chinese Communists have made no effort to cut off contacts with Arabia, and Chinese Muslims appear to regard the Sharif of Mecca as a saint with special authority, even over them.

We have already noted the rather contemptuous feeling about Chinese Islam expressed by one Pakistani, and there appears to be some truth to this judgment, for while many visitors have commented on the cleanliness of mosques in China, Western observers have also noted that the imams (a-hungs) in China are rarely learned, speaking Chinese primarily and knowing only segments of the Qur'an. Moreover, at the present time, congregations are seriously isolated from each other, so that there is little chance for supportive contact. Virtually no Chinese Muslims have been recognized outside China as religious authorities. The continuing problem, then, is one of self-identity: whom does a Chinese Muslim believe himself to be? Are the Hui really Chinese?

Curiously enough, there appears to be no lack of self-esteem among Chinese Muslims, for many observers have found them to be cocky and self-assured. (This feeling, of course, is common to most Muslims, since they regard themselves as having the final truth.) In the past, some have acquired great prominence in China in both government and the military. Many have expressed strong feelings about letting their children marry non-Muslim Chinese, and efforts continue to be made to retain Arabic names and to remember Middle Eastern origins—even to the point of assigning Arab names to Chinese locations and devising legends that will link Chinese mythology and Islamic history.

Nevertheless, the weight of evidence points to the fact that Muslims are, for a variety of reasons, out of place in Chinese society and victims of a good deal of Chinese hostility. All kinds of jokes and taunts involving the pig are hurled at Muslims (the Han, of course, love pork and make the refusal of the Hui to enjoy it a matter of continuing comment). More seriously, some significant differences must be pointed out: Chinese Muslims have always rejected ancestor worship, worshiping instead within the living community; Chinese Muslims have not recognized any state religious cult but have relied solely on their imams for leadership, and these imams have always enjoyed a much higher status than Buddhist priests. Moreover, because of the Islamic principle of almsgiving, Chinese mosques tended to have more substantial funds available to them than do Buddhist shrines, and the result of this comparative affluence is that Chinese Islam has developed a well-organized educational system. Superiority in these areas has helped Chinese Islam, but it also made it a target for many, the object of great hostility.[33] Ira Lapidus has also pointed to a difference between the two groups in social organization; Islamic society is based on voluntary association; Chinese society on a hierarchy descending from the emperor.[34] But the overarching problem is, quite simply, the fact that Muslims are not Confucianists, and in the eyes of Chinese, one cannot be Han without being loyal to the great sage of China and his teachings. Not to be a Confucianist has meant living outside the father-son framework; not to respect the ancestors has meant exposure to various evil spirits; the rejection of Confucianism has also meant being unable to partake, through the emperor, in the blessings of heaven; it has implied the claim of an authority above the emperor; in short, it has indicated a rejection of the traditional Chinese way.[35] At various times throughout history, Muslims have attempted to lean toward Confucianism and have made gestures of conciliation, but these have rarely amounted to much, and the degree of acculturation of Chinese Muslims continues to be strictly limited.

At the very start of this book we spoke about the enormous diversity of peoples and beliefs and landscapes that Asia encompasses. We see this diversity, too, in our examination of Buddhism, Hinduism, and Christianity, and we see it once again in our study of Islam. Here is a faith which has attracted adherents all the way across this vast continent, from Istanbul to Djarkata, and which has taken a different form and made a different contribution in every country. But despite all the diversity we have observed, Islam continues to express loyalty to one God, and one prophet, and one book. Islam is, indeed, an astonishing example of the power of human beings to create endless variations on a single great theme.

[33]For a summary of the differences, see Israeli, *Muslims in China*, p. 20.
[34]Quoted by Israeli, ibid., p. 52.
[35]Ibid., p. 20.

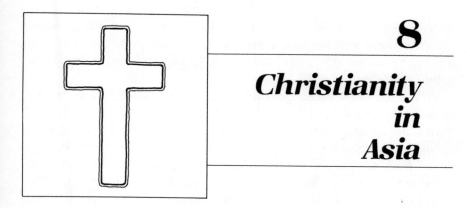

8

Christianity in Asia

Christianity is by origin a religion of Asia, of Southwest Asia specifically; but its most dynamic forms have developed in the Western world—Europe and America—and its strongest manifestations in Asia today—in India, Korea, and the Philippines—are all the results of Western missionary activity, sometimes going back for many centuries. However, we often fail to take into account the question of origins and the fact of the considerable strength of several native churches in the western parts of Asia and on its perimeters. Native churches include the Armenian Orthodox Church, which originated in eastern Anatolia, in the region of Mount Ararat, whose adherents claim to be the oldest surviving Christian group in the world; the Nestorian, or Assyrian, or Jacobite Church, which teaches the strict separation of the divine and human natures of Christ; and the Maronite Church, the Eastern Rite branch of Roman Catholicism, a denomination that has flirted in the past with the heresy that there was only a divine—not a human—will in Christ. The Greek Orthodox Church, one of the major divisions of world Christianity, is very active in western Asia, and its patriarch resides in Istanbul, where Europe and Asia meet. And the Coptic Church, centered in Cairo, an hour's plane ride from Jerusalem, embraces perhaps four million adherents in Egypt. But such indigenous bodies generally maintain a low profile, and Westerners are aware of them only when they read about Muslim-Christian conflict in Lebanon or Muslim-Coptic riots in Egypt, or when they visit the great Christian shrines in Jerusalem.

When that vast mosaic which is Christianity in Asia is scrutinized, tiny piece after tiny piece catches the light—the story of Paul's missionary activity in Asia Minor in the early years after Christ's crucifixion; the long journey of Nestorian missionaries from Iraq to China in the Dark Ages; the establishment of Christianity in the Philippines in the seventeenth century; the charitable work of Mother Teresa of Calcutta, which won her the Nobel Peace Prize in 1979; pictures of the great Roman Catholic Cathedral of Saigon, during the war in Vietnam; the daringly modern chapel, given by Henry Luce, on the grounds of Tunghai University in Taiwan; agricultural, nursing, and theological schools at Silliman University; Kagawa preaching the gospel in the slums of Tokyo; a book on my shelf called *Zen Sermons on Christian Themes;* a church in Pakistan that is Presbyterian, Congregationalist, and Methodist, served by a Lutheran who is a bishop in Anglican orders; Thomas Merton, the Trappist poet and theologian, dying in Bangkok at a Buddhist conference; and countless less well known witnesses who "muzzled ravening lions, quenched the fury of fire, escaped death by the sword" or "were tortured to death, disdaining release, to win a better resurrection" (Heb. 11:34, 35, NEB). What an enormous range of human experience is here!

The problem of saying something significant about such a variety of commitments across so many years and such a vast expanse of territory has compelled us to condense our remarks here to a few brief case studies—case studies which we hope will suggest something of the differing forms Christianity has taken in Asia, the differing problems it has had to face, and the differing triumphs it has enjoyed. First we discuss what has happened in Iran, where the Christian community, today under grave threat, is very small but very old; then we describe the situation in China and India, where Western missionary activity has been more vigorous and longer sustained than anywhere else in the world; and finally we comment on the situation in Japan, where there is a small but vital church, Catholic and Protestant.

C. G. F.

Christianity in Iran

Iran is the second largest country in West Asia; it is the land of the Aryans, whose history can be traced back for nearly five thousand years. In biblical times, under Cyrus and Darius, the Persians established an empire that stretched from the Aegean Sea to the Indus River, and it was during this period, of course, that the long Jewish experience in Persia worked itself out. Cyrus, the liberator, was seen by Isaiah as a prototype of the Messiah. Esther and Daniel, according to the Old Testament, served in the imperial court. The return of the Jews from exile was facilitated by Ezra and Nehemiah, who also had royal connections, and the Jews who did not return to Palestine formed a community in Persia that continued right up into the twentieth century.

Iran's connection with Christianity is almost as ancient. Some claim that the Magi, or Wise Men, those mysterious visitors who brought gifts to the infant Jesus, were Persian scholar-priests of the Zoroastrian tradition. Three decades later, according to the Book of Acts, "Parthians, and Medes, and Elamites"—all Persian peoples—were among those who heard Peter preach at Pentecost (Acts 2:9). Moreover, it is said that Thomas, the celebrated doubting disciple, labored in Persia on his way to India, and Bartholomew by tradition is held to have ministered in Persia as well as in Arabia and India. Still other ancient accounts have it that Simon and Jude went as a team to preach in Persia, where they were both martyred after thirteen years of work. Whatever may be the history behind these pious narratives, one reality is beyond question: Christianity has very ancient ties with Iran.

In the seventh century, however, Iran was conquered by Arab armies and the area became part of an Arab Muslim state stretching from the Atlantic to the Indian oceans. Although Islam was accepted, it was accepted in dissenting fashion, for Persians became Shi'ite, not Sunnite, Muslims. Even today, 98 percent of all Iranians are Muslim, but only 5 percent of them are orthodox. During the period of Arab domination, Persians won distinction in science, philosophy, and letters, all the time maintaining their own language and culture. In the middle of the eleventh century Persia was invaded by Turkish-speaking peoples from Central Asia, the Seljuks, and further mixing of cultures occurred. Then followed a period of domination by the Mongols and the Timurids, both groups converting to the very Islam they had conquered. Early in the sixteenth century, however, there began a revival of Persian nationalism under the Safavid shahs, who established their capital at Isfahan, made Shi'ite Islam the official faith, and created a Persian Muslim state that extended far into Central Asia.

By the nineteenth century, Persia was in a state of decline, at the mercy of Western nations that coveted the land's resources and sought to control the strategic crossroads at which she is located. The British and the Russians in effect partitioned Persia in 1908, but in the period between the two world wars, Reza Shah, a Cossack soldier and self-made shah, introduced the Pahlavi dynasty in an attempt to modernize and nationalize the region. Following the Second World War, Reza Shah's son, Mohammad Reza Shah Pahlavi, envisioned a new Iran, a great civilization, and this vision was becoming a reality by the mid-1970s, with the advice of Western and Japanese experts and the support of Iran's new petrodollars.

But the burden of change proved to be more than the fragile institutions of Pahlavi Iran could bear. Massive frustration developed. Within Iran, the successful forces of opposition to the regime were the Communists and the Muslim clergy. When the revolution came in 1979, it took a double form: the removal of the shah, which was the result of mass protests unprecedented in the history of the country; and the installation of a Muslim theocracy under the Ayatollah Khomeini. At the start of the 1980s Iran was struggling to become an Islamic civilization, but as of this writing, prospects for stability in Iran remain uncertain.

Even more uncertain is the fate of the Christian church in Iran, which, although small, has been representative of the major theological and cultural expressions of the Christian faith. In Tehran, before the two recent revolutions, there were Russian and Greek Orthodox churches; a community church of Presbyterian origins serving a wide range of Americans, Europeans, and Asians; and an Evangelical or Persian Presbyterian Church. Saint Abraham's Church, which was Roman Catholic, ministered to both nationals and expatriates, as did Saint Paul's Episcopal Church, part of the Anglican fellowship in the Middle East. Also represented were the Southern Baptists and Pentecostals, the Bible Believers and the Assemblies of God, as well as Christian groups from England, Germany, India, Korea, and Taiwan. In the midseventies, Christianity in Tehran was a miniature of world Christianity. Evangelicals and Anglo-Catholics, charismatics and liberals—all manner of perspectives on the faith were present. Tehran was a good city in which to study not only Islam but also comparative Christianity.

Let us consider some of the representative Christian denominations to be found in Iran.

What is perhaps the oldest continuing Christian tradition is represented in Iran by the Armenian Apostolic Church. In 1970 it was organized around three centers—Tabriz, with forty-five churches and perhaps 15,000 baptized members; New Julfa, with forty churches and more than 30,000 baptized members; and Tehran, with thirty-five churches and about 110,000 baptized members. The origins of this church lay, of course, in the neighboring nation of Armenia, which has now been absorbed by Turkey, Iran, and the Union of Soviet Socialist Republics. Armenians believe that their country was mentioned in the story of Pentecost (they substitute "Armenia" for "Judaea" in the list of nations in Acts 2:9). According to tradition, both Thaddeus and Bartholomew ministered in Armenia. It was not, however, until 301 that Christianity became the official religion of the land, as a result of the labors of Gregory the Illuminator. Armenians believe that theirs was the first kingdom on earth to have become Christian.

During the many tribulations in Middle Eastern history, Armenians began to emigrate to Iran. In the reign of the Il Khans, Armenians began to be established in western sections, and during the reign of Shah Abbas (1587–1629) Armenians were resettled in the center of the country, at Julfa, in the neighborhood of Isfahan. During the Qajar dynasty, Armenians began to settle in Tehran, now the capital of the country. By 1970 the majority of Iran's Armenians lived in the national capital.

Through the centuries, the Armenian community in Iran has suffered from three problems in particular. In the first place, they are a people without a country, a diaspora folk like the Jewish people before 1948, scattered from Iran to California. Moreover, they are a minority people in both Iran and Turkey, fearful of persecution by Muslim majorities, hopeful of coexistence as they maintain their own educational, social, cultural, and religious institutions. In addition, in Iran, they are a Christian people who have been subjected to proselytizing by Western churches, both Roman and Protestant. Roman Catholics, as early as 1330, sought the union of Armenians under the papacy, and starting again in 1604 Augustinians and then Carmelites and Capuchins came to preach among the Armenians of Julfa. By 1742 there was an Armenian Catholic Church, in fellowship with Rome.

The Assyrian Church of the East (Nestorian) traces its origin back to apostolic times. It is said that from the very earliest days there were Christians in Mesopotamia using the Aramaic language (as Christ did) and tracing their roots to such an illustrious apostle as Thomas. Disliking the name *Nestorian* (the Eastern church claims to have received this persecuted theologian into its midst but denies that he was the founder of the denomination), Assyrian Christians contend that in the Dark Ages their missionaries were active across the vast stretches of Eurasia from Mesopotamia to China and Manchuria. Around A.D. 1000 these people, who knew Arabic, Syriac, and Greek, performed an invaluable role in Baghdad as translators of the Greek classics into the Arabic tongue, in this way actually assuring the preservation of Greek philosophical and scientific writings during the Middle Ages.[1]

By 1970 it was uncertain how many Assyrian Christians lived in Iran. The main centers of the church were Tehran and Rezā'īyeh. Suffering from proselytizing efforts by Western civilization, from emigration to the New World (the Patriarchate of the Church of the East was moved to San Francisco), and from isolation among Muslims, the Assyrian Church, while proud of its illustrious history, feared its uncertain destiny.

The Roman Catholic Church in Iran in 1970 consisted of two Uniate Churches, dating from modern times, and a Latin archdiocese of Isfahan.[2] The first of the Uniate Churches is the Armenian Catholic Church. Although there were Armenians who sought fellowship with the pope in the late Middle Ages, this tradition

---

[1] See DeLacy O'Leary, *How Greek Science Passed to the Arabs* (London: Methuen, 1949), especially chapter 12.

[2] The Uniate Churches follow the liturgy and practices of the Greek Orthodox tradition and are loyal to the pope in Rome.

was not established under its own patriarch until 1742, and even then turmoil dogged this denomination. By 1970, the headquarters of the patriarchate were in Beirut, with most of the Armenian Catholics living in Tehran.

The second of the Uniate Churches is the Chaldean Catholic Church, founded in 1552. This church came into being as a secession from the Assyrian Church over the selection of an unpopular priest as patriarch of the Church of the East. By 1970 this small church was part of the Patriarchate of Babylon.

Finally, the Archdiocese of Isfahan of the Latins, established in 1632, was the direct result of missionary labor. Although Franciscans and Dominicans had been active in Iran from the late Middle Ages, it was not until the seventeenth and eighteenth centuries that French Catholic mission work began in earnest. By 1970, the members of the Latin Rite were predominantly expatriates.

Protestantism in Iran dates from Anglo-American missionary work begun in the nineteenth century. Although by 1970 less than 4 percent of the total Christian population was Protestant, their influence on the society was out of proportion to their numbers.

The Episcopal Church of the Middle East includes the Diocese of Iran, which was constituted in 1912, and by 1970 consisted of six congregations. The President-Bishop of the Episcopal Church in the Middle East was an Iranian. This church counts as its greatest figure Henry Martyn, an Anglican minister who worked in Shiraz in the early nineteenth century, translating the New Testament into Farsi.

The Evangelical (Presbyterian) Church of Iran traces its origins to the missionary work of the American minister, Justin Perkins, who arrived in Iran in 1834. Since then more than six hundred Presbyterian missionaries have worked in the nation, and by 1933 three presbyteries were organized, made up of eighteen congregations. Because membership in the Evangelical Church is 55 percent Assyrian, 21 percent Armenian, and 24 percent other ethnic groups, the presbyteries were organized along ethnic rather than geographical lines. Known for their educational work, the Presbyterians conducted the Armaghan Institute, Community School, and Damavand College, all in Tehran.

The Khomeini revolution has threatened all forms of Christianity in Iran. A faith that has as its central symbol the cross cannot despair, however, about the future. Out of loss will come gain; out of tragedy will come victory.   C. G. F.

Christianity in India

The apostle Thomas carried the Christian gospel to India, according to both ancient Indian tradition and the third-century Syrian Acts of Judas Thomas. The document tells of the apostles casting lots after the ascension of Christ to decide which were to proclaim the gospel to the various nations of the world. India fell to Thomas, but he refused to go even when the Lord appeared to him in a vision affirming the decision. But providence arranged that he was sold as a slave to an Indian king who needed a master craftsman to build a new palace. Thomas took the money for the mansion and distributed it to the poor, telling the king that he should seek rather to enter the mansions of heaven. The incensed king imprisoned Thomas, but soon found himself converted by the simple faith of the apostle. Released from prison, Thomas proclaimed the gospel throughout southern India until he was martyred by brahmins and buried outside of present-day Madras.

The legend is fanciful, but it has a basis in fact. We know that the king involved was a historical person, and we have evidence that Roman ships often stopped at Indian ports. A bishop, John, calling himself the metropolitan of India, was present at the Council of Nicea in 325. The sixth-century "Universal Christian Topography" tells of Christians from Persia sending missionaries to India to perpetuate a form of Christianity (Nestorian) considered heretical in the Roman West. Subsequently merchants, including Marco Polo, tell of Christians in India and Saint Thomas Mount as a place of pilgrimage. And the tradition persists among the Church of Thomas Christians that the apostle was their founder.

Whatever the facts of the apostolic origin and later presence of Christianity in India, by the sixteenth century this vast country was seen as a field ripe for the harvest of the gospel—and for colonial exploitation. When the Portuguese, among them Vasco da Gama, invaded western India, they found large communities of Christians whom they considered heretical, leaderless, and almost a caste within Hinduism. Claiming authority from the pope over all India, the Portuguese sought to correct these lapsing Christians and to convert Hindus to Christianity. But their religious intentions were seriously undermined by the irresponsible behavior of the conquerors. When in 1954 the Portuguese colony of Goa was annexed by India, its ambassadors to the United Nations insisted that "Portuguese Goa is essential to the Christianization of India." The Indian ambassador sardonically replied that there were by that time more Christians in India than there were in Portugal.

In 1542 Jesuit missionaries—also of Portuguese origin but not identified with the colonialists—arrived in India. Among these followers of Ignatius Loyola was the most famous Roman Catholic missionary, Francis Xavier. Within a short time conversions of entire villages were taking place, with tens of thousands baptized into Christianity. The Jesuits identified themselves most closely with the Hindu people, particularly brahmins, learning the languages and translating the Scriptures and manuals of instruction into the vernaculars, and establishing schools to train leaders for the church. This was the beginning of the missionary movement as we think of it today.

Protestants were late in arriving in India. In the seventeenth century chaplains of British, Dutch, and Danish traders ministered to the Hindu servants of the colonialist masters. But the British East India Company—the largest of the traders—was suspicious of any attempts to Christianize India. In fact, the company organized and supported temple foundations, hoping to keep the religious status quo while establishing economic domination over the subcontinent.

The first Protestant missionaries per se arrived in 1706 from pietist German Lutheran missionary societies. Their converts were made among Hindus and Roman Catholics. The first English missionary was William Carey, sent by the Baptist Missionary Society in 1793. He achieved remarkable success by translating the Bible into a number of Indian languages, and by establishing independent congregations with trained Indian leaders. Carey and his associates also translated the *Ramayana* and other Sanskrit literature into English with the hope that missionaries might enter into the thought world of the Hindus (even though it was non-Christian) in order to be more able to convert them to Christianity. The Scotsman Alexander Duff added a new dimension to the missionary enterprise by establishing schools of higher education using English, thereby eliciting sympathetic responses from Hindu intellectuals even if they were not converted.

As the East India Company's military and economic power unified large areas of the subcontinent, it permitted more missionaries to enter. By the middle of the nineteenth century the relatively small Christian population reflected the denominational divisions of Western Christianity as well as the variety of languages of the colonizing nations. A rumor spread among the Hindu people that plans were being made to force the conversion of Hindus to Christianity The tragic Sepoy Mutiny of 1857 grew in part out of this fear. The rumor was unfounded, but a significant change did take place. The British *raj* took over the government of India. Queen Victoria's goal was the transformation of India, not by force but by social reform, education, medical aid, different standards of morality, the civil service, and British civility and culture. Christian missions made enormous investments in personnel and institutions in the areas of medicine and education; but converting Hindus to Christianity was still their primary concern.

The impact of Christianity upon the Hindu tradition is difficult to assess. Some claim that the tradition was drastically altered by Christian influence more than fourteen hundred years ago: the development of the *bhakti marga* vis-à-vis obedience to *dharma* and animal sacrifice, the evangelistic fervor of bhakti gurus, the transformation of Siva into a gracious supreme being, the birth and childhood stories of Krishna, the loving "side" of Krishna in the *Bhagavad Gita*, the importance of pilgrimage and asceticism, the concept of Vishnu incarnate—almost anything similar to Christianity has been claimed by Christians to have been borrowed. Others suggest that such claims reflect more Christian arrogance than actual fact, and at present there seems no way to determine the truth of this matter.

Christian Western influence is clear, however, in such social reforms as the abolition of child marriage, the discouragement of *sati* (women ascending their husbands' funeral pyres as a final act of devotion; also known as *sutee*), the prohibition of temple "prostitution" (and the coresponding loss of traditional Indian dances), the institution of sabbath (i.e., Sunday) obersvance, and educational, agricultural, and medical changes. Moreover, it was a clear victory for Christians when India became independent in 1947 and declared itself to be a secular state: legally their rights were now equal with those of the overwhelming Hindu majority and many of the social reforms were made a part of the new country.

Today it is estimated that there are seventeen million Christians in India. In the enormous population of the subcontinent, however, that constitutes a mere 2.6 percent of the population. Eighty-three percent are considered Hindus, 13 percent Muslims, and 1.4 percent belong to other religions. The majority of Christians reside in South India, including Kerala, which is often identified as the most successful and prosperous state in India. It claims the highest percentage of Christians—and also of Marxists.

Indian Christianity has enormous problems because of its divided allegiance. On the one hand it continues to struggle with its Western heritage, that is, divided Christianity. Forces from both within and without have weakened or severed many of the ties with colonial and missionary founders; but becoming independent has often resulted in a poverty of faith, of leadership, and of money. The toll of this triple poverty has been immense. The stories of courage and sacrifice are inspiring; the stories of gross ineptitude and selfishness are equally striking—and often appalling.

A significant development in Christian ecumenicity came about with the establishment of the Church of South India (CSI) in 1947. It consists mostly of Protestant denominations of American and English origins; but remaining outside of the CSI are various Lutheran churches, Southern Baptist and American fundamentalist groups, as well as the Roman Catholic and Mar Thoma churches. Various levels of cooperation have developed at the one end of the ecumenical spectrum; at the other, "sheep-stealing" exists and proselytes are sought among other Christian groups as much as from non-Christian religions.

Of even greater importance are the problems that stem from the inevitable association of Christianity with the overwhelming religio-cultural Hindu tradition. Many Christians reject any relationship by trying to isolate themselves in urban Christian ghettos or in villages that have been Christian for centuries, but they find it is difficult to escape the Hindu tradition of caste, for example, despite Christian claims that it has been eliminated. Denominations and congregations are often constituted of persons from the same or related caste origins or from groups of outcastes or excluded classes. There is good reason to think that Lutheran participation in the CSI, for example, is prevented not so much by (Western) theological differences as by the nontheological factor of caste, that is, the low caste status of most Lutherans. Christians have become culturally a caste within a caste in the larger social context. Christians have been heard to say that if the choice arose between an arranged marriage with a Christian of a different caste or a non-Christian of the same caste, they would choose the latter.

Finally, some fundamental questions must be faced continually by Indian Christians. How are they to deal with the tension between the Hindu tradition of inclusiveness and the Western Christian concept of exclusiveness?[4] Can there be any accommodation between the once-for-all incarnation of God in Jesus Christ and the incarnations of Vishnu? How does one relate Jesus as the Way to the Hindu attitude that there

> Flow streams that come from hills on every side,
> Their names are various as their springs
> And thus in every land do men bow down
> To one great God, though known by many names.[5]

May the Hindu scriptures—for example, Krishna's "highest word, the most secret of all: You are loved by Me"—be used in Christian worship? May the All, the Whole, the One be related to the fullness of God or the cosmic Christ? Is Brahman without attributes comparable to, possibly identical with, the God-head who, according to Christian mystics, can be spoken of only by negating human terms in the presence of the unfathomable mystery? May indigenous symbols (e.g., Vishnu's mace or Siva's crown), be adapted as symbols of Christ's power and victory? May certain forms of the Hindu tradition of bhakti—offerings of food, circumambulations, prostrations, *ashrams*, *guru* leadership—be "Christianized"?

---

[4]Hinduism welcomes all traditions, even making room for Christianity; Christianity by contrast tends to be exclusive, to define precisely who "belong."

[5]From a Tamil folk song.

May Christians develop their own forms of *yoga* and *mantras* (e.g., "the Jesus prayer" of the Greek and Russian churches, *kyrie eleison*, "Jesus, Son of God, have mercy on me a sinner")? May images—in wood, stone, paint, or stained glass—of Jesus the baby or the crucified one, or the image of Our Lady of Fatima, be interpreted as containing the power of God within them? Can such Christian symbols be bearers of God's power, or are they idolatrous? Is Hinduism a false religion, a preliminary one, a true one? Is Christianity the true faith for all human beings and for all cultures? These are questions that may seem strange to Western Christians, but questions that arise, inevitably, in the Indian context. As Paul had to confront the Greco-Roman Empire, so Indian Christians must find some means of relating to the Hindu faith, which is the social context of their lives.   H. W.

Christianity in China

The story of Christianity in China extends from the time of a legendary visit of Thomas to China right down to a very questionable present—nearly two thousand years. As we know it, it is very largely a story of efforts by European and American missionaries to establish the church in China and the story of Chinese dealings with this powerful and persistent effort, sometimes in a friendly manner, sometimes with hostility. It is a vast story extending across thirteen centuries and occupying nine hundred pages in the standard history by Kenneth Scott Latourette,[6] a distinguished Baptist historian. It is an enormously moving story of great and heroic deeds and a story that raises many fascinating questions about the relationship between Christianity and other faiths and cultures to which it is a stranger. And it is a story, too, that forces us to ask questions about the methods and the goals of those who seek to spread the Christian message to foreign lands, a story that involves judgments—sometimes harsh, sometimes supportive and enthusiastic.

Nestorian Christians from Syria and Iraq appear to have reached China in the seventh or eighth century, but they were too

---

[6]*A History of Christian Missions in China* (New York: Macmillan, 1928).

few in number and too scattered to leave any lasting effects. Early efforts at missionary activity by Roman Catholic emissaries in the fourteenth century were also too early to be effective. In fact, it was not until the time of the religious awakening that accompanied the Renaissance that European missionaries began to have any permanent impact on China, in particular through the work of the great Francis Xavier, who died in China in 1552. In the same century, under the leadership of Matteo Ricci, the Jesuits sought to make contact with clerics and scholars and to adjust the Christian faith to Chinese culture—a key element in Jesuit strategy. At the end of the seventeenth century, French Catholics arrived and a Chinese bishop was actually appointed. At the same time, an edict of toleration protecting the church encouraged prosperity and permitted expansion.

But this rapid growth of Roman Catholic influence was eventually followed by the celebrated "rites controversy," the acrimonious debate over whether to allow Chinese Christians to worship their ancestors and to use various Chinese words to refer to God. After a bitter dispute within the church, the pope ruled that the church could not compromise its customs nor adapt itself to Chinese life. As Latourette observes, this fateful decision (on an issue that also dogged Protestants later) established a tradition of making the church "unadoptable to Chinese conditions and beliefs" and kept the church always a foreign institution. What is more, the Roman Catholic stress on infant baptism raised an issue that was definitely alien to Chinese culture and lessened the ability of the church to work real changes in the lifestyles of Chinese converts.

As a result of the papal decision about rites, there followed a period of persecution and retarded growth. At the same time, the growing spirit of rationalism in Europe was proving hostile to missionary activity. Thus, at the beginning of the nineteenth century, it appeared that the church might not survive in China. However, two wars at midcentury between China and Britain led to peace treaties that forced Chinese authorities to increase the degree of toleration that missionaries enjoyed and enabled them to further expand their mission. At this time influential boards in Britain and America sent missionaries, and a high level of cooperation among Protestant groups was achieved. But another serious reversal occurred as a result of the T'ai P'ing or "Great Peace"

Rebellion of 1850, led by a Chinese who had been deeply—if somewhat peculiarly—influenced by Christian doctrine. Although the rebellion was soon suppressed, untold lives were lost and missionaries experienced some suffering because of the ties between their foreign faith and the rebel leader.

The second half of the nineteenth century saw the emergence of the greatest names among Protestant missionaries—Samuel Scherechewsky, born a Russian Jew, who became a very influential Anglican bishop in China, with a remarkable mastery of the language; Timothy Richard, of the Baptist Missionary Society, whose work in Shantung province was influenced by his own deep appreciation of Chinese culture and whose ambition was nothing less than to convert the empire; and Hudson Taylor, of the China Inland Mission, which placed more missionaries in China than any other board, always with a distinctly evangelical emphasis. By 1889 there were approximately thirteen hundred Protestant missionaries in China, carrying out a wide variety of tasks with great devotion, cooperating to achieve common goals, and seeing as their chief concern the task of changing the lives of Chinese by preaching the gospel. Great emphasis was placed on organizing and nurturing a national church, on the translation of Scripture, and on the preparation of hymnals, tracts, and dictionaries. But in these processes the social consequences of the gospel were not forgotten: through work with opium addicts and lepers, campaigns against gambling and footbinding, the expansion of medical missions, the founding of schools and colleges, a concern for the emancipation of women, and a ministry to the poor.

Despite such important contributions to the well-being of the Chinese, missionaries continued to find themselves in conflict with Chinese officials, the missionaries being seen by many as disturbers of existing customs and institutions. Sometimes agitation against them was generated by Chinese scholars, who saw themselves as upholders of traditional ways. And it must be admitted that missionaries often did see themselves as agents of change who were preparing China for a new age; many Chinese in fact welcomed the changes that missionaries brought, seeing that only by learning Western ways could China cope with Western influence. In particular, mission schools were seen as an excellent source of the kind of knowledge China needed so badly. To some extent, as Latourette observes, "they were helping to steady and direct the occasionally bewildered and often inexperienced reformers as the latter attempted to guide a huge Empire into untried and dangerous paths."[7]

The most serious case of antimissionary sentiment broke out in 1900, in the celebrated Boxer Rebellion, named after one of many anti-Western groups, the Righteous Harmony Fists. Like many similar organizations in China at the time, this group was made up of young men angry over mission intervention in lawsuits, mission purchases of land, mission rejection of many time-honored Chinese customs. The Boxers won the support of the Dowager Empress, who apparently felt that they, with the help of magical powers, could dislodge the foreigners. The rebellion, suppressed by foreign troops, was over by the fall of 1900, but it constituted the most serious persecution ever suffered by missionaries in China. Some missionaries took advantage of what had happened to them to secure indemnities from the Chinese government, but most intervened with the authorities on behalf of their persecutors.

Following the Boxer Rebellion, missionaries found many new opportunities open to them, in part because in 1905 the civil service examination system gave way to a new school system that stressed Western learning. Even more important was the fact that in 1911 the inept and corrupt Manchu dynasty was swept away and a republic established, the leaders of which were far more open to Western influence than their predecessors had been. As new ideas came in, the hold of Confucianism was weakened and China became increasingly open to new ideas.

Because Protestants generally held ideas more in keeping with the spirit of the times than the Roman Catholics did, the greatest growth at this time took place within the ranks of the former group. One particularly significant Protestant institution was the YMCA, an organization that has had a far greater impact in China than it has in the West, nurturing many important leaders across the years. YMCA leaders, both in China and America, were very sensitive to the problems of an emerging China, and local native leaders were picked with great care—at the same time that outstanding graduates of American colleges and universities were

[7]Ibid., p. 496.

being recruited for service in China. John R. Mott, the famous philanthropist, went to China in 1907 as a YMCA organizer, and Sherwood Eddy preached to hundreds of thousands in the decade that followed. Before long, Chinese YMCA organizations were supporting language and industrial-arts schools and a variety of medical-education projects. Mission interests also included social-service work with orphans; the deaf, dumb, and blind; and famine victims. Critics are now decrying the alleged secularization of the mission movement, but there can be little doubt that as a result of such activities, Christian missions played a much larger role in the emergence of modern China than would have been the case had they confined themselves to purely "spiritual" issues.

World War I brought suffering to German and Russian missionaries in China, and although the United States, with newfound wealth, emerged as the great new mission force, missions of all countries had to face the ever-growing challenge of Chinese nationalism. In particular, the New Tide movement was intolerant of foreign influence, its members urging the Chinese to take responsibility for their own reforms. Withal, the number of native Chinese clergy was increasing and the responsibilities for fundraising and decisionmaking were being transferred to nationals. In this postwar period, too, there was an interesting case of cooperation between Protestants, Roman Catholics, Buddhists, Taoists, and Muslims to defeat a government attempt to declare Confucianism the basis for national moral training.

The postwar period also saw the mission enterprise in China besieged by the same great theological questions that at the time were devastating the Christian church in Europe and America. Many Christians in the Western world were realizing how far their own lands were from being Christian. They concluded, rightly or wrongly, that they had best set their own houses in order before undertaking to convert others. Domestic social programs often loomed larger than the evangelical concern that every living human being have a chance to hear the gospel. Knowledge of and appreciation for the great religions of Asia developed, and some missionaries were questioning how to relate Christianity to the cultural and religious heritage of China. This was also the period when such noted skeptics as Bertrand Russell and John Dewey were traveling and teaching in China, and their writings, widely

read in England and America, evidenced great sympathy for
traditional Chinese culture (and the role of modern science in
reshaping that culture) and very little respect for the work of
Christian missionaries.[8]

The revolution of 1949, in which the forces of the Nationalist
leader Chiang Kai-shek were defeated and forced to flee to
Formosa (now Taiwan) was the effective end of foreign missionary
work in China.[9] By this time a fairly large body of Christians had
developed in China;[10] many of these people remained true to their
faith and bore eloquent witness to their commitment during the
chaos of the revolution. Most observers are willing to attribute
some of China's readiness for modernization to the earlier work of
the missionaries, who promoted literacy, raised moral standards,
and generally introduced useful Western ideas. It has even been
suggested that missionary activity led to significant reforms
within the Buddhist and Confucian traditions. For America, an
important but little recognized side benefit has been a large
number of important educational and cultural leaders who grew
up in China, children of missionary parents.

Information on the state of the church in China following the
departure of Western missionaries is hard to come by and often
contradictory. One author argued, in 1960, that the church had
survived with vitality and strength, and that it had not been
liquidated by Red leaders. Schools, hospitals, and other socially
useful institutions were of course taken over by the totalitarian
government, but the Communist constitution guaranteed (for
whatever reason) "freedom of religious belief." (Perhaps, it has
been suggested, because the Red leadership did not want adverse
publicity or because the number of Christians was too small to
fuss over.) However, any who had been converted in the belief that
Christianity could save China realized that their hopes had been
dashed and that the Communists were carrying out (by force, and

[8]See Bertrand Russell's *Problem of China* (New York: Century Company, 1922), especially
the chapter on higher education in China. Here Russell has a number of points to make
about missionary-related institutions which he finds to be more devoted to preaching
Americanism ("clean living, clean thinking, and pep") than Christianity.

[9]Chiang Kai-shek was a Christian, but his faith was a minor influence on his life; his
support for Confucianism was much more enthusiastic. His wife, Mei-ling Soong, from a
famous and influential family, was an active believer.

[10]Latourette estimates that there were twenty-one million Christians in China in
1927.

Oura Tenshudo Cathedral in
Nagasaki.

therefore very effectively) some of the same reforms Christianity
had promised. But it was the conclusion of Earle Ballou, in 1960,
that many Christians did not defect, the church in 1960 being at
least three-quarters of the size it was in 1949. There was no doubt,
however, that radical changes had occurred, the number of places
of worship in Peking having been reduced from sixty-five to four.
In his opinion worship was the only visible expression of belief
that remained.[11]

Eight years later, after the church had been virtually liquidated
by the Red Guards, only half a dozen congregations continued to
hold services, leadership had virtually disappeared, and transmission of the faith from parents to children was proving virtually
impossible. Some Protestants did apparently try to work through

[11]See *Christianity and Crisis*, July 11, 1960.

the three-self reform movement,[12] but it proved to be too much of a government arm to serve as a vehicle for evangelical Christianity. Much the same experience faced the Roman Catholics: some leaders saw a possibility of adjustment to Communist goals, but ultimately found it impossible, given their obligation of loyalty to the pope in Rome. Priests were expelled and tortured, and all members of the church were subjected to overpowering propaganda. In 1968, there was evidence that Communists were working toward a church independent of foreign control which would eventually disappear within the Communist monolith.[13] And in 1977 John B. Wang, an American observer, reported that churches and temples were gone, Taoist and Buddhist monasteries closed, and Chinese children "indifferent, uninterested, and ignorant" when religious matters were discussed.[14]   J. R. K.

Christianity in Japan

Japanese Christians number approximately 1 million in a total population of just over 112 million. Divided about evenly between Roman Catholic and Protestant, they are mostly of the urban and upper middle class. They constitute about 1 percent of the Japanese population, but make up well above 1 percent of the physicians, college professors, legislators, judges, and corporate and government managers.

For both historical and cultural reasons the Christian tradition in Japan is generally perceived to be an alien presence. The Christian faith made entry into Japan during three eras of crisis and rapid social change: the period of the civil wars (1482–1558), the Meiji period when the decision to modernize the government, military, education, and commercial structures was being implemented (1868–1912), and the seven years of the American occupation after World War II. In each of these periods the persons attracted to the Christian faith were those who had been made rootless by the social changes. The converts were largely from the groups who were no longer served by the old social order. For example, in the early Meiji period the new members of the church

---

[12]The church was to be self-propagating, self-governing, and self-financing.
[13]*Christianity and Crisis*, May 13, 1968.
[14]*Christianity Today*, November 18, 1977.

were drawn from the warrior class (*samurai*) who had served under the feudal rulers of the fallen Tokugawa regime. As a consequence an antiestablishment sense characterized the new Christians coming into the church.

Second, the Christian faith was and remains at variance with several values common to Japanese culture. Shintō perceives a continuity between the sacred and the human, in contrast to the Christian faith, which teaches a basic discontinuity. An openness to all religious traditions, for all are believed to be valid relative to the needs and perceptions of the worshiper, characterizes the Japanese generally, whereas the Christian community insists upon the uniqueness and truth of its faith. In Japan a person's relationship to the sacred is primarily a group or family relationship, in contrast to the Christian tradition with its emphasis upon the individual who stands alone before God. Japanese culture is essentially optimistic about the nature of human beings. The Christian heritage teaches that mankind is sinful, even depraved.

Because it is in conflict with basic Japanese values, the Christian community in Japan is still thought of as foreign. In response, Japanese Christians feel they are not accepted and have developed a citadel mentality. They have close ties among themselves, are prone to criticize the establishment, and often work with members of another minority group who are also perceived as professing foreign values, and who are of the urban upper middle class, the Marxists.

The Yasukuni Shrine controversy illustrates these differences. Today protesters often gather around the Diet building to demonstrate either for or against legislation to provide national government funds for the maintenance of the Yasukuni Shrine.

After the Pacific war the American occupation government established the separation of church and state as an article in the new Japanese constitution. No shrines could any longer depend upon financial support from the government. This policy included the great shrine in Tokyo, Yasukuni, established as a memorial for Japan's military dead by the Meiji government. During the last one hundred years tens of thousands of soldiers and sailors have been enshrined at Yasukuni, which in this regard bears some resemblance to Arlington National Cemetery. With disestablishment, however, Yasukuni Shrine was suddenly dependent upon voluntary contributions from the families of the deceased who are enshrined there, and from veterans' organizations. This was a satisfactory arrangement for many years, but in the early 1970s as the veterans became aware that, after they and the immediate relatives were gone, there would be no source of support for the shrine unless special legislation was enacted. The numerous veterans' organizations and family associations throughout Japan have lobbied strongly on behalf of the Yasukuni Shrine bill. Opposing them is an active coalition of Christians and Marxists. Both Christians and Marxists were forced to worship at Shintō shrines during World War II as a demonstration of their loyalty to the nation and many Christian and Marxist leaders were jailed for either the failure to cooperate or the suspicion that they might not cooperate. Both have bitter memories. The issue is not resolved, but from the viewpoint of the majority of the Japanese two foreign ideologies are working together on behalf of an American idea (the separation of church and state) to prevent proper respect being shown toward Japan's war dead. The Yasukuni Shrine controversy reinforces the general Japanese perception that the Christian faith is an alien presence in their culture.   E. R. S.

Factors Influencing Christianity in Asia

These brief sketches have introduced a large topic: Christianity in Asia. In these vignettes we have suggested some dimensions of the rich history, cultural diversity, spiritual vitality, and theological identity of the churches of the Asian East. As a conclusion it is appropriate to indicate some of the issues affecting the destiny of Asian Christianity.

Although it is difficult to generalize concerning the world's largest religion as it fares on earth's biggest and most populous continent, and conditions faced by the churches in contexts as contradictory as Korea and Kerala, Turkey and Thailand, will be quite contrasting, there are, we feel, several common factors confronting the Christian churches.

One of these is nationalism. Forty years ago Western imperialism was still very evident in Asia, as revealed by the Dutch presence in Indonesia, the British in the Indian subcontinent, the French in Indochina. Western imperialism has not totally disappeared, as was dramatically demonstrated by the Soviet invasion of Afghanistan. One hopes, however, the Russian action is a relapse into the recent past, not the advent of neocolonialism. Certainly the prevailing pattern for two generations has been the emergence of new nations with old civilizations. Pakistan and India are examples of this phenomenon. The Christian churches are challenged to relate creatively and critically to this development. This is not always easy. Sometimes the churches are the product of Western missionary activity in modern times (like the Episcopal and Evangelical churches in Iran), or they date from witnessing by Middle East expatriates in antiquity (like the Mar Thoma Church in India). The churches may have an "Occidental orientation" or be composed of converts from "minority populations." Whereas in Korea the churches have been able to identify with the new nationalism, this has not been as readily accomplished in Pakistan (where nationalism takes on an Islamic flavor). Because of the inherent universalism of Christianity, believers are challenged to balance the often conflicting claims of loyalty to one nation-state with citizenship in the kingdom of heaven. Often national churches have been created, with ties of affection and conviction to sister denominations in the West. Occasionally regional and even ecumenical churches have been formed (e.g., the Church of South India). Efforts to "indiginize" the church have often been combined with the struggle to maintain a firm confessional identity (as in the Batak churches in Indonesia). Christians try to be patriotic and to participate in the work of the nation-state. Sometimes this is not possible. Exclusion or even persecution occurs. As Jesus ministered as both King of the Jews and Savior of the world, so Christians in Asia will strive to be both Koreans and Presbyterians, Iranians and Episcopalians, Baptists and Vietnamese.

Industrialization is another force transforming Asia. Westerners have long regarded Asia as a "traditional" society. The images that come to mind are of rice paddies, water buffaloes, or thousands of isolated villages. Certainly that is still one of the many Asias of the late twentieth century. Beside it, however, is another Asia—one that has moved beyond custom and caste, agriculture and tradition, to become highly technological. This is industrialized Asia. Oil refineries and steel plants, car factories and textile mills can be found everywhere from the Persian Gulf to the Straits of Tsushima, but the main concentration of industrialism has been in Japan,

Korea, Taiwan, Singapore, and other portions of the Pacific littoral
of Asia. Collectively these countries are called the East Asian
industrial complex. Many believe that China is now in the throes
of its own Industrial Revolution. The significance of "the Asian
challenge" to the older industrialized nations of America and
Europe has been noted by economists. Consumers are aware of it
in the marketplace, as they buy Japanese cars and transistors,
Korean shorts and skirts, toys from Taiwan or Singapore. Christians in Asia are aware of the change in other ways. Although
Christians sometimes have been in the vanguard of industrialization, others remain in the rear guard of social and cultural
traditionalism. The trend toward industrialization, however, causes all Christians to consider the implications for faith and life of
this great transition from a traditional to a technological society.
Industrialization brings urbanization—as illustrated in Tokyo,
Shanghai, Hong Kong, and Singapore. It means rising levels of
expectation and frustration—shown in a thousand and one ways,
from crowded classrooms to streets congested with new cars. It
invites social mobility, a new emphasis on individualism, and
leads to new expressions in personal and social living. The moral
implications of these are enormous—and the pastoral responsibility of the churches is great. As Jesus preached both in urban
synagogues and in the countryside, working miracles of healing
in the crowded streets of Jerusalem and giving his great ethical
discourse, the Sermon on the Mount, in a rural setting, so the
Christians of Asia are invited to minister effectively to peasant and
executive, soldier and statesman, factory worker and intellectual.

The struggle of authoritarianism and freedom is an issue facing
Asian Christians also. Asia in the late twentieth century is a place
of enormous political ferment. At the conclusion of the Second
World War many felt that Western-style democracy would come to
prevail from Istanbul to Kyoto. Turkey was experimenting with a
multiparty political system. India emerged as earth's most populous democracy. Japan, in the wake of the American occupation,
became a constitutional monarchy. Many outside observers believed that "the four freedoms" enshrined in the Atlantic Charter
would become the political foundations of the new Asia. In part
those hopes have been fulfilled. In part, however, they have been
dashed. Authoritarianism has also prospered in postwar Asia.
China embraced Marxism, as did Indochina. Fascist regimes have

appeared elsewhere. Experimentation with Islamic theocracies has occurred in Iran and Pakistan. The result is that Christians in the 1980s live in Asia under regimes as varied as a liberal monarchy in Japan, an Islamic republic in Iran, dictatorships in South Korea and the Philippines, Communist states in China, Vietnam, Cambodia, Laos, and North Korea, military regimes, as in Turkey, traditional tribalities, as in the Persian Gulf, and city-states such as Singapore. The churches face these emerging patterns with different traditions. Some Christians in Asia, whose origins date to Western missionary activity, are accustomed to the church-state pattern brought from the Continent by Lutheran or Reformed missionaries. Others, the product of Anglo-American missionary endeavor, are more familiar with the free-church system that evolved in a mass-participatory democracy. Yet others, whose roots are in the Mideast, have long been familiar with being a Christian minority in a Muslim theocracy (the classical Arab or Turkish empires). Still others, such as the Orthodox Christians of Russian background, are accustomed to the two extremes of the Czar-Protector (and Head of the Church) on the one hand and Marxist persecution on the other (since the establishment of the Soviet regime in 1917). These mixed backgrounds are now being severely tested in an Asian context where Christians experience a variety of reactions from the state ranging from toleration to persecution, from opposition to full participation in the ruling process. Christians, like their Lord, will need wisdom to know how to render to Caesar what is his and to offer to God what is his due portion. The shape of the church in Marxist China, Muslim Iran, democratic India, and socialist Burma will be one of the main concerns of the future.

Another force sweeping Asia is that of revivalism—not simply the revival of Christianity (as in Korea), but also the resurgence of the traditional religions of the East. Reinvigorated by contact with Christianity, many of the ancient faiths, long regarded as dead or dying, are now awakening. Buddhist Sunday schools are not unknown; the Hindus have Boy Scouts; Shintōism is gaining new respect in Japan. Missionaries from the Eastern faiths are now active in the West, witnessing from Chicago's Loop to London's Strand. Signs abound of the religious revival sweeping Asia. An Islamic revolution in Iran is but the most dramatic evidence of this "religious renaissance" of the late twentieth century. The response of the Christian churches to this phenomenon has been varied. It has been variously viewed with alarm, with apathy, with concern, and as an opportunity. Certainly it has raised for Christians of Western heritage the issue of contextualization; that is, how a church nurtured in Occidental culture can both maintain its spiritual integrity and relate significantly to the culture of its host nation. For Christians of Mideast origin—such as the Mar Thoma believers in India—a similar issue is posed. Often the churches of Oriental or Orthodox origin have been "ghetto communities," intent on preserving a minority counter-culture. Can Armenian and Assyrian Christians, for example, both effectively communicate their faith to the majority population and preserve their own historic communities? As Jesus lived in a pluralistic society, ministering among Romans, Greeks, Syrophoenicians, and Samaritans, and yet sustained his own relationship to the biblical tradition, so Christians in Asia are challenged to be both scriptural—loyal to their sources in the Bible—and contextual, able to speak persuasively in a largely non-Christian environment.

The experience of Asian Christians will be of great value to their coreligionists in the West. Often we have forgotten that Jesus was Asian, as were his first followers, and that the earliest communities of faith were gathered in what is now Palestine and Israel, Lebanon and Syria, Turkey and Cyprus. In similar fashion we fail to remember that the initial theological controversy to shake the church was the issue of "Europeanization," or how to adapt the gospel to the needs of a gentile (primarily Hellenistic) population. Judaizers (at home in the Asian environment) opposed Paul's efforts to "Westernize" the church. Today the issue, we feel, has been reversed. Canadians, Germans, Swedes, Mexicans, New Zealanders, and New Englanders feel at home in Christianity, an Asian religion. The challenge of the coming years is allowing Christianity to make a "homecoming" to its Asian roots. In such a manner it can once more minister effectively to the people of the East—and from this experiment in applied Christianity we in the West can better learn how to sort out our own religious heritage, to discover what is truly "of the gospel" and what is certainly culturally acquired. As a result of this painful but invigorating process, believers, whether in Korea or Kansas or in India or Indiana, will learn once more that Christ is the "Alpha and Omega, the first and the last" (Rev. 1:11).   C. G. F., J. R. K.

Bibliographic Essay

Christianity

A classic study of Christian missions in Asia is *The Great Century in Northern Africa and Asia, AD 1800–1914*, volume 6 of Kenneth Scott Latourette's *History of the Expansion of Christianity* (New York: Harper, 1944). A recent work is *The Church in Asia*, edited by Donald G. Hoke (Chicago: Moody, 1976).

Evangelism and ecumenism have been two major concerns in twentieth-century Asian Christianity. Hans-Ruedi Weber's *Asia and the Ecumenical Movement* (London: SCM, 1966) offers an assessment of the role of the Asian contribution to the world church. Morris A. Inch, *Doing Theology Across Cultures* (Grand Rapids: Baker, 1982) takes up the issue of "how should the Christian conceive and express his faith in a particular cultural setting." Specific examples are drawn from Sinhalese, Chinese, and Muslim contexts. J. Herbert Kane's *Concise History of the Christian World Mission: A Panoramic View of Missions from Pentecost to the Present* (rev. ed., Grand Rapids: Baker, 1982) places the Asian experience in the broader setting of world Christian outreach. The issue of contextualization is addressed in Dean S. Gilliland, *Pauline Theology and Mission Practice* (Grand Rapids: Baker, 1983) and in Arthur F. Glasser and Donald McGavran, *Contemporary Theologies of Mission* (Grand Rapids: Baker, 1983).

Asian reactions to Christianity are found in *Christianity: Some Non-Christian Appraisals*, edited by D. W. McKain (New York: McGraw Hill, 1964), containing a series of essays, some sympathetic, some highly critical, by adherents of other religions. Efforts to bridge the barrier between Christianity and Buddhism are seen in Winston L. King, *Buddhism and Christianity: Some Bridges of Understanding* (Philadelphia: Westminister, 1962) and D. T. Niles, *Buddhism and the Claims of Christ* (Richmond: John Knox, 1967). A Christian appreciation is found in

Confucius and Christ: A Christian Estimate of Confucius (New York: Philosophical Library, 1951). Also informative is Winifred Nelson Beechy's *New China* (Scottdale, Penn.: Herald, 1982), which one reviewer described as "wise advice for Western church leaders as they seek to renew contacts with the Christian church in China." Phil Parshall, *New Paths in Muslim Evangelism: Evangelical Approaches to Contextualization* (Grand Rapids: Baker, 1980) indicates ways in which Christianity can adapt to a Muslim context. A theoretical volume is *Protestant Crosscurrents in Mission,* edited by Norman A. Horner (Nashville: Abingdon, 1968), giving liberal and evangelical points of view. David M. Paton's "Christian Missions in Asia," in *Asia Handbook,* edited by Guy Wint (Baltimore: Penguin, 1969) contains a balance of both optimistic and pessimistic views about the future of Christianity in Asia, stating that "the facts allow for several interpretations." Langdon Gilkey's *Shantung Compound: The Story of Men and Women under Pressure* (New York: Harper and Row, 1966) is a fascinating account of the witness and the general response of Christian missionaries in a Japanese prison camp in China during World War II. Chapter 10, "More Saints, Priests, and Preachers," is an especially valuable statement about the strengths and weaknesses of these missionaries.

Islam

Asia Handbook, edited by Guy Wint (Baltimore: Penguin, 1969), is a useful source of information about the history and politics of Asian countries where Islam has been a force. For material on the various religious groups of these countries, an invaluable source is edited by Richard V. Weekes, *Muslim Peoples: A World of Ethniographic Survey* (Westport, Conn.: Greenwood, 1978), which contains nearly one hundred articles by specialists, with up-to-date, scholarly bibliographies. *Islam: A Survey of the Muslim Faith,* by C. George Fry and James R. King (rev. ed., Grand Rapids: Baker, 1982), describes basic Muslim beliefs and customs and offers annotated bibliographies. On India, see Wilfred Cantwell Smith, *Modern Islam in India: A Social Analysis* (London, 1946; Lahore: Shaikh Muhammad Ashraf, 1963) and Annamarie Schimmel, *Islam in the Indian Subcontinent* (Leiden: Brill, 1980). W. T. DeBary edited *Sources of the Indian Tradition,* 2 vols. (New York: Columbia University Press, 1958), which includes both texts and background material, in a chronological arrangement, devoting considerable space to Islam. Syed Ameer 'Ali's *Spirit of Islam* (1891; reprint ed., London: Methuen, University Paperbacks, 1967) and Mohammad Iqbal's *Six Lectures on the Reconstruction of Religious Thought in Islam* (1930) are both still readily available. Clifford Geertz has important observations on Indonesian and Moroccan Islam in *Islam Observed* (New Haven: Yale University Press, 1968), and Wilfred Cantwell Smith, in *Islam in Modern History* (Princeton: Princeton University Press, 1957), makes a number of important comments on Indonesian Islam and updates his earlier study of Islam in South Asia. Marshall Broomhall's *Islam in China: A Neglected Problem,* originally published in 1910, was a pioneering study, especially valuable on the influence of the Christian missionary movement. It was reprinted in 1980 (New York: Gordon). More recent is

Raphael Israeli's *Muslims in China: A Study in Cultural Confrontation* (London: Curzon, 1980). It is written from an anthropological point of view. Andrew Forbes, in "Muslim National Minorities of China," *Religion* (Spring 1976), pp. 67–87, reviews the literature and offers a valuable analysis of the topic, and two of Edgar Snow's volumes, *Red Star over China* (rev. ed., 1968; New York: Bantam, 1978) and *Red China Today: The Other Side of the River* (1962; rev. ed., New York: Random, 1971) comment on the situation of Muslims in China. Two journals, *Religion in Communist-Dominated Areas* and *Religion in Communist Lands*, publish articles from time to time on both Islam and Christianity in China.

Index of Subjects